— A GAME OF EXTREMES BUNDLE

75 EXCEPTIONAL

SPORT STORIES

ROY LINGSTER

A GAME OF EXTREMES BUNDLE

75 EXCEPTIONAL SPORT STORIES

ABOUT WHAT HAPPENS ON AND OFF THE FIELD
BASEBALL/BASKETBALL/FOOTBALL

ROY LINGSTER

CONTENTS

A GAME OF EXTREMES: 25 EXCEPTIONAL BASKETBALL STORIES

A GAME OF EXTREMES: 25 EXCEPTIONAL FOOTBALL STORIES

ABOUT THE AUTHOR

Roy Lingster is a military sports instructor and the author of *The Baseball Player's Guide to Hitting Like a Pro* and the *A Game of Extremes* series.

Much of his work is devoted to exceptional stories in sporting history, delving deep into the world of baseball, basketball, and football, but he also writes about developing specific sporting skills.

Roy's passion for sports began with baseball, which he describes as 'a hobby that got out of hand'. He has spent 25 years in the game as both player and coach, but his interest in sports has led him to branch out into basketball and football. The expertise he's built throughout his career is evident in his writing, and his books provide a rich source of information and advice for sports enthusiasts who want to learn the history behind their game and develop their skills at the same time.

Roy's journey may have begun with baseball, but when he began writing about exceptional stories, he uncovered fascinating tales behind every sport, and the books seemed to write themselves. His research has informed his technique and coaching style, and he's fascinated by how developing knowledge in one sport can lead to greatness in another.

Roy has a drive for helping others overcome their setbacks and achieve their dreams, which stems from battling with a setback of his own. His commitment to overcoming this and getting his mind back in the game saw him break down the elements of how to achieve success in baseball, and he's now passionate about sharing everything he's learned with others.

Roy lives in the Netherlands, where he spends most of his time soaking up anything to do with sport.

A GAME OF EXTREMES: 25 EXCEPTIONAL BASEBALL STORIES

ABOUT WHAT HAPPENS ON AND OFF THE FIELD

A
GAME
OF EXTREMES
25 EXCEPTIONAL
BASEBALL
STORIES

ROY LINGSTER

INTRODUCTION

Baseball is a sport of legends. For fans, drama and strategy hang on every pitch. Two teams face each other in a grueling marathon that spans 162 games where only one can come out on top. The players and coaches are involved in a battle that may start with physical talents, but very much involves psychological and emotional aspects that draw fans in with its complexity and competition.

Early in its history, George Herman "Babe" Ruth became one of the first true international celebrities due to the prowess of his play, but also because of his larger-than-life personality and the particular time in history that he was in the limelight. The world was looking for a hero. Even with his records being slowly eclipsed in the modern day, Ruth is still remembered as the face of baseball—the one who elevated the status of the game. He brought baseball and its rich history along with him and helped turn it into a glamorous pastime. He was one of the five inaugural Hall of Fame members. In that Hall, warriors from the field are enshrined in perpetuity with stories that rival those of courageous heroes of ancient battles—their memory is emblazoned upon the fans of the game.

Celebrating that richness are stories of courage, overcoming adversity, hope for the underdog, as well as tragedy and failure. In this book, we look at more than twenty-five stories of men who took the field and played a game to the joy of millions of fans. Arguments often occur between fans as to which player is the best, using statistics and the play that occurs on the field. *A Game of Extremes* attempts to reach beyond that boundary of baseball being just a "game of inches" to look deeper at the special moments created by the heroes, situations, and drama of the game.

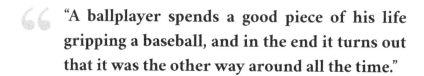 **"A ballplayer spends a good piece of his life gripping a baseball, and in the end it turns out that it was the other way around all the time."**

— JIM BOUTON

THE 168 MPH FASTBALL

Baseball has its share of myth and legend. People, to this day, argue whether Babe Ruth called his home run in Game 3 of the 1932 World Series by seemingly pointing to the fence before lifting a ball over it with his next swing. The shot gave the Yankees the lead in the game. They went on to win that game and the World Series. It was the Babe's last time in the fall classic and that moment of the "called shot" left an indelible mark on the history of the game. Ruth, himself, encouraged the claim by providing a voice-over for a newsreel where he says he pointed toward the fence and it was later confirmed by Lou Gehrig.[1] There is a point where much of myth and legend is based on fact, even if it is exaggerated.

Stories that we hear can be like a game of telephone,[2] where a message gets passed down a line of players and comes out the other end. The truth may be a lot different than the stories you hear.

One curious baseball story emerged in *Sports Illustrated*, released in late March for the April 1985 issue of the magazine, showcasing a baseball protégé that the New York Mets had signed. The prospect was a yoga master from Tibet who had the unprecedented ability to throw a baseball as fast as 168 mph with pinpoint accuracy. After the article was released, Mets' players were interviewed on major news stations corroborating the story and taking pictures of the locker that awaited his arrival between George Foster and Daryl Strawberry. The team's fans were overjoyed with the news and amazed at their good luck in finding such a rare star. They looked forward to the rookie taking the field to amass a string of victories where the opposing team barely had a chance to see the ball before it was by them.

On April 2, the Mets held a press conference in which they gave the sad news to fans that Sidd Finch, who obviously had an amazing career ahead of him, had decided to pursue his love of playing the French horn instead of baseball. On April 15, the details of the hoax were officially announced. There was no Sidd Finch. The whole Mets' organization had played along with the April Fool's joke—the official publication date of the magazine was indeed April 1. Despite the numerous absurdities in the article (he threw with one foot in a work boot and the other bare), no one saw through the hoax. The player who threw with unbelievable accuracy and speed was a complete fabrication played as an elaborate prank on the readers of the magazine. Because it was a respectable resource and long-standing sports publication, readers had no reason to question the story.

The stranger part of the story of Sidd Finch is that not everything about him can be considered a complete fabrication. His name, of course, was made up, as was his existence in reality as a pitcher; but, like all good stories, the myth has some basis in fact.

The October 1970 edition of *Sports Illustrated* had a story about a player who was touted by the coaches and players around him as the fastest flamethrower to ever take the field. Steve Dalkowski spent most of his professional pitching career in the minor league system of the Baltimore Orioles from 1957 to 1965.

Earl Weaver had the chance to manage him in the minor leagues. Weaver said definitively that Dalkowski was clearly faster than Nolan Ryan. There is a rumor that Ted Williams once stepped in the batter's box against him, saw one pitch. and said Dalkowski was the fastest pitcher he'd ever faced and he'd be damned if he ever stood in against him again.

Many players, coaches, and announcers have memories of facing or watching Dalkowski deliver the ball.

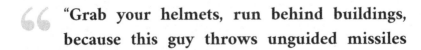 **"Grab your helmets, run behind buildings, because this guy throws unguided missiles**

and [even] he doesn't know where they're going."

— LOU BROCK

Part of the problem with Dalkowski's speed was that—unlike Sidd Finch—he lacked the pinpoint control that Finch was said to have. Over 956 innings in the minor leagues Dalkowski amassed an incredible 1,324 strikeouts, an average of 12.5 Ks per nine innings. That rivals the greatest strikeout pitchers of all time. The bigger problem was that he also walked 1,236 batters over that same number of innings and roughly twice as many batters as were able to get a hit off of him. It meant he almost always had at least one man on base.

Several things besides merely the speed contributed to Dalkowski's seeming inability to control where the ball went once it left his hand. Earl Weaver had Dalkowski's intelligence tested, but it is hard to say whether the score reflected his actual intelligence or that his inability to focus gave him no chance to do any better on the test. Weaver did recognize that Dalkowski would lose focus not only between innings or pitches but also as he was throwing the ball. As a means to keep Dalkowski focused, Weaver would take a bucket and bang on it to get his pitcher's head back in the game. Another contributing factor to Dalkowski's wildness may have had something to do with his propensity to drink to excess, even on the nights before ball games. Dalkowski admitted it may have had something to do with the downfall of his career.

But even with testaments from Weaver, Williams, and Brock, Dalkowski was never officially clocked on a radar gun. Using radar to measure pitches didn't come into vogue until the mid-'70s. Before that time it was a matter of relying on word of mouth, myth, and legend.

Cal Ripken Sr., father of the Hall of Famer Cal Ripken Jr., was a respected baseball man, coach, and minor-league catcher. Ripken Sr.'s playing time overlapped with Dalkowski's in the Orioles' farm system. He had the opportunity to catch Dalkowski along with other Oriole greats in the minor leagues such as Jim Palmer and Steve Barber. Ripken Sr. got to know him well enough to have respect for the velocity that was coming at him.

> "If you... put [him] on a radar gun today, I think that you'd probably see where Dalkowski threw the ball maybe 110, maybe 115 miles an hour."[3]
>
> — CAL RIPKEN SR.

Dalko was said to be the inspiration for Nuke LaLoosh in the movie *Bull Durham*, as well. LaLoosh was a hard and wild pitcher who lacked control of the ball. It is interesting that a minor league pitcher like Dalkowski would be used, not only as a character in a movie but also as inspiration for one of the biggest pranks in baseball history. It is strange that no one ever thought to turn a camera on Dalkowski to capture his motion just to study it and figure out what he was doing. Still, Dalkowski reigns as the inspiration for Sidd Finch and they both hold a seat, if not in Cooperstown,[4] in the annals of baseball lore.

---

1. In an audio clip from an October 6, 1932 episode of "The Fleischmann's Yeast Hour," Lou Gehrig confirmed the called shot.
2. Generally thought of a children's game, it demonstrates how a message can get scrambled when passing it from one person to the next in a line.
3. *Far From Home—The Steve Dalkowski Story*. https://youtu.be/ Kzh42wir_Ms
4. The location of the Baseball Hall of Fame in New York State, USA.

2

HOME RUNS WERE NO FUN

The ongoing power surge in baseball, counted as the number of home runs per year, is attributed to a lot of things. Some say the surge is happening because the players are better trained to hit a long ball. Some claim the ball is being progressively juiced. Some say that the speed pitchers now throw at contributes to the speed of the ball off the bat. Some opt for more obvious factors, like the fact that the season was extended[1] or that there are simply more teams and more players on the field.[2] In all, 2019 saw the greatest number of long balls coming in at 6,776—1,191 more than the previous year. It seems obvious that more than one factor is at play as there were no changes in the number of teams or games.

Changes seem to be adopted to thrill the fans who like to see home runs. But there was one familiar old-timer who didn't often agree with fans—or practically anyone else. He didn't much like losing and was responsible for creating chaos on the base paths. He spiked other players, fought with his own teammates, with umpires, and the police, and is rumored to have killed a man. In 1912, at a game where Detroit was playing the New York Highlanders, he rushed the stands to pummel a fan for shouting insults. But make sure you keep this in mind: Ty Cobb was so famous in his time that a lot of the things he was blamed for were actually done by other people. Some things that were said about Cobb were exaggeration or even pure fiction.[3]

The game of baseball was something Ty Cobb played with an intensity that has rarely been matched in modern-day ball. And although he played life just as hard, not all of his achievements or contempt are accurate depictions of the real man.

It is easy to create a myth when there is nothing to verify it. However, when you go by statistics that are verified by multiple reliable sources, it seems much harder to go wrong. Cobb has one achievement that is in one way or another indelible as it sits as one of many of his triumphs in the record books.

Cobb was not very happy with the new direction the game of baseball had taken since Babe Ruth came on the scene. As Cobb watched Ruth take batting practice once, he reportedly remarked:

"The old game is gone. I guess more people would rather see Babe hit one over the fence than see me steal second. I feel bad about it, for it isn't the game I like to see or play... A lot of these kids, in place of learning the true science of hitting or base running, are trying to knock every pitch over the fence."[4]

— TY COBB

The rumor that emerged from this quote was born as Cobb was sitting with a reporter before a game on May 5, 1925. Perhaps prompted for a response by the reporter, Cobb said: "I'll show you something today. I'm going for home runs for the first time in my career."[5] It seemed as if Cobb suggested that he could just flip a switch and turn on his power to crank the ball over the wall. He just didn't think home runs were as exciting as really playing the game. Here he was, already 38 years old, known more for his unparalleled batsmanship, and suddenly he declared he could become a power hitter at will.

Although the name of the reporter was not revealed beyond the note in Cobb's biography, it is hard to argue with the box scores. That day, on May 5, with his Detroit Tigers mired in a 4–14 slump, Cobb had one of the most memorable offensive games in the history of baseball. He went 6-for-6 with three home runs, a double, and two singles. But that was not the last of it. In the following game on May 6, he went 3-for-

6, collecting two more home runs and raising his season batting average to .526 in the process. Cobb went out and clubbed five home runs in two days, something the "Sultan of Swat"[6] never did in his career. It seemed to make the statement that if all fans wanted was home runs, Cobb could hit them practically at will, but the game wasn't going to be as much fun. To say whether that was strictly fun for himself or the fans would be conjecture.

In all, during the 1925 season, Cobb hit a total of only twelve home runs. That is only seven more over the other 138 games he played in that season and none were multi-homer games. It seems such a coincidence that he hit the bulk of his home runs in a period of two games. About 40 percent of the home runs he hit in his career were inside-the-ballpark. Every one of the five home runs hit over those two days went over the fence. It could simply be that he wanted to single-handedly raise his team out of its slump or live up to his boastful prediction. All you have to do is look up the box scores from the games to confirm that it happened, and the boast clearly seems in line with his result.

———————————————

1. From 1904 to 1960 (AL) and 1961 (NL), teams played 154 games. Both added expansion teams and increased the season to 162 games.
2. There has been an ongoing expansion in the number of franchises since the beginning of baseball history. The last expansion, from twenty-eight to thirty teams, was in 1998. The American League expanded to fourteen teams in 1977, and the National League followed sixteen years later in 1993.

3. Cobb's biography by Al Stump was released almost immediately after his death and researchers say that it contains many fallacies.
4. Grantland Rice quoting Cobb in Rice's 1954 autobiography *The Tumult and the Shouting.*
5. Cited in Charles C. Alexander's biography of Cobb, *Ty Cobb.*
6. Another Babe Ruth nickname. There are many.

DON'T LOOK BACK, SOMETHING MIGHT BE GAINING ON YOU

Many players throughout the history of the game have had long careers. Most of these players started their pro careers at early ages and not all of them were stars. Others, perhaps, were not ready to give up the game simply for the love of it.

The fact that aging normally affects performance would make you think that anyone who started a career in their 30s was destined to be a short-lived prospect. But a prospect breaking in as a rookie at the age of 42 would certainly be a relic waiting to be put on the shelf. After all, most players retire before they are 40.

Leroy Robert "Satchel" Paige was a truly unique character. In a career that spanned from 1927 in the Negro leagues to his debut as an MLB player in 1948, and into his final appearance in 1965, Paige stayed in the game for as long as anyone.[1] In his final appearance at the age of 59, Paige sat in the bullpen in a rocking chair being served coffee by his nurse. The running joke was that no one really knew how old he was. In that last start for the Kansas City Athletics, Paige went three scoreless innings giving up just one hit to the Boston Red Sox icon Carl Yastrzemski.

 "Age is a case of mind over matter. If you don't mind, it don't matter."

— SATCHEL PAIGE

Part of Paige's longevity was his showmanship which made his appearances extravagant and exaggerated like the antics of a circus performer. He attracted crowds for barnstorming games[2] that filled stadiums around the US as they traveled from place to place playing teams in non-league scrimmages.

His windmill windups were a flurry of arms and legs that ended with his high leg kick and delivery. But, from pitch to pitch he varied his arm angles, sometimes hesitating at various points in his delivery. He might windmill three times on one pitch and not the next to sneak in a quick pitch. At times he'd come set with his hands above his head and just freeze. In his stride forward he would sometimes land hard and delay his forward arm movement. It's been reported that he'd even bear down like he was coming with a fastball and just hold the ball as it wrapped around his back and float it in toward the plate. He always had the ability to throw hard and put the ball where he wanted just about every time.

He used these antics in his delivery to intentionally throw off a batter's timing. His windup was practically the opposite of the monotonous, consistent mechanics that is drilled into the head of modern-day pitchers who are taught efficiency and simplify every step of their motion to get the ball where they want it to go. Paige's delivery was anything but simple and efficient. His hesitation pitch[3] became somewhat notorious as being so unconventional that players and coaches thought it must have been illegal. When brought to the attention of American League President Will Harridge, he declared that the hesitation pitch would be charged as a balk. As a balk could only hurt with runners on base, Paige continued with his antics and deceptive deliveries.

 "I never threw an illegal pitch. The trouble is, once in a while I toss one that ain't never been seen by this generation."

— SATCHEL PAIGE

Ted Williams faced Paige once, only managing a .222 batting average in 11 at-bats, frustrating the batting master. The great hitter found the pitcher's unconventional approach confounding and could recall the one time that Paige struck him out. After Paige got two strikes on Williams, Williams watched carefully to try to pick up what was coming on the next pitch. As Paige started into a double windup, he lifted his hands up behind his head where Williams (and everyone else in the ballpark) could see them and turned his wrist tipping off that the next pitch was going to be his curveball. Williams got ready to swing at the curve and a fraction of a second later couldn't turn on the ball when Paige uncorked a fastball. Paige being the ultimately confident showman said to Williams: "You ought to know better than to guess with ol' Satch."

Paige's trickery was something he developed using a creative mind and his extensive experience. Success with his deliveries only led to more experiments and tools to add to his articles of deception. According to Paige, he probably pitched over 2,500 games in his career and won 2,000 of them. The claim is really impossible to verify because of the number of years he played, suspect record keeping in some leagues (when records were even kept), and the fact that not every appearance he made was scheduled. He played baseball like a rogue and a vagabond, filling in holes in his contracts and schedule by playing in other leagues and barnstorming. He never considered resting his arm to be important like they do in modern times.

"I sure get [my] laughs when I see in the papers where some major league pitcher says he gets a sore arm because he's overworked, and he pitches every four days. Man, that'd be a vacation for me."

— SATCHEL PAIGE

This mild-mannered clown, showman, craftsman, and magician of the pitching mound was a philosopher as well. The length of his career, long bus rides, and the time he spent in reform school[4] allowed him to be introspective. He used the time to learn about pitching and about himself. While some youths might consider that time as stolen from their childhood, Paige believed it was responsible for his success.

 "I traded five years of freedom to learn how to pitch. At least I started my real learning on the Mount.[5] They were not wasted years at all. It made a real man out of me."

— SATCHEL PAIGE

His confidence showed on the mound. It is widely rumored that during games in the Negro leagues, Paige would sometimes call in his outfielders to have a rest and get ready to hit while he finished off the opposing team on his own. While that is easier to believe for a single inning of a regular-season game, Paige's favorite recollection was of a Negro league World Series game in 1942.

According to Paige in his autobiography,[6] he came into Game 2 of the series when the Monarchs led the Grays by two runs. Paige got two outs and let up a triple to the Monarchs' lead-off man, Jerry Benjamin. Paige huddled with his manager and decided to load the bases by walking the next two batters to face the most feared bat in all of the Negro leagues: Josh Gibson. Gibson was known as the Black Babe Ruth and later was a Hall of Fame inductee alongside Paige. This could have been a strategic move to create a force at every base, or just for the sake of the show. But Paige had shown good success against Gibson in the past, so it could be that he saw facing him as an advantage. He went on to intentionally walk two batters as planned, and then up stepped Gibson.

Paige taunted Gibson by telling him what he was going to throw and where he was going to target each pitch with phrases like: "this one's gonna be a pea at your knee." Three pitches later, the mighty Gibson had struck out.

Though published in books and well-publicized, that bit of lore was later debunked by researchers.[7] It seems that Paige had merged parts of two stories and gotten them both wrong. He did face Gibson in that series in the seventh with the bases loaded and two out. After the first batter got out, Paige let up a single—a fielder's choice—and then two more singles to load the bases. When Gibson stepped up, it is likely Paige faced him with confidence, but the news reports mention nothing of taunting. However, in another game that season Paige did walk the batter in front of Gibson with a man on second and two out to induce a weak fly ball. As the autobiography was written twenty years after the event, it is easy to see how the showman in Paige preferred the better story to the right one. In any case, he did beat Gibson both times, so in the win and loss column, the difference doesn't matter. In the end, the myth seems so much more like the man.

One of Satchel's claims to greatness was indeed his ability to stay young and experience a superbly long career. His character and charisma are probably part of the reason for his myth and legend. The true test of that is the observation of his fellow teammates and opposing players who attest to his greatness. It is the reason he was the first Negro league inductee to the Hall of Fame.

Paige left behind a set of six simple rules that he said he lived by to enhance his longevity and life-long success. You may find them useful as you journey through life.

Satchel Paige's Six Rules for Staying Young

1. Avoid fried meats, which angry up the blood.
2. If your stomach disputes you, lie down and pacify it with cool thoughts.

3. Keep the juices flowing by jangling around gently as you move.

4. Go very light on vices such as carrying on in society. The social ramble ain't restful.

5. Avoid running at all times.

6. Don't look back, something may be gaining on you.

---

1. Minnie Minoso, Nick Altrock, and Charlie O'Leary also made guest appearances in MLB games in their later 50s. But Paige currently holds the record for being the oldest active player.
2. A form of traveling exhibition game usually with a hand-selected and star studded team.
3. Paige named some of his pitches and the associated deliveries. Most of them were fastballs.
4. He was sentenced to six years in reform school at the age of 12. Various sources report different reasons, but the most popular notion seems to be that it was for petty larceny.
5. Refers to the location of the reform school in Mount Meigs, Alabama.
6. Paige's autobiography is *Maybe I'll Pitch Forever.*
7. The debunk: https://www.baseball-reference.com/bullpen/1942_Negro_World_Series

4

JAKEY, THE SAUERKRAUT-FACED BOOB

In a day where large shepherd hooks were used to drag acts being pummeled with rotting vegetables off the stage, there lived a jakey,[1] sauerkraut-faced boob[2] who aspired to be in vaudeville. While his bawdy and sour jokes often failed to fill the air with applause and laughter from an audience, he achieved some success on the vaudeville circuit and was not alone in a group of baseball players who turned to the stage to fill out their offseason. His antics on the field and his skills as a multi-positional player did win him praise. He played second fiddle to a famous group of players known as the greatest double-play combination in baseball. He was the odd man out playing alongside the infamous Tinker, Evers, and Chance, whose induction into the Hall of Fame by the "Old-Timers' Committee" left some wondering exactly what the criteria were for being enshrined.

Apparently, some purists did not think it only required having someone remember you in a song.

But if fame could come from a song, it might also arise from a player's ability to entertain a crowd. The plethora of stories that follow in Herman "Germany" Schaefer's wake are stacked so high that it was difficult to know if they were true or just another instance where his over-active imagination ran wild. His mind was always tuned to humor, both on and off the field. It ran the gamut of pranks from the simple to the elaborate.

The incorrigible prankster is charged with throwing his own shoes out the window of a train. He thought he was pulling a stunt on a compartment-mate, having mistaken whose shoes were whose as they rode on through the darkness. When it rained on a game that an umpire refused to call, he walked onto the field in a raincoat and galoshes to hint that it might be time to stop play. A similar thought crossed his mind when stars began to peek out of a twilight sky at old Wrigley Field when he appeared on the field in the light of a lantern. Wrigley didn't have lights on the field until August 8, 1988, so he was clearly ahead of his time.

The winning moments for this clown star were when he earned undeniably memorable achievements. One instance was so infamous that a new rule was created in the official rule book. Another was the rival of a famous at-bat by Babe Ruth. A third was so clever that he won his entire team an extra payday.

Schaefer showed how his mind worked on the serious as well as the absurd at the start of the 1907 World Series. Under the rules at the time, players shared in the gate receipts of the first four games. Schaefer, then captain of the Tigers, thought about what might happen in the unlikely scenario of a tie. He brought up the possibility to officials, wanting to know if the players would be entitled to a share of the fifth game. His reasoning was that the rules called for a game to be played over again if the result was a tie due to rainout or darkness. The issue had never come up before as there had never been a tie game in World Series play. Thinking that the odds of a tie were practically nil, the officials agreed with Schaefer. On the following day, the Tigers and Cubs played to a 3–3 tie in front of the largest crowd to watch a game up until that date. Both teams enjoyed the extra share of the gate.

One Ruthian play that has been well-debated is the Babe's called shot. Some believed it turned from myth to legend after Ruth made the claim he called the shot and Lou Gehrig backed him up. But one player called a shot that was never in dispute, and it was the merry Germany Schaefer. He had been sidelined since May 26 of 1906 after injuring his thumb and was relegated to the coaching box where he took the opportunity to entertain the fans. Down to the final out and losing 2 to 1 with a man on first. The Tiger's pitcher was the next one scheduled to bat. Red Donahue was not particularly known for his batting prowess having hit a mighty .123 that season, so the Tigers manager called on Schaefer to pinch-hit as the White Sox fans began filing out of the stadium.

Catcalls and mockery rained down on Schaefer who had been taunting the crowd himself from the coach's box all game. Before stepping into the batter's box Schaefer turned to the crowd and, according to teammate Davy Jones, he bellowed in his best theatrical voice:

> **"Ladies and gentlemen, you are now looking at Herman Schaefer, better known as "Herman the Great," acknowledged by one and all to be the greatest pinch-hitter in the world. I am now going to hit the ball into the left-field bleachers. Thank you."[3]**
>
> — GERMANY SCHAEFER

Although it seemed completely unlikely for a player who hit a total of nine home runs in his fifteen-year career, Schaefer promptly sent the first pitch over the left-field wall. As he rounded the bases Schaefer called his progress around the diamond like a horse race. He slid into each bag hamming it up in a way that probably would have gotten the opposing team to do some head-hunting in his next at-bat in the modern day. As he crossed home he slid in, leaped to his feet, and shouted "Schaefer wins by a nose!" and then kindly thanked his audience for their attention. The homer had put the Tigers ahead and they stayed there to the great dismay of the Sox fans who had returned to their seats. Although this was the only home run Schaefer called, it is said that he called other hits during his career. He was said to often be wrong, but accuracy isn't anything if you are a legend for getting one right.

 "Nobody remembers those times, they only remember when you're right."[4]

— DAVE NIEHAUS

His antics were indeed admirable on and off the field, but the one play he instigated that was cause for a change in the rule book is probably the best known. It was August 4, 1911—the first game of a double-header. Schaefer became one of the few professional baseball players to ever be recognized for stealing first base. Sort of. According to the box score, he was only credited with one steal in that game; it must have been great confusion for everyone involved, including the official scorer.

With the score tied 0–0 in the bottom of the ninth and two out, Schaefer was on first and Clyde Milan on third. Schaefer broke for second hoping to draw a throw from the White Sox catcher, but Fred Payne did not take the bait. With the winning run on third, there was no reason to try and nab Schaefer at second. Having failed to draw a throw, Schaefer apparently called out to Milan saying they should try it again. On the next pitch, Schaefer broke for first, again disappointed not to have drawn a throw.

The White Sox manager came out to complain about the shenanigans on the base paths and as the manager was arguing with the umpire, Schaefer broke for second again. This time he drew a throw and got into the rundown he was looking for. Milan took advantage of the confusion and the rundown but was tagged out on the throw to the plate and the game went into extra innings.[5] A lesson to be learned is that if it is not specifically disallowed in the rule book, it is an option during play.

Herman "Germany" Schaefer permanently left his mark on the game as the legend who stole first base with what was officially known as Rule 52, Section 2, which states:

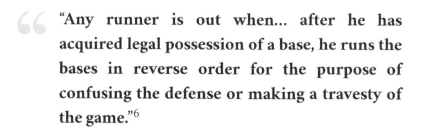

> **"Any runner is out when... after he has acquired legal possession of a base, he runs the bases in reverse order for the purpose of confusing the defense or making a travesty of the game."[6]**
>
> **— OFFICIAL BASEBALL RULES**

---

1. At the turn of the twentieth century, this was a term used to describe a chronic alcoholic. "Jake" refers specifically to methylated spirits.
2. The unfortunate subject of this story suffered from smallpox scarring, and he was often called a "sauerkraut-faced boob" by hecklers.
3. Lawrence Ritter, *The Glory of Their Times*.

4. Hall of Fame baseball announcer.

5. Various accounts of the story differ. Some claim Schaefer pulled the stunt more than once. Supposedly, the first time was May 30, 1907, when Detroit was playing at Cleveland and it was successful. Schaefer was credited for a stolen base in both the 1907 and 1911 games, and both were 1 to 0 games that went into extra innings, so if the play occurred in the bottom of the ninth it failed both times. Further problems arise in the story claiming the play was a success is that Schaefer's team lost in 1907 and won in 1911. If the play was successful in 1907 Schaefer's team would have won; if the play was successful in 1911, it would have had to occur in the eleventh inning. No other player on Schaefer's team was credited with a steal on those dates, so a successful outcome is likely a stretch of reality. Milan did score the winning run in 1911, it just was not likely via a stolen base unless the official scorer did not give Milan a stolen base because of an error on the play. The version used here most closely resembles what was also recounted in both the *Washington Post* and the *Chicago Tribune*.

6. Rule 5.09(b)(10) of the Official Baseball Rules: http://mlb.mlb.com/mlb/official_info/official_rules/foreword.jsp

5

TEN TONS OF GUACAMOLE AND A SAMURAI SWORD

S ome baseball players are odd because they try to be. Others are just naturally gifted in the art of eccentricity. Players don't have to be from the early 1900s to claim the right to peculiar notions and colorful personalities. Maybe when you are a star and you play a game in front of a camera where your every word has a chance to come off with a twist, you have more opportunity to seem different. Or maybe you just are.

In 2004, a player who would later go on to win six Gold Gloves, play in the All-Star game six times, earn two Silver Slugger awards, a Cy Young, and win the ERA title twice was called into the Kansas City Royals office at their Triple-A affiliate. The 20-year-old was informed that they were sending him to the big league club—the dream of every minor league player was just dropped in his lap. The young player paused a moment contemplating the news and then said to his manager:

> "I don't know. Do you think if we asked them, they would let me go back to Single-A and be a shortstop? I think I can be a pretty good shortstop."
>
> — ZACK GREINKE

The idea took his manager aback. It would not be the strangest thing Greinke said or did in the career that has him edging close to the Hall of Fame as a pitcher. His manager encouraged him to take the opportunity.

It seemed Greinke wanted what he had in high school: a chance to play every day and keep himself occupied. In his own words, he doesn't think hitting is that hard. He was, after all, a .400 hitter in high school and had only turned into a pitcher in his senior year. That's when he started turning heads with his arm to the tune of a 0.55 ERA in sixty-three innings with 118 Ks.

The Royals took him sixth overall in the draft as a pitcher who had only logged those sixty-three innings. Instead of playing all the time, he was filled with doubts about his career choice. Along with that grew a latent and crippling anxiety that came on him so badly that he considered quitting the game for good. He didn't want to be around people anymore and preferred being in nature.

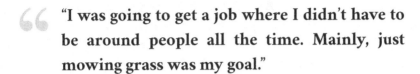
"I was going to get a job where I didn't have to be around people all the time. Mainly, just mowing grass was my goal."

— ZACK GREINKE

It turned out Greinke was suffering from social anxiety disorder. Some people with the condition go a lifetime without being diagnosed or treated. Even things that were once a great joy are no longer stimulating for those with the condition. The fear it can bring on is crippling, and it nearly ended his career. His managers saw that something was wrong. They sent him home to seek treatment and after treatment he was able to rekindle his love for the game. Then he set about becoming the best player he could be. Like in everything else, he adopted a burning sense of competition, became a student of pitching, and developed his talents. He seems to have settled back into his body in a way that lets his personality flourish.

He grew into a player that people think can do just about anything he wants to with a baseball. He can tell batters what is coming and they still can't handle what he throws. He is a player who has already made over $300 million dollars in his career, and it was because he came back with hope.

> **"Hope is a good thing, maybe the best of things, and no good thing ever dies."**[1]

— ANDY, *SHAWSHANK REDEMPTION*

Some think that Greinke has become as famous for his quirks as for his play. Before signing a record-breaking contract with Arizona for $206 million over six years—an average of a little over $34 million a year—the curious things were the reported riders. The team and Greinke's agent haggled for weeks over the terms before hammering them out in one day. It made no sense to Greinke why they couldn't just go in a room and get it done the first time. The complications may have to do with how unusual the rider requests were. The contract reportedly includes the following:

- Ten tons of free, high-quality guacamole
- Minority stake in one Chipotle franchise
- *The Shawshank Redemption* on Blu-Ray
- At least five games per year as a position player
- Samurai swords[2]

These are the kinds of demands that an event organizer might expect from a rock star. Perhaps in a way he has become one to the fans who love the way he plays the game. His response, when asked about the restaurant and guacamole, made Greinkian sense. He was upset that they had raised the prices $0.30 on the menu item from $1.50 so that the guacamole which he already thought was overpriced now set him back $1.80. Never mind trying to tell him about the millions he is making. Even with pricing food on menus, Greinke needs to compete.

> **"I don't really love the guacamole... It's not about the guacamole itself, I just don't want to let them win."**
>
> — ZACK GREINKE

It may confuse some people to follow the curvy lines of logic. For example, winning the Cy Young may have played a part in Greinke's request for samurai swords. When he received the actual award, he wasn't as impressed as he was with the gift Mizuno gave him. He gave the award to his parents, as he had always done with his awards.

> **"I've only kept one award in my whole life, and it's the coolest thing ever. Mizuno gave me a samurai sword for winning the Cy Young. It's awesome... It's got a hanger thing and everything. I'm going to hang it up and, maybe, start a collection. Not a gun collection, but a samurai sword collection."**
>
> — ZACK GREINKE

Greinke is a very giving guy. He shares his trophies like he shares his knowledge with other players, especially when he thinks he can help his team. Once, when rookie Alex Gordon was having trouble at the plate, Greinke offered to help the youngster out. Gordon accepted the offer. Greinke was a pitcher, but he had to know something about hitting. Didn't he?

They went off to the video room where Gordon expected Greinke to reveal a great secret that would get him out of his funk. Greinke popped in a favorite video of his fourth at-bat in the major leagues. During that at-bat, he hit his first MLB home run. He played it for Gordon several times without saying anything then he said: "Do more of that."

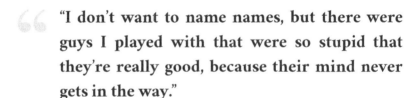

> **"I don't want to name names, but there were guys I played with that were so stupid that they're really good, because their mind never gets in the way."**
>
> — ZACK GREINKE

In a way, that may seem like a session that would have done Gordon absolutely no good. But maybe it was Greinke's own unique way of communicating to Gordon that he was over-thinking at the plate. It seems you can never tell with Greinke.

1. One of Zack Greinke's favorite films.
2. Taken from an official announcement by Major League Baseball: https://www.mlb.com/cut4/zack-greinke-signs-with-arizona-diamondbacks/c-158874402

6

THE STEAK AND POTATO OF
RETIRED NUMBERS

Ace Bailey was a hockey player who doesn't belong in a book on baseball. That is except for one unprecedented achievement. He was the first professional sports player to have his number retired (number 6). Retiring a number has since become the ideal way to honor a player. It may be for their contributions and achievements as a player, sometimes as a marker of a career cut tragically short, and usually stands as a symbol of respect, pride, and emotion. Usually.

The first number ever retired in baseball was number 4, belonging to baseball's Iron Horse. Lou Gehrig played 2,130 straight games before taking himself out of the Yankees lineup as he felt his capabilities as a player had diminished too much to continue to play. The date that his number was retired, July 4, 1939, is one that any true baseball fan remembers as the day the fading star gave his speech.

 "Today, I consider myself the luckiest man on the face of the earth... I might have been given a bad break, but I've got an awful lot to live for"

— LOU GEHRIG

The day was an emotional outpouring for a great star and competitor that happened to fall under the shadow of Babe Ruth but rose to his own immortality in the sport.

This chapter could well be full of great heroes, and here we find Dave Bresnahan. This career minor leaguer was a backup catcher with a minuscule batting average, but he managed to have his number, 59, retired by the Williamsport Bills in 1987. The Bills were Cleveland's Double-A farm team, and four retired numbers hang on the outfield fence at Bowman Field. You might think this is a lackluster background for a player to achieve the honor of having his number retired. It does seem that way.

Maybe it had something to do with his baseball heritage, which is significant. His great-uncle Roger Bresnahan was a Hall of Famer who had a long playing and managerial career. Also a catcher, he worked behind the plate as battery mate to Christy

Mathewson[1] and was the first catcher inducted to the Hall. He was instrumental in incorporating shin guards and batting helmets into the game as an innovator in player protection. But, certainly pedigree isn't enough to see your number retired.

Here is how it happened.

In the second game of a double-header on August 31 in 1987 against the Reading Phillies, Bresnahan had the opportunity to play in a game rather than warm his usual spot on the bench. In the fifth inning, the opposing team had a player reach second with only one out. For some reason, Bresnahan was calling breaking balls and change-ups as if to induce a ground ball to the right side of the infield. Not a typical strategy if you want to win a game by keeping the runners from advancing. But, with only a few weeks to play and the Bills some twenty-eight games out without a chance to get back in the race, winning wasn't the only thing on Bresnahan's mind.

After successfully helping the other team advance their runner to third, Bresnahan called a time out for an equipment malfunction. He claimed that his mitt was damaged and he needed to get his backup from the dugout. He trotted off the field and returned a moment later and got in his crouch. He called a slider low and away off the plate and tried to pick the runner off third as he had against the same team a few games ago. Even though the throw was good, it somehow got by the third baseman and went on into left field. The runner on third, thinking that the ball had gotten away, started to dash toward home.

Bresnahan stepped up to the runner flying in from third and reached out to tag him before he reached the plate. He revealed the ball in his glove to the runner and the umpire and started to make his way off the field having manufactured the last out of the inning.

Lots of confusion emerged at that moment. The third-base umpire went into the outfield and retrieved what he knew went flying by him. He lifted it up and yelled out: "It's a *[expletive]* potato!" Bresnahan had schemed to carve a potato to look like a baseball and fool everyone on the field—except his teammates, who already knew about the gag.

The umpire behind the plate was being evaluated that day by a supervisor in the stands, and he was pretty unhappy to have a situation where he had to make a call that wasn't in the rule book. He was sure the section on deceptively substituting a ball with a potato was missing. However, Rule 8.01 (c) covers pretty much every other instance not already accounted for in the rule book:

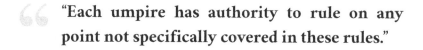

> **"Each umpire has authority to rule on any point not specifically covered in these rules."**

The umpire made his decision and chose to let the runner score. Bresnahan's manager pulled him from the game immediately and fined him $50. The next day the team released him and he never played another game in pro ball. With his release, Bresnahan saw no reason to pay the fine to a team for who he no longer played. Instead, he bought two sacks of potatoes, dumped them on his former manager's desk, and left behind a note.

"Of course you don't expect me to pay the $50 fine, but here's at least 50 potatoes. This spud's for you."

— DAVE BRESNAHAN

While the current management was pretty distressed with his behavior, the team's new General Manager, Rick Muntean had a very different view. The Williamsport Bills held "Dave Bresnahan Potato Night" in 1988 where the play was reenacted and Dave's number was retired in front of 2,734 fans who each paid $1 and a potato to get in. It was the second-highest attendance of the season.

"Baseball purists ask why he made a travesty of the game. But we think Dave did something that is the essence of baseball—he had fun with it. At a time when the business of baseball dominates the headlines, he brought baseball back to the field."

— RICK MUNTEAN

The saddest part of this story is the true history of spud substitution. It could be that Dave Bresnahan thought he was being unique, but he himself may have heard hand-me-down stories from his great-uncle about players who had pulled off spud tricks long before. There is a story from the *Dallas Morning News* in 1895 (coincidentally in Williamsport) that reports of a potato being put in play in a game between the Williamsporters and Lock Haven by a pitcher who duped a runner at first base into trying to take second by throwing a spud wide of first on a pick-off. The ump called the player out, but the Williamsporters protested the play and the game ended.[2]

In 1889, a player on the Staten Island Athletic Club attempted a similar play in a game against Yale. The runner was successfully put out, but the player was asked to resign from the Athletic Club.[3] Umpire Bill Klem called it "an old gag." Regardless of the age of the prank, in a D-League Lafayette White Sox game in 1934, a catcher did the same exact maneuver as Bresnahan, throwing the "ball" over the third baseman's head, then tagging out the runner with the real ball he had in his glove.[4]

Regardless if he was aware of the play from stories handed down through the pedigree of generations, Bresnahan is the man who was honored by having his number retired for just one play in his otherwise lackluster career. His own words close the story well.

"Lou Gehrig had to play in 2,130 consecutive games and hit .340 for his number to be retired, and all I had to do was bat .140 and throw a potato."

— DAVE BRESNAHAN

---

1. Hall of Famer, considered one of the best pitchers of all time.
2. Peter Morris, *A Game of Inches: The Stories behind the Innovations That Shaped Baseball.*
3. H. Allen Smith and Ira L. Smith, *Low and Inside.*
4. Also from the book by Peter Morris.

7

LEGEND OF SURPRISE WITH DOMINANCE

The record for most consecutive batters hit by a pitch is three. One pitcher did it within his eleven-pitch start on May 1, 1974, in the first five pitches of the game. In fact, he almost hit Pete Rose with the last warm-up pitch as he stood looking on from outside the batter's box. It took two pitches to hit Pete Rose, one to hit Joe Morgan, and two more to hit Dan Driessen. He followed that with a four-pitch walk to Tony Perez which found Perez dodging balls all aimed at him. The walk knocked in a run and put the Reds in the lead. When Johnny Bench came up, he dodged two pitches thrown close to his head.

Danny Murtaugh, manager of the Pittsburgh Pirates, came out to talk to his pitcher and when he had no excuse for being so wild, decided to take him out of the game.

Now that might be the type of performance you might expect if a pitcher was extremely impaired or suddenly found himself with the yips. Eleven pitches to five batters, none of them strikes, and apparently, the pitcher was unable to control where the ball was going—except that it kept going directly at the hitters. It seems especially true that the performance was unusual for a pitcher who normally showed good control.

Such a poor performance might be what you would have expected to happen for a player when he was high or drunk and then went out and pitched a game anyway. In reality, the pitcher Murtaugh removed from the game had vowed that he would hit as many Reds in his May 4 start as possible days before he took the field. He looked at the Reds as the arch enemies of the Pirates, and he wanted to show them who was boss.

> "I've pitched some good games at Cincinnati, but the majority I've lost, because I feel like we weren't aggressive... We gonna get down. We gonna do the do. I'm going to hit these motherfuckers."[1]

> — DOCK ELLIS

Dock had simply gone out to knock down the opposing batters one after the next to put the fear back into the games they had against the Reds. It was a plan he put in place and his control was practically impeccable. It just wasn't accurate according to the typical rules of balls and strikes. The performance was to the score of Ellis' own concerto.

Let's say you take this same pitcher and put him on the mound when he is actually impaired and high on LSD and Benzedrine. It seems impossible that a pitcher could navigate through the effects of hallucinogenics and speed while pitching a game. But that's just what Ellis did on July 12, 1970.

By his own admission, he never took the field without being high. He also claimed that the majority of players in the league took the field with some level of Dexamyl in their system. It was the stimulant of choice in those days, used as a performance enhancer.

> "I was so used to medicating myself. That's the way I was dealing with the feeling of failure. I pitched every game in the major leagues under the influence of drugs... It was just a part of the game, you know? You get to themajor leagues and you say 'I got to stay here. What do I need?"
>
> — DOCK ELLIS

The day Dock pitched on LSD and "benzos," started on June 10—two days before his scheduled start. Ellis went to visit a friend in Los Angeles after a game in San Francisco because the team had the next day off. By his account, he dropped some acid at the airport in anticipation that the dose would hit him just when he was where he wanted to be. It is unclear if he partook in other drugs or alcohol over the next day, but that would explain his strange response to his friend's wife on the afternoon of the 12th.[2] Still at his friend's house, his host reminded Ellis he needed to get to the ballpark because he had to pitch that evening. He was sure she was wrong and that it was still the 11th. He had another whole day before he was scheduled, and told her she was crazy. She grabbed the newspaper and brought him the sports page. It seems our hero had lost all track of time. To make matters worse, he had already taken some more acid when he awoke that morning. Being two in the afternoon with game time at six, all he knew was he had better get to the airport.

He arrived ninety minutes before the first pitch and was still quite high from the LSD he had taken that morning. He went to visit a lady in the stands who had a "pretty little gold pouch." She was his golden fairy in the stands who used to always supply him with Benzedrine, another stimulant, when he came to play in San Diego. After he got what he went to see the good fairy for, he downed the pills before he reached the dugout, adding a more typical dose of speed to his lingering acid experience. He started to feel elated from the pills just in time for the team to take the field.

"[I am sure] the opposing team and my team-mates knew I was high but they didn't know what I was high on. They had no idea what LSD was other than what they see on TV with the hippies."

— DOCK ELLIS

Ellis claimed that when the game started that evening there was a fine mist in the air that lasted all through the game. The historic weather report doesn't agree.[3] When he looked where the catcher was supposed to be, Ellis couldn't see the hitters, let alone the signs. All he could tell was if there was a batter on the right or left side of the plate. The catcher put reflective tape on his fingers so Ellis could see the signals.

Whenever he recounted his drug-induced experience to various writers, his consistent memory was that he could only remember bits and pieces of the game. He had a distinct feeling of euphoria. At times he couldn't feel the ball. When he could, the ball was sometimes too small or too large. Sometimes he saw the catcher, and sometimes he didn't. The chewing gum in his mouth felt like it turned into powder. Richard Nixon took over calling balls and strikes as the home plate umpire. Jimmy Hendricks came to bat holding a guitar to take his turn at the plate.

There were times when the ball was hit back at Ellis and he jumped because he saw it coming at him fast. Every time the catcher threw the ball back it was so big he had to use two hands. One time he had to cover first base on a grounder to the right side and he probably surprised himself by not getting lost on the way. He ran the play perfectly, catching the ball and tagging the base all in one motion. Then he said: "Oooh, I just made a touchdown."

> "I didn't pay no attention to the score, you know. I'm trying to get the batters out. I'm throwing a crazy game. I'm hitting people, walking people, throwing balls in the dirt, they're going everywhere."
>
> — DOCK ELLIS

The Pirates had a rookie on the team at that time named Dave Cash. After the first inning Cash teased Ellis saying he had a no-hitter. Around the fourth inning, Cash said it again. The rookie should have known better and sensed, like Ellis did, that the other players wanted Cash to shut up. It's a superstition that you are not supposed to say anything if somebody's throwing a no-hitter.

Ellis finished the wild outing with 8 walks, 6 strikeouts, and one hit batsman; he let up three stolen bases, but even with all those base runners, he didn't let up a run. Willie Stargell commanded all of the offense with 2 solo home runs, and the Pirates won 2 to 0. But that was it. No balks. No wild pitches. Oh, and the Padres didn't manage a hit all game. Ellis pitched his one and only no-no on LSD.

Ellis claims he never used LSD during the baseball season again, but still used amphetamines. He later admitted to regretting being so high that day because it robbed him almost entirely of any memory of his greatest professional performance.

One curious quote by fellow teammate Al Oliver suggests that if Dave Bresnahan deserves his number retired for pegging a potato into left field, Ellis deserves something even greater.

 "I know this: if you can pitch a no-hitter on LSD, you should be in Cooperstown."

— AL OLIVER

---

1. Quoted from two different parts of Donald Hall's, *Dock Ellis in the Country of Baseball.*
2. It is hard to believe that there is a credible report from anyone if Ellis could not remember the entirety of June 11, and he is the one mostly responsible for reporting the story.
3. According to weather history there was no mist or precipitation on the date of the no-hitter. https://www.wunderground.com/history/daily/KPIT/date/1970-7-12

8

BASEBALL'S NAMELESS HEROES AND HYPOCRITES

M ythic heroes sometimes draw attention to themselves by attempting to outperform the gods. The gods then typically throw a hissy-fit and subject the daring heroes to scrutiny because no human can be like a god.

However, heroes still dare to challenge the gods as if they don't know what is coming. The typical hero is endowed with powers lesser than the gods but far greater than typical human abilities. In order to get these powers they turn to PEDs[1] as if they were PEZ.[2]

Heroes have goals. Odysseus[3] battled with the gods and other beasts in order to end up in epic poems and celebrated in songs so that people remembered his name. The real message is to step up and risk your life so people make movies about you after you are dead.

> "*Messenger Boy:* **The Thessalonian you're fighting. He's the biggest man I've ever seen. I wouldn't want to fight him.**
>
> *Achilles:* **That's why no-one will remember your name.**"
>
> — FROM THE 2004 MOVIE, *TROY*

Greek gods, in particular, can be colossal jerks. Tantalus, a demigod,[4] cooked up his son to serve at his father's dinner party. It was an unusual choice but he was tasked with cooking dinner and, considering the guest list, it would have been bad to screw it up. Maybe Tantalus burned the pig or goat or calf or whatever he was supposed to serve and the only thing handy was the kid. You get hired to cater a party to the gods and you need to step up.

When his daddy, Zeus, found out that his son served everyone "grandson fricassee," Zeus got a little pissed. He punished Tantalus by sending him to Hades for eternity to stand in a pool of water that he couldn't drink, with a fruit tree just out of his reach. The only thing Tantalus did was cook his son to fill his contractual obligation and make daddy's guests happy.

It turns out that the kid getting cooked was no big deal. The gods looked at the stew, got suspicious, found out what happened, and they just took the bits of grandson out of the stew and stuck him all back together as they might do with a jigsaw puzzle. Gods can do that sort of thing. A chunk of arm here, a little liver there, and voila. They resurrected Pelops (the grandson) and he got to hang around with Poseidon, learn how to drive the divine chariot, and he got to sport a really cool shoulder made of ivory. The shoulder had to be replaced because Demeter—some goddess invited to the grandson BBQ—ate the kid's shoulder absentmindedly while crying about losing her daughter. Weep, weep, weep. Apparently, you can't unchew a body part. Consider the replaced shoulder something like Tommy John surgery or bone chip removal.

You may start to see what all this blather about Greek gods being crazy has to do with baseball. Hypocrisy. In Greek mythology, that would be Hippocrates: the god of silence, secrets, and confidentiality. That's where "hypocrisy" comes from. Hypocrites claim to have all these high standards when part of what they "achieve" is keeping their mouths closed.

Unless you are some kind of baseball historian, you may never have heard of James Francis "Pud" Galvin.[5] The guy is in the Hall of Fame.[6] Pud won forty-six games in 1883 and 1884. That is not a total of forty-six games, which would be good enough. It is two years in a row winning forty-six games for a total of ninety-two wins. In each season he threw more than 630 innings. 1,260 innings in two years. That is a career for some Hall of Fame pitchers.[7]

In those two seasons he had more than seventy complete games, with over 140 complete games in two years. He ended his career with 365 wins, a 2.85 ERA, and more than 6,000 innings pitched in fifteen years. That's an average of 400 innings a year. Nolan Ryan, who is considered an iron man for playing baseball for twenty-seven years, came up about 400 innings short of Pud's total.

Just putting up those numbers made Pud a serious stud-muffin. If that kind of endurance and longevity came in a bottle, every player would be drinking it. Time to learn about Brown-Séquard Elixir.[8] The late 1800s were still the age of snake-oil salesmen. People went from town to town selling magic potions to cure what ailed you. This particular elixir was different than a lot of concoctions in that it was developed by an actual doctor through research. It was originally made from the testicles of guinea pigs and dogs and was supposed to prolong life, enhance energy, and preserve youth. How did you take it? By injection. What did you get from it? Testosterone. Testosterone is a PED. Taking PEDs is now illegal in baseball.

If that statement is setting off alarms in your head at the moment, it means that PEDs were being used in baseball at least as early as 1889. This is recognized by Pud's participation in using the elixir before a game where his team, the Pittsburgh Alleghenys, played the Boston Beaneaters on

Tuesday, August 13, 1889. The test was practically celebrated by the news.

> **"[Pud] Galvin was one of the subjects at a test of the Brown-Sequard Elixir at a medical college in Pittsburgh on Monday. If there still be doubting Thomases who concede no virtue of the elixir, they are respectfully referred to Galvin's record in yesterday's Boston-Pittsburgh game. It is the best proof yet furnished of the value of the discovery."**

— *THE WASHINGTON POST*, AUGUST 14, 1889

Galvin had openly participated in a test of the elixir. He took a shot in the thigh that contained testosterone. In that game, the day after the shot, Galvin pitched a two-hit shutout, winning 9 to 0, and was unusually successful at the plate hitting a double and a triple to help his own cause. His vitality had been failing since his dominance years before, and it appeared the elixir helped Galvin turn back the clock. He'd been looking for a way to get back to his heyday of '83 and '84 because in '88 and '89 he'd only been able to muster forty-six wins total—twenty-three two years in a row.

Some believe the result was psychosomatic and equivalent to the confidence gained from taking a miracle sugar pill. Galvin, *The Washington Post*, and more than 12,000 physicians who distributed Brown-Sequard's Elixir after the documented test probably believed in the effects. One thing was clear: after the test, everyone wanted to use the elixir, find something like it, or find something even better.

Even in the early 1900s, baseball players turned to cocaine and other substances that are on the current PED list to play to their potential. There were no rules against it. But baseball is not where performance enhancement started. Greek Olympians—the heroes of their time and gods on earth—used performance enhancers.[9]

> "The ancient Olympic champions were professionals who competed for huge cash prizes... Most forms of what we would call cheating were perfectly acceptable to them, save for game-fixing. There is evidence that they gorged themselves on meat—not a normal dietary staple of the Greeks—and experimented with herbal medications in an effort to enhance their performances... The ancient Greek athletes also drank wine potions, used hallucinogens, and ate animal hearts or testicles in search of potency."
>
> — SALLY JENKINS, "WINNING, CHEATING HAVE ANCIENT ROOTS," THE WASHINGTON POST, AUGUST 3, 2007

It would probably shock most people to know Babe Ruth took a shot of sheep testicle extract to enhance his performance. That he tried at least once suggests that it wasn't the only thing he did as he felt his skills start to decline. It would not be a surprise that soldiers who returned from war in the '40s and '50s—who used amphetamines to counteract fatigue, elevate mood, heighten endurance, and fight for their lives and American values—figured those same drugs might help them on the ball field. What player wouldn't want to heighten alertness and improve their ability to see the ball?

The most important thing that happened to draw attention to PEDs was when a few athletes tried to push the boundaries of how far they could go in taking them. Deaths started happening. The alleged motto of Tommy Simpson, a champion cyclist who died in 1967, was:

 "If it takes ten to kill you, take nine and win."[10]

— TOMMY SIMPSON

Simpson made no denials about taking drugs. On the day of his death, during the thirteenth stage of the Tour de France on July 13, 1967, he had amphetamines with him and they were detected in his system.

Even horses were testing positive for banned substances.[11] Surprise steroid testing at the Pan American games in 1983 found nineteen athletes failed testing while two dozen more simply left the competition with no explanation. Let's guess what the reason was for their departure.

The use of PEDs reflects the mindset of high-performing athletes. Winning is everything. Individuals may take almost anything in the belief that it will give them a physical or psychological advantage over their opponents.

Widespread use of "greenies" by major league players for decades before MLB issued a list of banned substances[12] did not put fans or the press in a tizzy. If modern rules were applied to former players, it would remove many of the plaques hanging in the heralded Hall of Fame. No player has ever been removed from the Hall, even after admitting to using drugs that are now considered illegal.

According to Tom House,[13] he remembers how a teammate joked that they didn't lose a game so much as they were "out-milligrammed." In other words, players respected each other's elite talents but may not have been taking the right drugs or enough of them. Rumor has it that when they found out what drug defeated them, they took that too.

Players were prone to taking performance enhancers as a means to level the playing field, maximize their performance, and compete. With advances in science and technology, players had access to more efficient enhancements than hamster balls. There was no official rule change in baseball until 2005,[14] and HGH was not specifically banned until

2011. If you want to create a giant or a god, HGH is the drug you would give to the scrawny kid who gets beat up on the playground. It is known to speed healing and build muscle and bone. That sounds like a benefit in treatment of injuries.

> "Shouldn't amphetamines—or 'greenies'—which were widely used in the majors for decades before modern steroids became prevalent, be classified as 'performance-enhancing drugs'? If so, shouldn't we penalize players that came to prominence during the pre-steroids era? When should the guilt-by-association end?"
>
> — ISAAC RAUCH, FILED WITH THE BASEBALL HALL OF FAME, 2013

In a 2001 interview, when asked how Hall of Fame voters should treat the likes of Bonds and Clemens, Hall president Jeff Idelson referred to the "character clause"—a rule that demands "voting shall be based upon the player's record, playing ability, integrity, sportsmanship, character, and contributions to the team(s) on which the player played." The curious point is whether "integrity" and "character" have changed in meaning with time. But there is also a question as to if a player's "record," "ability," and "contributions to the team" come at the expense of a single element for which no rules were enforced.

Elite players in different eras compiled some of the most ethereal and unbelievable achievements that dwarfed the best in the game and will likely never be approached again. The gods of the game who have achieved the most hits (Pete Rose, 4,256),[15] won seven Cy Young awards (Roger Clemens), the most home runs (Barry Bonds, 762 career; 73 in a season), and may be a descendant of other baseball gods like, say, Willie Mays. Or at least have one as a godfather.[16] Players whose forefathers admitted to using PEDs that are now banned[17] have to suffer their accomplishments being belittled because the rules have changed. All they wanted to do was match the advantages taken by the competition. Their biggest mistake was often to stand out enough to come under the microscope because their "ability," "record," and "contributions to the team(s) on which the player played" were outstanding.

 "You can give a [mere mortal] all the PEDs you want, but you still have to make contact."

— SKIP BAYLESS, TALKING ABOUT BARRY
BONDS ON *UNDISPUTED*

You can't hit a baseball without the skill to hit one. A pill does not give you the recognition to be so respected that you are walked with the bases loaded just to avoid the possibility of having you swing a bat.[18] What minimal gain does a player actually get when they stalk a mountain like Tommy

Simpson or drop like a fly from heatstroke because of a bad calculation in a dose like Steve Belcher?[19] To them, the greater risk might be not using every advantage available to perform.

The influence of media and the ability to misinform, create sensationalist positions, and distort perception is something looked at broadly in the pages of this book. The cheating starts when a rule is in place. It is dishonorable not to follow it. Rules change with time and they are meant to affect play going forward, not looking back. Originally marijuana use by baseball players was prohibited. Now that laws have changed, players who previously tested positive for recreational use would not be flagged today. Tantalus should have had other reasons not to put his own kid in the oven, but the rule was not established until after there was no way to take it back. He went to hell.

In the years that are to come, players who are committed will find ways to compete. The practices they take on to achieve their edge might be more sophisticated and later come into question. For example, some people think it is criminal to use PEDs although it seems to have been done all throughout the history of baseball. But now players even associated with that era of baseball's indecision end up at fault.[20]

If it is considered unfair to take drugs that enhance performance, where does the line get drawn in the sand? There are other things that enhance performance. Tommy John was 13 and 3 in 1974 before ending his season to have surgery to reconstruct his ulnar collateral ligament. He came back to continue his admirable career and won 288 games with a 3.34 ERA.[21] It doesn't seem quite right that operations get to slide under the radar. Since Tommy John acted as a guinea pig for the surgery, more than 500 MLB players have had the procedure—it is not documented whether each one was needed or not. Even Tommy John spoke out against the surgery being used for performance enhancement.[22] If you look at performance enhancement surgery and compare it to the risks and objections of PEDs, the lists are similar:

- The person having the procedure is taking a risk and can die from the surgery.[23]
- The procedure can be used inappropriately instead of as a means to fix a clearly identifiable problem.[24]
- The procedure is legal.[25]

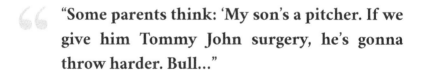

> **"Some parents think: 'My son's a pitcher. If we give him Tommy John surgery, he's gonna throw harder. Bull..."**
>
> — TOMMY JOHN

It is not enough to condemn performance enhancement without considering its history, reason, definition, and rules. Players who are pressured to perform may not always make the right decision—end up putting their own children in the oven. But it is likely that they never did so without a motivation to be more like the gods.

---

1. Performance Enhancing Drugs.
2. PEZ is a candy made by an Austrian candy company. The candy became famous more for the collectability of the candy dispensers than the candy itself. The dispenser has a head which gets tipped back to release one candy at a time.
3. All you have to know is this guy was a bad sailor who got lost for ten years trying to get home from a war and gouged out the eye of a cyclops.
4. A child born of procreation between a human and a god.
5. "Pud" stood for "Pudding," because Galvin was said to reduce hitters to pudding at the plate.
6. Elected in 1965 by the Veterans Committee.
7. Mariano Rivera threw just 1,283 innings in his nineteen-year career.
8. Developed by Charles-Édouard Brown-Séquard, a 72-year-old physician seeking a solution to his own decline.
9. The longer history of this is available online: https://sportsanddrugs. procon.org/historical-timeline/ , "History of Performance Enhancing Drugs in Sports."
10. Mr. Simpson is referring specifically to a type of amphetamine he used.
11. Dancer's Image, May 4, 1968 was disqualified from a win at the Kentucky Derby for phenylbutazone. The drug is an NSAID and was later made legal in horse racing.
12. The official updated list: https://en.wikipedia.org/wiki/ List_of_banned_substances_in_baseball
13. A pitcher with an eight-year career in the '70s who observed the use of performance enhancing drugs first-hand.
14. Fay Vincent sent a memo to teams in 1991 stating that the use of steroids was illegal. It was a moral statement. Who knows how and if that memo was passed on to players and coaches. Barry Bonds could not have even gotten word of the memo for the first five years of his career, and substances were not officially banned until he was 40.
15. Yes, Pete Rose is officially banned for gambling. But it is naive to think that Pete didn't take every advantage he possibly could on the field, especially if he knew everyone around him was doing it.

16. Mays is Barry Bonds' godfather.
17. Many MLB players in the Hall of Fame have admitted to PED use, including Mays, Aaron, and Mantle.
18. Buck Showalter walked Barry Bonds with the bases loaded on May 28, 1998 when the Giants were playing the Arizona Diamondbacks. Arizona had a two run lead, and Showalter guessed it was better to give up one run than four.
19. An Oriole player who dropped dead in 2003 from organ failure brought on by PED use and the pressure to perform.
20. Baseball sent a memo. They did not change the rules or institute testing until 2005. That is clearly not standing up to conviction. They could easily have laid down the law.
21. He is probably better when comparing stats to many pitchers already in the Hall, like Jim Palmer, Bob Feller, Sandy Koufax, Dizzy Dean, Catfish Hunter, Bob Lemon, and Mike Mussina.
22. In an interview with *Sports Illustrated*, Tommy John spoke out against parents using him to help promote their children's careers in baseball.
    https://www.si.com/mlb/video/2019/03/05/tommy-john-speaks-out-against-tommy-john-surgery-youth-sports
23. Sang Ho Baek died in 2021 at the age of 20 following Tommy John. Any surgery comes with risk.
24. HGH shows benefits in recuperating from injury, but now that it is banned that benefit cannot be realized by any player. Just like PED use in young players was a reason to display a responsibility to the public.
25. Regardless of what you think about abortion and lobotomy, these procedures are restricted or banned in various countries and jurisdictions.

9

LARGER THAN LIFE AND GROWING IN MYTH

There are a lot of baseball stories that are hard to believe. Some players have more of the mystique of crazy than is likely their fair share. In this category, one player seems to stand practically alone on the stage when it comes to trying to separate truth from fiction. The storm of stories and antics that follow in his wake like debris from a tornado all together make him seem less real than even Sidd Finch.[1] It is this way because the reality of this player was already so large that it became possible to believe he would be capable of absolutely anything on or off the field.

Take the intellect of a 10-year-old, place it in the body of a hulking farm boy who has ADHD. Now give him an alcohol addiction and a lifelong love of fire engines that he was supposedly drawn to chase like a dog chasing cars. Let it sink in that he was a selfless, gentle, valiant man who saved the lives of thirteen or more people and one "drowning" log while unthinkingly putting his own life in danger as if he were indestructible. When a levee broke in Hickman, Kentucky that held back the mighty Mississippi, he jumped in like a superhero to help sandbag the gap as if he alone could stop the flow. When the gap was patched, he rowed for hours through the floodwaters looking for people in distress that he might save.[2] When the levee broke again the following year, he sacrificed himself again to move the river back to where it belonged—probably by just lifting it and putting it back in place. Never mind that the hours in the cold water and exhaustion from exertion gave him pneumonia that weakened his immunity which allowed him to contract tuberculosis that eventually claimed his life.

As kind and helpful as he was, he had at least one incident while carrying a gun that discharged accidentally. He beat his father-in-law badly with an iron because the man asked Rube for board that was owed. When the man's wife tried to stop Rube, he beat her away with a chair. Rube joined the circus to wrestle alligators in the offseason to fill his time,[3] and was the leading man in a vaudeville show. As he couldn't remember his lines he ad-libbed them every night to the delight of the audience and chagrin of the crew. While traveling with the show, he came to a town where there was a lion exhibition. When he went out of curiosity, he confronted the lion which either bit or swiped at him.[4] As he became known for crowd-pleasing, he later attempted a bigger stunt at an aquatic attraction by climbing in the tank with a walrus which he tried to hypnotize. He failed in the attempt and lost his trousers in the scuffle but emerged unharmed.[5]

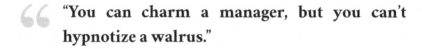

> **"You can charm a manager, but you can't hypnotize a walrus."**
>
> — GEORGE "RUBE" WADDELL

His contract included a clause where he was forbidden to eat crackers in bed because his munching left his bed-mate losing sleep because of the crumbs. Connie Mack, the wise owner of the team Rube played for over much of his career, wouldn't pay him more than a few dollars at a time as it was the only way to control how much he drank. Rube was a fountain of unpredictability who was born on Friday the 13th and died on April Fool's day thirty-seven years later. Those dates, at least are no ruse.

Many of these anecdotes need to be considered a bit like taffy in that they have stretched and changed with time. Some parts of them may have been fabricated by a man who would be quickly dismissed from the stand by the worst of lawyers as being an unreliable witness to his own life. Just as he couldn't remember his lines as the lead of a play, he couldn't remember he'd not divorced his first wife before marrying his second. He sometimes forgot where he needed to be at game time, which didn't mean just the start time of the game, it may have meant which team he was supposed to play on and in which city. Freely following his muse to concentrate on what he was already involved in, he might be found fishing, playing games with kids, posing as a department store mannequin, or following a fire truck. These demonstrations of forgetfulness all put aside his copious craving for the mugs of beer and shots of delight that compromised the little brain power he naturally possessed.[6]

"He often missed school, but I could always find him playing ball, fishing, or following a fire engine."[7]

— RUBE WADDELL'S SISTER, MARGARET

The swirl of misinformation surrounding Waddell continues to circulate, swell, and grow, which makes it hard to sift fact from fiction. Even when his adventures and accomplishments can be verified by newspapers, relatively reliable eyewitnesses, and box scores, they are sometimes amended with poetic license.

Some things are irrefutable in the record books. This same man spent ten solid seasons in the major leagues striking out 2,251 batters over 2,835 innings while winning 183 games.[8] Rube won the pitching triple crown in 1905[9] while missing an entire month of the season that would likely have extended his leading totals. In the end, his relatively short career was deemed good enough to gain election to the Hall of Fame.

"Good enough" is a bit of an understatement if you look at some of the particularly shining moments which solidified his image as a hero of the sport. He twice pitched both ends of a double-header (August 19, 1900 and August 21, 1903), accounting for a total of twenty-seven and seventeen innings in those appearances. Across those four starts, he went 3 and 1. In the 1900 twinbill, he pitched seventeen innings in the first game and was conned by his manager into pitching the second game with the reward of a fishing trip following the second game. Luckily the second game went only five innings before Rube was off on his trip.

These were iron-man accomplishments, but Waddell most admired and reveled in his outing against Cy Young on July 4, 1905. The game went twenty innings and both pitchers pitched a complete game with Waddell winning the game. After letting two runs be scored in the first, Waddell put up nineteen straight innings of goose eggs. It is rumored that a softly hit ball by Waddell drove in what was to be the winning run when it was misplayed in the top of the twentieth. The Boston Americans did make six errors on the day so the story is plausible even with Waddell showing no RBI on the day's box score. Boston did muster a threat in the bottom of the inning, but Waddell escaped the threat without letting up a run.

His nickname was "Rube," which refers to a farm boy who is stupid and lacks culture and manners. Hardly a compliment, the label was placed on him by a catcher during his short tour of the minor leagues. Most likely it was for his childlike manner, the fact that he was easily distracted, and his lack of knowledge about the game which he was not shy of displaying brilliantly. He never learned the basic rules, even though he'd played college ball on a scholarship. He went for the pay—rather than the academics—which was $2 a game, plus room and board.

> **"Rube had a bad habit of throwing to bases without looking at the base to which he was throwing... the ball would go half a mile before it would be recovered, and every man who happened to be on the bases would score... he delighted in throwing to the basemen with all his strength."**
>
> — DR. THOMAS H. GEORGE, MANAGER, VOLANT COLLEGE

Rube believed he could record an out by throwing the ball directly at a runner and hitting him rather than to the base where the runner was advancing. In one game, Waddell was batting in the eighth inning with a man on second. After a pitch, the catcher threw to second in a pick-off attempt and the ball sailed into the outfield. The A's runner took off and rounded third to score, and the center fielder fired home. Waddell, with bat still in hand, swung at the incoming throw and hit the ball back into play. He was called out for inter-ference.

 "They'd been feeding me curves all afternoon, and this was the first straight ball I'd looked at!"[10]

— RUBE WADDELL

One thing quite notable about Waddell was his outstanding arm. The is partially attributed to his brute strength from mining.[11] His accuracy may have something to do with his pastime of throwing stones at birds that gathered on the planted fields. It is understandable how throwing stones all day could have contributed to building his mighty endurance.

The love of fire trucks started at an early age and lasted through his life. It seems from various descriptions that he just felt the thrill and responsibility to be on hand in case he could jump in and save someone's life. Rumor suggests that he was witnessed running off the field during at least one game to chase a fire truck down the road to follow it to its destination. A lot of how he is portrayed as a person seems bent on making him a caricature and even more soft in the head than he may have actually been.

> "Rube Waddell was the greatest pitcher in the game, and although widely known for his eccentricities, was more sinned against than sinner."

— CONNIE MACK

The problem with Rube's ever-growing legacy is that the stories began being fabricated even while he was still playing. Stories contained some elements of reality but writers either tended to embellish them or simply create fantasy. In the end, the lovable character's actual life ends up a soup of what is real, what is stretched, what is misread, and what is totally imaginary.

If you scour the internet, Waddell's history is practically treated like a set of Legos where he is assembled more by what will make him look funny and get likes than to take his legacy seriously. Every lie printed becomes a fact. One instance with an accidental discharge of his pistol in the lobby of a hotel becomes a story about how Rube plotted an attempt to murder his manager and good friend, Connie Mack. Facts are cherry-picked, unchecked, and end up printed for all to see just to perpetuate the mistakes and create new ones.[12] If he were scrapping with his father-in-law and the family dog jumped into the fray to defend his owner, Rube may have punched the dog to get him off after the dog bit Rube's pitching hand. That might be crossed up and morphed with Rube's visit to a lion on exhibition where

Rube jumped into the cage and punched a lion instead. If one time he led a parade when he was supposed to be at the ballpark, in the minds of writers, he did it many times. And those are the stories that get fed to the voracious minds of the fans that swarm to the myth.

The trend to bend Rube's reality started at the very core of his history. For example, there was an article in Philadelphia's *North American*, from August 12, 1903, that reported this headline: "Rube Caused a Bean Factory to Blow Up." The event was fitted within the actual events of a baseball game on August 11 where Rube pitched and lost against the home team 5 to 1. Rube came to the plate according to the box score and batted three times. One of those may have been in the seventh inning. The story goes on to say how Waddell fouled off a ball in that inning of that game and the ball flew out of the stadium. It landed in Boston's largest bean cannery.[13] This is where reality left the stadium.

Apparently, the ball jammed in the steam whistle causing it to sound, which to most workers would have signaled quitting time. Hearing it go off, they began shutting down and heading toward the door. When the whistle didn't stop, neighboring factories began blasting their horns thinking it was some type of emergency. Panic ensued and workers rushed from the buildings without properly closing down their stations as the fire trucks, which had been summoned by police, began to arrive. One of the vats of beans—which the in the worker's haste to leave the building was left cooking and untended—over-heated and exploded. The explosion showered fans still in the stands nearest the factory with a scalding rain of beans and molasses. A fan, fearing for his life, deafened by the explosion, and torched by the searing rain went insane with panic during the deluge from the sky and shouted:

> **"The end of the world is coming and we will all be destroyed."**
>
> — ANONYMOUS BOSTON AMERICANS' FAN

There were some strange footnotes about this story starting with the fact that the Philadelphia paper was the only newspaper in the country to carry the story. There is no record of a bean factory explosion reported on that date in Boston in any popular news source or record. Rube was not reported to have run out of the stadium chasing the sound of the sirens and the fire trucks to the place he would be needed to save humanity as he would have been in the commotion even if he were pitching the game. Oh, and the story was penned by Charles Dryden. Dryden was considered a masterful sports humorist during his time writing for the paper. Even in the accounting above, I have had a hand in smoothing out the rough edges of the events described in the article just to maintain the tradition.[14]

Regardless of the fact that it can be proven to be false with relative ease, the bean incident is reported now in accounts of Waddell's legacy as the truth when "researchers" find it and fail to look below the surface. Rest assured that many more of the "facts" you can dig up about Waddell are false and morphed and probably not as endearing or important as the reality of the man who earned the respect of his fellow players by being great at the game. In the end, even a heartfelt message that was supposedly crafted for young baseball fans is in question.

> "I had my chance, and a good one it was. Many boys may have a better one ahead of them than I had. If they will leave the booze alone, they won't have any trouble. I am not a very good preacher, but... keep away from booze and cigarettes."[15]
>
> — RUBE WADDELL

This message sounds virtually the same as one given by Hack Wilson on the radio just days before his death, and similar to one by Mickey Mantle expressing his regrets of excess. There also seems to be no record of who the recipient of this letter was. Regretfully, the origin is in as much doubt as much of the rest of his story and his last words to teammates as he lay dying.

> "I'll be over tomorrow and show you bums how to run. My weight is down to fighting trim now. I'm in shape."

— RUBE WADDELL

In the end, what holds is his place in the Hall of Fame, and the numbers in the box scores. Those markers are no myth.

---

1. Something needs to be said here about the general recklessness of research that exists on the internet for this particular character. The fluid imagination—even by authors who are supposed to represent his life faithfully in biographies—seems to be willing to make this particular player into a bigger circus than he already is.
2. *The Hickman Courier*, Thursday, April 4, 1912.
3. Macht, Norman L., 2007. *Connie Mack and the Early Years of Baseball.*
4. October 31, 1903 *Cincinnati Enquirer*. This account is considered questionable as it conflicts with other reporting and Waddell's own recounting.
5. *The Wilkes-Barre Record*, Thursday, March 28, 1912.
6. At least one resource notes that Waddell did well in school:
    https://pabook.libraries.psu.edu/literary-cultural-heritage-map-pa/bios/Waddell__Rube
7. There is remarkably little information about Waddell's family.
8. This is inclusive of only 1900 to 1909. Over that period Cy Young struck out 1,365, pitched 3,341 innings, and won 231 games.
9. 27 Wins, 1.48 ERA, 287 Ks.
10. Unconfirmed response.
11. Some accounts say Waddell lived and worked on a family farm, but his father was in the oil industry. The town he lived in was a farming community. This is the kind of fact that readily gets jumbled.
12. William Braund calls his book about Waddell, *King of the Hall of Flakes*, a novel. The reason for that is because it is mostly fiction. He takes complete liberty with the facts or doesn't even bother with them. Many

people will pick up his work thinking it is a biography and reference. It isn't.

13. Boston's baked beans were a thing, which is why a Boston team was named the Beaneaters.

14. A resource online does have a clipping of the original article as well as a breakdown of some investigation into its validity. Find that here:
    https://www.thefreelibrary.com/Consider+your+sources%3A+base ball+and+baked+beans+in+Boston.-a0144201875

15. Alan Levy, *Rube Waddell: The Zany, Brilliant Life of a Strikeout Artist*

I NEVER SAID MOST OF THE THINGS I SAID

Imagine being one of the best players ever to play your position in the history of baseball and having your career take a back seat to some words you supposedly said. It is almost a tragedy. This baseball oddity quit school at a young age to go to work and help support his family by working in a shoe factory. He later said he'd still be there if it wasn't for baseball. He enlisted to serve in the Navy and earned a Purple Heart in WWII after being wounded on the beaches at Normandy and missed two years of his career due to service.

In his seventeen-year career, this star played in fourteen World Series, helping to win ten titles—the most by any player in baseball history. Playing in a record 75 World Series games, he contributed with more than just the twelve home runs he hit in those fall classics. He was a fifteen-time

All-Star[1] and three-time AL MVP. He shares the distinction of winning three MVP awards with such well-known stars as Mickey Mantle, Joe DiMaggio, Stan Musial, Jimmie Foxx, Mike Schmidt, Alex Rodriguez, Albert Pujols, Roy Campanella, and Mike Trout.[2] His player stats for the regular season include a lifetime .285 batting average, 358 home runs, 2,150 hits, and 1,430 RBIs. He was inducted into the Hall of Fame in 1972.

Barely remembered for his exclusive talent on the field, this guy struck out only 414 times over 7,555 at-bats. He was considered an amazing "bad-ball" hitter and somehow combined a relatively tiny five-foot-seven frame with power and contact to become an offensive force.

 "[People said to me] you're a bad-ball hitter. No, the ball looked good to me [so I hit it]."

— LAWRENCE "YOGI" BERRA

Through the course of his career, he moved from player to player-manager and finally ended up managing the Yankees in 1964 bringing them all the way to the World Series. That year they lost to St. Louis but it took all seven games. Then in 1973, Yogi managed the team across town: the New York Mets. They sat in last place in the division until August 30. Questioned by a reporter in July if the season was over, Yogi made a sort of prophecy.

 **"It ain't over till it's over."**

— LAWRENCE "YOGI" BERRA

The Mets went from last place to first and clinched the division on their second to last game of the season, taking the division in front of the surging Cardinals who won their final five games. Moving on to the World Series, Berra's "Ya Gotta Believe"[3] Mets went the full seven games in the series outscoring the A's, but losing in the final game 5 to 2. These successes just added to the record number of times he reached the World Series.

What is the player who has appeared in the most World Series as a player and manager remembered for?

"I wish I had an answer to that because I'm tired of answering that question."

— LAWRENCE "YOGI" BERRA

Accidental philosophic and paradoxical quips, his welcoming demeanor and a TV commercial promotion with a duck.

The Four Balls Story (An introduction to Yogi-isms as told by Whitey Ford)[4]

"The White Sox came into Yankee Stadium in '59 and I was pitching ... Up comes Luis Aparicio. The first pitch I throw to him he bunts down third, beats it out. One pitch, man on first. Nellie Fox gets up; first pitch, double down the left-field line. Two pitches, second and third. Minnie Minoso, I threw him a really good curveball but it hit him in the kneecap, so he walks down to first. I've thrown three pitches and the bases are loaded. And up comes Ted Kluszewski... First pitch, high fastball off the right-center field wall. Three runs scored. I have thrown four pitches. Casey comes out to the mound and Yogi doesn't want to miss that, so he gets out there. Casey says to Yogi: "Does Ford have anything tonight?" and Yogi says: "How the hell do I know, I haven't caught a pitch yet!"

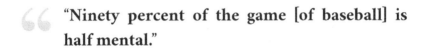

> **"Ninety percent of the game [of baseball] is half mental."**

> — YOGI BERRA

On the field, behind the plate, Yogi flapped his gums. A lot. He talked to the players in the batter's box and with the umpires, casually stirring up a dialogue. Yogi was kind and personable, yet in his subtle manner, he used his conversations to the advantage of his team. He might ask a player about their family, wonder what they had for lunch. Then when Yogi had made them comfortable, he might say what he called "helpful things." He might warn them that the pitcher was a little wild that day and seem concerned with their personal safety. In a teasing way, he might try to convince them to step back from the plate a little or to be careful not to lose sight of the ball in the white of the pitcher's uniform as the ball sailed toward them.

He admitted to once trying to get thrown out of a game by riding the umpire. Why? Because it was hot and his team was winning by a lot and he didn't want to be there anymore.

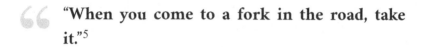 **"When you come to a fork in the road, take it."**[5]

— YOGI BERRA

One of the most popular Yogi-isms was supposed to have been said one of the ten times in 1961 where Mickey Mantle and Roger Maris hit back-to-back home runs. During the 1961 season, Maris and Mantle were having a duel to chase what was then thought to be an insurmountable record of sixty home runs in a single season, smacked by Babe Ruth in 1927.[6] In Yogi's classic style, his reaction to one of the ten back-to-back performances would certainly be the type of malapropism that he would effortlessly coin. But like many things from the lore of baseball, there is rumor and no record to substantiate it.

 "It's deja vu all over again."[7]

— YOGI BERRA

Once Yogi had become known for his quips, he continued to distort language into humorous kaleidoscopes. Having gained a reputation for his use of language, people were always on the lookout for him to say something clever and thought he could just make up Yogi-isms on the spot. Probably because people kept an ear out for his whimsy, the library of his quotes grew and he ended up getting credit for a lot of things he never said.[8] True to his form and under the constant scrutiny, his persona would come out with a language-twisting phrase when no one was expecting it. It brought him a lot of attention in the press and won him contracts for product endorsements.

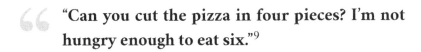

"Can you cut the pizza in four pieces? I'm not hungry enough to eat six."[9]

— YOGI BERRA

One such endorsement left Yogi a bit miffed. He was signed to do a commercial with an insurance company called Aflac that used a duck as a brand mascot. The talking duck was somewhat mischievous and said the name of the company instead of quacking. The company wanted to use Yogi-isms in their scripting to inject some additional humor into the plot of their commercials.

By this time (2002), Yogi was getting up in age but still enjoyed working with the guys in spring training and continuing his life-long journey with his love for the game.

He was not at all pleased to find out he had to take a break from the team to fly out to California for a Friday shoot and he let it show.

On the morning Yogi found out about the commercial, Ron Guidry went to pick him up to take Yogi to spring training as he usually did. Guidry acted as Yogi's chauffeur[10] during spring training for years, and he could tell Yogi was upset. He usually waved to everyone and smiled as he walked out of the hotel but was clearly in a grumpy mood and cursing as he got into the car. Guidry asked Yogi what was wrong and Yogi said:

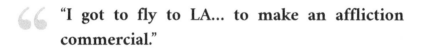 **"I got to fly to LA... to make an affliction commercial."**

— YOGI BERRA

Guidry was a bit puzzled wondering what affliction Yogi was talking about and began to drive off toward the stadium. As Guidry was trying to figure out what question to ask, Yogi turned to him and said:

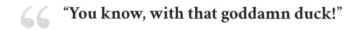 **"You know, with that goddamn duck!"**

— YOGI BERRA

Guidry began laughing so hard that he practically lost control of the truck. He pulled off and asked Yogi if he meant

Aflac. He and Yogi had a good laugh before getting back on the road.

When Yogi came back from the trip, Guidry was there to pick him up at the airport. He asked Yogi how it went and Yogi looked at Guidry and said:

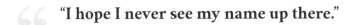 **"Gator.**[11] **You realize that duck really doesn't talk?"**

— YOGI BERRA

Everyone seemed to have their own stories about Yogi as if his wellspring of accidental insight were inspirational. George Bush, famed for his clumsy presidential speeches, claimed people thought Yogi was one of his scriptwriters. Reggie Jackson remembers standing next to Yogi at an old-timers' game as they scrolled through the names of baseball greats who had died that year as a final farewell. Yogi tugged at Reggie to get his attention and said:

"I hope I never see my name up there."

— YOGI BERRA

Yogi's legacy ends up not being just his accomplishments on the field. It ends up being his dedication to his country, team, family, and friends. It is about sitting by the bedside of Phil Rizzuto as he lay in an assisted living facility; watching over him in his final days and sharing stories that may not have been perfectly remembered. He spent the last moments of his life-long teammate's final hours playing cards and comforting him playing the game of life the only way he knew how.

Yogi is a celebration of living life to the fullest, enjoying the moment, and spreading his kindness, humility, and innocence. He was one small man who became bigger than baseball and a champion of life, living, and respect.

 "You should always go to other people's funerals, otherwise they won't come to yours."

— YOGI BERRA

---

1. He actually played in eighteen all-star games as there were two in 1959, 1960, and 1961.
2. Trout still has plenty of time to tack on another award.
3. The Mets had a surprise run to the World Series in 1969 with the slogan "The Miracle Mets," and again the Mets fans latched on to the underdog.
4. This account (https://youtu.be/aiJSpq6v-GY) is apparently of a game on April 30, which is the only one that comes close to what happened. Whitey gets just about every possible detail wrong beside the fact that Luis Aparicio bunted a single to third and that he hit a player on the third pitch (Jim Landis). First of all, they were in Chicago, not New York. Aparicio got on with the bunt, and then Nellie Fox grounded out to second base and Aparicio advanced on a fielder's choice. Whitey hit only one player that year, and it was in this game, but it was not Minnie Minoso. Although Minoso led the league in getting hit ten times in his thirteen full seasons in MLB, he was playing for Cleveland in '58 and '59

106 | ROY LINGSTER

between two stints with the White Sox. The fourth pitch went to Ray Boone, not Ted Kluszewski. Boone had only 21 at-bats for the White Sox that year. Kluszewski did play for the Sox in '59, but was only on the team after August 25. The one game Kluszewski faced Whitey Ford was on September 15. He got a walk and a single in four plate appearances. No doubles. Ford also faced the Sox at Yankee stadium on May 15 and Aparicio and Fox were on third and second in the first inning, but Landis grounded out. Aparicio scored on a fielder's choice. Yogi's version of the same story is different (https://youtu.be/rCqrvLBQxwo?t=932). Yogi claimed that Fox hit a single when the bases were loaded because the next guy got hit and the fourth hit a grand slam. So Yogi said four runs scored in that same story.

5. Directions he gave to his boyhood friend, Joe Garagiola, to get to his house. While Joe was a friend and player, he became more well-known for his own crusades as a baseball announcer and baseball blooper reels. He was instrumental in perpetuating the promotion of Yogi's quips.

6. People like to debate whether the record was really challenged, because in 1961 the season was lengthened to 162 games from 154. Maris hit #61 on the final day of the 162 game season.

7. Supposedly Berra referring to the fact that Maris and Mantle frequently went back-to-back that season.

8. The title of this chapter refers to a quote that Yogi used more than once to express the idea that people ultimately put words in his mouth.

9. Yogi was ordering a pizza and the waitress asked how he wanted it cut.

10. The adventures were chronicled in a book called *Driving Mr. Yogi*.

11. Ron Guidry's nickname.

11

JARABE TAPATÍO, OR DANCING AROUND THE GOLDEN SOMBRERO

This chapter is here for stat nerds. It is the sole *raison d'etre*. If you hate statistics, skip to the next chapter.

Striking out four times in a game is such a notorious flop that baseball has a sarcastic and spirited name for the achievement. It is called the Golden Sombrero.[1] A sombrero is often associated with its negative stereotype of a lazy Mexican having a siesta with his wide-brimmed hat pulled down over his face to shade him from the sun as he sleeps in the afternoon. Maybe that stereotype of "asleep at the plate" was what Carmelo Martinez was thinking when he was credited with coining the term.[2] According to lore, he had a particularly bad day at the plate and is said to have kept his sense of humor when interviewed by a reporter.

"[That was a] big hat trick... a sombrero... probably made of gold."[3]

— CARMELO MARTINEZ

Somehow his words were remembered and spread through locker rooms and polished with time. The achievement of a Golden Sombrero lends levity to a ballplayer's failure. It reflects a bad day at the plate and has achieved a name and recognition. A more notorious and rare "achievement" is not distinguished with a name, and that is hitting into four double plays in a single game. That means that in just four swings a single player accounts for 30 percent of a team's outs for the day.

The difference is that you have to swing and hit into a double play. In a samurai way, it is more honorable to hit into an out, even if it is more than one of them. A player can strike out by hitting the snooze button. Striking out does less to kill a rally. Achieved only three times, hitting into four double plays might be called offensive indifference.

- Goose Goslin, April 28, 1934, killed four Detroit rallies and ended each inning taking his turn at bat to whack groundballs to the right of the diamond and contribute more than his share of the outs. Despite Goslin's best efforts to thwart his team's chances of winning, Detroit won the game 4 to 1 over Cleveland.

- Joe Torre, July 21, 1975, completely killed only two rallies by ending the inning with his batted balls. The Mets failed to score in each of the innings where Torre contributed two-thirds of the outs while effectively negating Felix Millan's otherwise very productive 4-for-4 day at the plate (Millan was always the runner who was forced out). The Mets were probably not surprised to lose to the Astros 6 to 2.
- On September 11, 2011, Víctor Martínez killed two potential rallies by ending the inning but with slightly more style than the other two players in this exclusive club. He at least managed a line-out into an unassisted double play along with his three ground ball inning killers. One of his groundouts scored a run, though he was not credited with an RBI because of an error on the previous play.

Two of these players are already in the Hall of Fame, so you don't necessarily have to be a chump to ground into a double play.

Achieving the shameful badge of the Golden Sombrero has become more frequent in the era of the home run when it seems each at-bat is an all-or-nothing escapade of putting the ball over the fence or striking out—as if nothing else mattered. Hits outnumbered strikeouts in every season until 2017 where there were 2,111 more hits than strikeouts. Then the strikeouts outpaced hits for the next four years.

Year	Hits	Strikeouts	Strikeouts Exceeded Hits By
2018	41,018	41,207	189
2019	42,039	42,823	784
2020	14,439	15,586	1,147
2021	39,481	42,145	2,664

Strikeouts are becoming so popular that new names have been invented to describe the spectacular achievements of being unable to put the ball in play. Striking out five times in a game is called a Platinum Sombrero. Striking out six times in a game is a Titanium Sombrero.[4]

Aaron Judge once struck out eight times on June 4, 2018, using both ends of a double-header to perform that feat. Eight strikeouts in one day seems to deserve a name of its own. In one of those two games he earned a Platinum Sombrero which is another rare feat of striking out five times in a nine-inning game. No one has ever struck out more in one day than Judge did during that double-header.

It comes as no surprise that the players who have so far achieved the most Golden Sombreros is a list of power-hitting one-trick ponies. If they hit it, it goes a long way. If not, they whiff. Ryan Howard has the most Golden Sombreros as of this writing with 27. Chris Davis Follows close behind with 26. Their lifetime stat lines are remarkably similar.

Another strikeout award that is not named is one that was achieved by Joe Sewell. In 1925, 1929, 1930, 1932, and 1933, Sewell struck out five times (or less).[5] Five times or less—

over the course of an entire season. It was not some statistical anomaly where he played a limited number of games. During these five seasons he averaged 513 at-bats. In other words, it took him all of 1932 and 1933[6] to strike out one less time than Aaron Judge did in one day in 2018. Sewell repeated that same spread of striking out only seven times in 1929 and 1930.

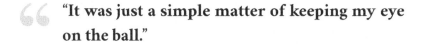

"It was just a simple matter of keeping my eye on the ball."

— JOE SEWELL

In 7,132 official at-bats (8,333 plate appearances) during his career, Sewell struck out a total of 114 times. The average strikeout rate for all of MLB in 2021 was one strikeout per 3.84 at-bats. Over the course of 513 at-bats in one year, the average 2021 player would strike out 133 times, or nineteen more times than Sewell did in his entire fourteen-year career.

- Trea Turner led all of MLB with a .328 AVE and 195 hits in 2021. He struck out 110 times in 595 at-bats. He was awarded a Golden Sombrero for his performance on May 31.
- Juan Soto led all of MLB with a rather ridiculous .465 on-base percentage. He struck out only ninety-three times in 502 official at-bats. He never won a

sombrero but did have three hat tricks (three strikeouts in one game) on three occasions.

- Kevin Newman—hardly a star—led the majors in at-bats per strikeout in 2021. He kept his grand whiff total to only 42 Ks in 517 at-bats which amounts to 1 strikeout every 12.6 at-bats. His rate is two at-bats better than the nearest contender (David Fletcher, 60 Ks in 626 at-bats). Still, there were five times Newman struck out twice in a game. Sewell struck out twice in a game a total of two times in his career. It happened seven years apart.

The list of great players who never achieved a Golden Sombrero is relatively long and includes some of the greatest players of all time along with some of the most recognized power hitters: Babe Ruth, Hank Aaron, Lou Gehrig, Ted Williams, Ty Cobb, Honus Wagner, Joe DiMaggio—and even current stars like Albert Pujols. None come close to Sewell's ability to put the ball in play. The closest runner-up in the history of post-1900 baseball[7] was Lloyd Waner who struck out 173 times in 7,772 at-bats, or 50 percent more than Sewell.

> "[In 1925], I had a record. I went to bat 600 times. I struck out four times. I didn't swing at three of the four. One was a bad call. [The pitcher] threw a ball right at my cap bill and [the umpire] Bill McGowan said: 'Strike three you're out—oh my god, I missed it!' He came up and apologized to me the next day."[8]

— JOE SEWELL

Sewell claimed he could see so well that he saw the spiraling seams on a baseball when pitched and watched the ball come off his bat. The one bat he used for his entire career was a 40-ounce bat modeled after one used by Shoeless Joe Jackson throughout his career. These bats were made of wood from the north side of a hickory tree and stained with tobacco juice. Sewell's one Black Betsy lasted through all fourteen years of his career.

As the art of contact hitting fades into history as a lost art in the game, it looks like there's no need to name the achievement of striking out only four times over 600 at-bats as it probably will never happen again. The award might as well be known as "a Joe Sewell."

---

1. The Mexican hat dance is typically a symbol of pride and romance.
2. Some reports say he struck out four times, but that isn't correct. He had two games in 1984 where he struck out three times. In both those games he had at least one hit and one RBI. 1988 was the only time he struck out

four times as a pro and that was long after the term had been used in print.

3. The Cub's Leon Durham was quoted by Steve Daley using the term saying that he was happy to have escaped winning a golden sombrero by hitting a triple and walking in his fourth and fifth at-bats after striking out in his first three plate appearances in a game on April 13, 1984.

4. Also known as a Double-Platinum Sombrero and a Horn, named after Sam Horn of the Baltimore Orioles achieved this in an extra inning game (fifteen) on July 17, 1991. It took him eight plate appearances that included a walk, reaching base on a strikeout(!), and hitting a double. Eight players have achieved the feat of striking out six times in a game. All of those were extra innings.

5. Statistical comparison between game logs and Sewell's totals show an inconsistency. Sewell has five strikeouts in the game logs, but is credited with only four in his totals according to baseball-reference.com.

6. During these years Sewell was with the Yankees and roomed with Lou Gehrig.

7. Wee Willie Keeler, playing from 1892 to 1910 did manage only 136 times in 8,591 at-bats. He had one year where he edged out Sewell in striking out only two times in 570 at-bats in 1899. However he also had the advantage of different rules that helped him achieve his record.

8. From an Oral History recording of Joe Sewell, August 1, 1986. https://collection.baseballhall.org/islandora/object/islandora%3A268693

12

105 GAMES WITHOUT TOUCHING A BAT, A GLOVE, OR A BALL

There comes a time when a chapter has to be as short as a player's career, or at least fitting to the depth of skills he had in playing the game.

Of course, there were infamous players whose baseball careers were really short. The one at-bat career of Eddie Gaedel was probably the shortest if taken by all standards. Standing at three feet, seven inches, Gaedel was paid—minimum wage, of course—to take the field on August 19, 1951, for the St. Louis Browns. Sporting the number 1/8, the smallest positive number ever on a jersey in baseball history,[1] Gaedel was given a specific role to play. The manager, Zack Taylor, instilled confidence in our hero—as he tied the man's shoes like a father holding a small boy in his lap—that he need not fear that the other team would throw at him.[2] General Manager Bill Veeck went a step further in cementing what Gaedel was paid to do. He warned Gaedel to crouch as they'd practiced, and not attempt heroics at the plate by moving the bat off his shoulder.

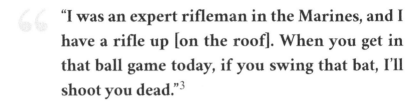

> **"I was an expert rifleman in the Marines, and I have a rifle up [on the roof]. When you get in that ball game today, if you swing that bat, I'll shoot you dead."**[3]
>
> — BILL VEECK

Veeck's words promised that Gaedel's career would be even shorter had he gone even slightly off-script.

Fearing for his life, Gaedel was sent in to pinch-hit for the first batter in the bottom of the first inning in the second game of the double-header. Gaedel took his curtain call, and the defense took a huddle wondering how to play a little person. The catcher lay on the ground to get his target low enough, and the grumpy umpire would have nothing to do with making a mockery of the game. No, this was pushing the limits far enough.

Detroit's Bob Cain threw four pitches that sailed past Gaedel's eyes that would have been strikes for any normal-sized player. Gaedel just sat and watched the balls fly by until he was told to take his base by the ump. He stopped several times on the way to bow to the admiring crowd which had roared into a frenzy. When he arrived at first, he was promptly lifted from the game for a pinch-runner. It could have only been slightly funnier if he played for the Giants.

But in this short chapter, we are not talking about Eddie, who at least touched a bat and took a plate appearance in his major league debut. We can put aside the sequel to his first appearance where he was put on a baseball field to play an alien in a staged abduction of players on the White Sox.[4] What we are talking about instead is a man who played a total of 105 major league games, scored 33 runs, stole 31 bases, and was a member of the 1974 World Champion Oakland Athletics. He never touched a bat, a glove, or a ball. He never stood at the plate, never threw a pitch, and never played in the field. All he really did was act as substitute legs for other players. With those opportunities, he achieved a few average base-running stats while creating some unnecessary outs. And for that, he earned a World Series ring.

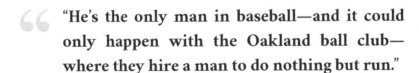

> **"He's the only man in baseball—and it could only happen with the Oakland ball club— where they hire a man to do nothing but run."**
>
> — CURT GOWDY

Herb Washington was signed by the Oakland A's who took him on strictly for his speed. He was a sprinter who broke the world record for the 50- and 60-yard dashes several times in his track and field career.

Ready to sign his contract to play speedster for the A's, his contract negotiation was held back by a small detail. He was going to be signed to a $45,000 deal with a $20,000 signing bonus with one caveat.

> **"You have to grow a mustache by opening day and I'll give you another $2,000."**[5]
>
> — CHARLIE FINLEY

Washington was unable to grow much facial hair and his mustache, by opening day of spring training, was little more than a feathering. His sister offered the advice that he just "pencil it in" with makeup as women did with their eyebrows. Herb gave it a try, but when the bench manager inspected him for the bonus, he told Herb that the mustache was not credible.

Later that day Herb extorted some resources and went back to visit the bench coach again. He waived $200 at him, then asked him to take another look at the mustache which he must not have seen in good light. The manager somehow now saw the mustache as passable—prominent even—and Herb ended up winning his bonus money for the small bribe.

Regretfully, what Herb was able to conjure up as a clever manipulator of circumstance, he was not able to deal on the base paths. His speed did win him 31 stolen bases but over a total of 48 attempts. That's 17 outs for anyone counting. In the end, he was 1/10 of 1 percent better at stealing than the league average. His performance in the postseason led to a total of five appearances recording two caught stealing attempts, one pick-off, and no other offensive production except being the out in a fielder's choice.

In other words, his only benefit to the A's winning effort in the World Series was to record three or more outs. One in pinch-running for Reggie Jackson and making the first out in the eighth inning of a three-run inning in a 5 to 0 win over the Orioles. The second was pinch-running for Gene Tenace who stole a base in the previous game during the inning where Herb was thrown out.[6] The third was picked off for unsound base running skills.

The crowning achievement of Herb's visit to the postseason was in Game 2 of the World Series against the Dodgers. Behind 3 to 0, the A's scored two runs in the ninth inning when Sal Bando got hit by a pitch and Reggie Jackson doubled. Joe Rudi hit a single to score Bando and Jackson. Rudi, on first, represented the tying run. After Gene Tenace struck out for the first out of the inning, Rudi, not known for his speed, got lifted for Herb who pinch-ran for him. Herb got picked off first base, effectively ending the rally by making the second out and clearing the bases. Angel Mangual, pinch-hitting for Blue Moon Odom, struck out ending the game with the Dodgers winning by a run.

Oakland won the next three games and took the series despite the fact that Herb appeared two more times. He pinch-ran for Gene Tenace in the third game to no benefit as the next two batters made unproductive outs. He also pinch-ran for Jim Holt and got forced out in a fielder's choice in the fourth game (effectively another base-running out, but let's not be picky).

Eddie Gaedel may have been a little person, a Martian, and a parody, but he had a 1.000 on-base percentage and never sapped a rally. Herb Washington was a failure as a baseball player but holds world records, had a successful career as a McDonald's franchise owner, sports the only Topps baseball card where the position is Pinch Runner, and is the only player in major league baseball who has appeared in more than one hundred games, yet never held a bat, never touched a ball, never played the field as a defender, and has a World Series ring.

----

1. Several players have worn the number zero or double zero.
2. Peter Golenbock, *The Spirit of St. Louis: A History of the St. Louis Cardinals and Browns*
    St. Louis sportswriter Bob Broeg
3. Veeck speaking to Gaedel.
4. Bill Veeck put four little people in alien costumes and had them abduct players from the White Sox team during the game.
5. This part of the story comes directly from a recorded interview available in various places around the internet and can be verified in Herb's own words. https://youtu.be/LVkigDj0HEw
6. In the same pitching and catching battery, Tenace stole a base. Tenace was 36 for 78 stealing bases in his entire fifteen-year career.

13

FIRED FOR A SONG

Sometimes a different kind of champion steps on the field. Billy Martin was not a great baseball player. He was cherished by some as a teammate because of his scrappy, clutch playing style when he was on the field. In 1953, he was the World Series' MVP putting up 12 hits in the six-game series, batting .500 with 8 RBI. He ended the series by knocking in the winning run with one out in the bottom of the ninth in the final game. That year he was a force in pushing the Yankees to win a record fifth straight World Series. At the age of 25, he was playing on a team with many future Hall of Fame players like Mickey Mantle, Yogi Berra, Whitey Ford, Phil Rizzuto, Johnny Mize, and Casey Stengel, and he lifted them on his shoulders and lived the dream of every child who swings a bat in a game of their imagination.

"I'd rather be a Yankee than the president of the United States."

— BILLY MARTIN

He played with the New York Yankees from 1950 to 1957 on teams that made appearances in five World Series, and they won four of those under the leadership of Casey Stengel. But almost as if his meteoric rise had caused him to use everything he had in the tank, his career started to sputter. Management saw his scrapping and drinking off the field was negatively influencing his teammates and especially his roommate Mantle. During a trip to Kansas City on June 15 during the 1957 campaign, Martin got traded to the Kansas City A's between the first and second games of the series and was set to switch dugouts the next day. He, Mickey Mantle, and Whitey Ford sat up all night drinking and reminiscing until dawn about the legendary run these friends, teammates, and brothers had in their years together in the game.

Martin played for four more years and five more teams, seeming to always get moved because of his roughhousing and because he rubbed management the wrong way. But leaving his Yankees behind took some of the spirit from his play. After his eleventh year, his career as a player ended in 1961 at the age of 33 when he was released by the Twins.

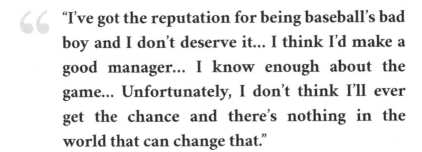

> **"I've got the reputation for being baseball's bad boy and I don't deserve it... I think I'd make a good manager... I know enough about the game... Unfortunately, I don't think I'll ever get the chance and there's nothing in the world that can change that."**

— BILLY MARTIN, *BASEBALL DIGEST*, JUNE 1961

It turns out Billy was wrong. He went on to manage five different teams over sixteen years, getting fired eight times over that span. It takes a special kind of attitude to get fired eight times by five teams. It was almost nine, but in one instance he quit before it happened.

One moment that helps define Martin's personal lore and personality came in one of his many documented and fabled off-field exploits. Mickey Mantle wanted to bring Billy out to hunt with a new gun he'd been given. Mickey had a friend who owned some land so the two took a four-hour drive out to the ranch.[1] When they got there, Mickey went up to the doctor's door and asked his permission to go hunting. The doctor agreed but asked Mickey to do him a favor and put down an old mule that was aging and had gone blind. Mickey agreed and then decided to pull a prank on Martin who was still in the car.

When Mickey returned to the car he acted upset that they'd taken the trip for nothing. The doctor didn't want them hunting on his land. Mickey took his gun and told Martin he was going to kill the doctor's mule. Martin tried to convince Mantle that it was a really bad idea, but Mantle insisted and walked off toward the barn and put down the mule. A moment later Mantle heard a few shots and found Martin with his smoking gun. Martin, always the team player, told Mantle he killed two of the doctor's cows. Mantle was left to explain his prank and Billy was left to pay for the cows.[2]

 "[Those cows] cost me $800."

— BILLY MARTIN

Billy's first tour as manager started with the Twins in 1969. In 1968, the Twins finished in seventh place, twenty-four games out of the running. Looking for a change and noting Martin's success as a manager of their minor league affiliate, Calvin Griffith offered the big-league job to Martin. Continuing his aggressive style, Martin led the Twins to first place in the first year of division play.

 "I feel like I'm sitting on a keg of dynamite."

— CALVIN GRIFFITH, GIVING HIS IMPRESSION
OF MARTIN AS A MANAGER

Even though the Twins took first place under Martin in 1969, management felt Martin's risk outweighed his benefit and did not sign him for 1970.

Martin spent 1970 out of baseball, and Jim Campbell signed Martin to take the helm of the ailing Detroit Tigers in 1971 which had a star-studded lineup that underperformed in the previous two years. Martin led the team to a second-place finish in 1971, first in 1972, and third in 1973. But Martin was already gone before the end of the '73 season. With twenty-eight games left to play, Martin encouraged his pitchers to throw spitballs in protest of umpires not calling Gaylord Perry for throwing the illegal pitch. Martin went on record with the press, was suspended by the AL president, and before the suspension was over, Martin was dismissed from his responsibilities as manager.

Bob Short, owner of the Texas Rangers saw Martin's release as a great opportunity. In a back-handed apology, Short told his current manager Whitey Herzog that he would fire his own grandmother to have a chance to hire Martin. Days later Herzog was dismissed when Martin was hired, inheriting a team that had stumbled to a 47 and 81 record. The team finished in last place.

 "I'm fired. I'm the grandmother."

— WHITEY HERZOG

In 1974, Martin changed the prospects of the Rangers considerably. They finished second in the league with an 84 and 76 record, improving by twenty-seven wins. But the team was sold by Short to Jim Corbett at the beginning of the season. Corbett was much more hands-on than Short and reduced Martin's managerial control. Corbett also found Martin's behavior and attitude difficult to deal with. Their grievances with each other continued to mount and came to a head on July 20 of 1975, the day after Corbett told Martin he was considering firing him. Corbett obviously did not understand that Martin wasn't one to fool with.

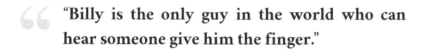

"**Billy is the only guy in the world who can hear someone give him the finger.**"

— MICKEY MANTLE

Martin stewed over the threat and an issue from earlier in the season bubbled up to the surface. In the sixth inning of the next game, Martin called the public address announcer and demanded that he play "Thank God I'm a Country Boy" instead of the traditional "Take Me Out to the Ball Game," during the seventh-inning stretch. This was something Martin and Corbett argued about at the beginning of the season, and Corbett insisted on the more traditional song rather than Martin's push for what would please the crowd. Corbett blew up when the song came on and fired Billy immediately after the game.

By this time, one positive aspect of Martin's reputation was his ability to turn a ball club around. Because of that reputation, Martin was hired by George Steinbrenner for his first tour as manager of the Yankees. Billy led the team to a pennant in 1976, and then to a World Series win in 1977, all the while battling with Steinbrenner and the new "star" Steinbrenner hired in the likes of Reggie Jackson. A summary of the events seems in order.

- Reggie claims to be "the straw that stirs the drink," suggesting disrespect for both Martin and team Captain Thurman Munson.
- On June 18, in a nationally televised game against the Red Sox, the Yankees trailed 4 to 7 having fallen half a game out of first place on the previous day's loss. Martin felt Jackson didn't hustle on a one-out base hit by Jim Rice, turning the single into a double. Instead of it being one-out with first and second, it was one out with second and third. During a pitching change, Martin lifted Jackson before another pitch was thrown, replacing him with Paul Blair to show up Jackson, and a well-known altercation ensued.[3]
- Jackson hit three homers on three pitches from three different pitchers, winning the sixth and final game of the World Series to become a legend of the postseason. His stats that year earned him the nickname Mr. October.

- In the 1978 season, with the Yankees tied 5 to 5 in the tenth inning of a game against Kansas City, Martin gave the sign to have Jackson put down a sacrifice bunt after Munson hit a lead-off single. Jackson became defiant and bunted the next two pitches ignoring the signs to swing away, even after a visit from the third-base coach. He popped out to the catcher on the third pitch and may have cost the Yankees the game because his ego was bigger than the team.

- Martin called for Jackson's suspension for the rest of the season for ignoring signs but Jackson only got five games. Martin learned from Bill Veeck that Steinbrenner was trying to work a manager swap with the White Sox, and on the advice of his lawyer, quit on July 24, 1978, before he was traded or fired. This meant the Yankees had to pay him.

- Steinbrenner almost immediately regretted pushing Billy, and after hiring Bob Lemon to a two-year contract, brought Billy back for Old-Timers' Day just five days after he resigned. The Yankees announced Martin as their new manager for 1980, leaving Lemon as a lame duck.

- Martin came back early after the Yankees got off to a sour start in 1979, and got fired later that year five days after having a brawl with a marshmallow salesman who he mocked because of his profession.

"**All I know is, I pass people on the street [of New York City] these days, and they don't know whether to say hello or to say good-bye.**"

— BILLY MARTIN

- Hired by the Oakland A's before the 1980 season and true-to-form, he turned the team around going from dead last in '79 to a respectable second-place in '80. In 1981, the season was split by a strike, and the A's took first place in the first half, but later lost to the Yankees in a three-game sweep. 1982 did not go well, and rumor had it that he'd been contacted by Steinbrenner who offered his job back if he could manage to get fired from Oakland. Martin obliged by displaying reprehensible behavior, demoting gay players, traveling with his mistress, and trashing his office when the team refused him a loan to pay off tax debts.

- In 1983, the Yankees hired Martin with a long-term contract, but Steinbrenner fired him at the end of the season, moving him to a scouting job. Billy was back in 1985 and managed a second-place finish, but second was not good enough for the impulsive Steinbrenner. Steinbrenner fired Billy as manager but raised his salary (!) keeping him on as an advisor and retiring his number 1 (!)

> "I may not have been the greatest Yankee to ever put on the uniform, but I was the proudest."
>
> — BILLY MARTIN

- Billy again took the helm in 1988, but off-the-field troubles plagued the dynamic personality. A brawl in a nightclub, looming marital troubles, and an ejection that led to a suspension for throwing dirt at an umpire contributed to Martin being dismissed halfway through the season. He was again moved to a consultant position marking the eighth time he managed to get fired from his position as manager.
- Penciled-in to manage the Yankees again in 1990 for his sixth tour as manager, the hopes of fans and management were thwarted by Martin's untimely death in a car accident near his home on Christmas day.

> "[Martin was] one of the most magnetic, entertaining, sensitive, humane, brilliant, generous, insecure, paranoid, dangerous, irrational, and unhinged people I had ever met."
>
> — BILL PENNINGTON

Being feisty is not really a prerequisite to being a successful manager. In fact, managers come in all flavors from the silent tacticians to the Napoleonic governors to the masters of chaos. The one thing all great managers seem to possess is a passion and knowledge of the game, a notion that nothing less than winning is acceptable, and a curious ability to inspire players and fans with their passion. Martin's monomaniacal desire to win—especially as a Yankee—drove him to unmatched highs and lows in his career and personal life. But certainly, he is an extreme in the game of baseball.

---

1. Whitey Ford is sometimes included in this story, but it seems unlikely.
2. The validity of the entire story is sometimes questioned because similar tales have been told by comedians, writers, and in the press. It suggests these pranksters may have appropriated the story and adapted it for their own purposes.
3. This clip shows the altercation: https://youtu.be/HHctFAj1ywI

14

DO NOT GO GENTLE INTO THAT GOOD NIGHT

The title name comes from a poem by the Welsh poet Dylan Thomas that is meant to acknowledge that every life ends in death but that should not be a reason to quit. In this case, the use of the title is meant to suggest that a warrior in the game recognizes they have been a champion and do not give in to a slow and dismal fade into obscurity.

Of all the storied careers that seem improbable, impossible, or flat-out lies, there is a rare breed of players who end their careers on a high note—a place where they seem to play their best moments before bowing gracefully into retirement. Mike Mussina's underappreciated eighteen-year career ended with his first twenty-win season at the age of 39, and that achievement probably got him into the Hall of Fame. Ted Williams came back after a disappointing season in 1959 as if he had something to prove, redeemed his reputation, and walked off the season with his final at-bat being a home run at the age of 41. In that season, he eclipsed the cherished 500 home run pinnacle even though he missed about five years of his prime due to military service. David Ortiz retired in 2016 after hitting a record 38 homers—the highest number by a player in their final season—at the age of 40. Each of these players had all but announced their retirement in their final year. Each achieved commemorable goals.

One far more improbable figure absolutely dominated baseball for a period of just six years. Entering what he acknowledged to himself as his final season at the age of 30, he pitched to his lowest career ERA (1.73), won the most games of any season he played (twenty-seven), and won his final of three Cy Young awards in the years where only one Cy Young was awarded annually. His career started late, ended early, and as a shooting star blazed into the annals of baseball legends battling the demise of his own body which had encumbered him with crippling arthritis. But it was not to happen before he left his mark on the game.

 "There are two times in my life the hair on my arms has stood up: The first time I saw the ceiling of the Sistine Chapel and the first time I saw Sandy Koufax throw a fastball."

— AL CAMPANIS, DODGERS' SCOUT

Koufax was not even a baseball star in his early days. Sandy excelled in basketball. He did play baseball but was a position player, gravitating to catching, and was moved to first base. He pitched only four games in his college career and did play well (3–1, 2.81 ERA, 51 Ks in thirty-two innings) but it was hardly the focus of his athletic endeavors.

The eyes of scouts somehow did the improbable and recognized his more unique talents and promising arm. Despite the fact that he could be relatively wild, Koufax threw hard. So hard that in a tryout with the Pirates, Koufax threw a fastball that broke the thumb of Sam Narron (a bullpen pitching coach).

> **"When he first came up, he couldn't throw a baseball inside the batting cage."**
>
> — DUKE SNIDER, HALL OF FAME CENTER FIELDER

Koufax took a flier and signed with the Dodgers. Because his signing bonus was over $4,000 dollars, the club was required to keep Koufax on the major-league roster for two years. He saw little action during this time and made just as little progress as a player.

"My first two years in the big leagues I did very little except watch... [I] realized [I] was not trained for my job. I pitched four or five sandlot games and four games in college. That was it."

— SANDY KOUFAX

Between 1955 and 1960, Koufax amassed a less-than-stellar record of 36 and 40, never once with an ERA less than 3.00. Then, in the offseason, Koufax came to a sort of realization.

"I really started working out. I started running more. I decided I was really going to find out how good I can be."

— SANDY KOUFAX

From 1961 to 1966, Sandy Koufax struck out more batters than innings pitched. He went 129 and 47. Three times he threw to an ERA of less than 2.00, leading the league in ERA in five straight seasons. He was a perennial all-star for six straight years. Won two consecutive Cy Young awards in his last two. He was in the top two in MVP voting in three of his final four years, winning one nod in 1963, and losing to Willie Mays in 1965 and Roberto Clemente in 1966. In two of three World Series wins as a player, he was twice named

MVP for his ability to take the ball and shut down the opposition.

Over those six years, Koufax also threw four no-hitters and a perfect game. He tamed the wildness that plagued his early career and broke out his potential.

> **"My first recollection of Sandy Koufax is in Vero Beach—his first spring—and it was like 10 o'clock in the morning and Sandy's first pitch went sailing over the backstop landed on the roof of the press room—'clunk'—and it woke up a 65-year-old sportswriter who was in there take a morning nap."**
>
> — JACK LANG, SPORTSWRITER

Sandy had to exit the game as a baby-faced player at just 30 years of age because his body took up against him. No more cursed than Gehrig, he faced the reality of life and purposely threw a dominant season that would mark his achievement, feeling the pain of every pitch but coming through as a giant on his field of dreams so he could hold his head up because of his accomplishments. Too many try to push beyond.

"The man who stands alone is the most dominating pitcher I ever saw—without a doubt, and with no equal—Sandy Koufax."

— DON SUTTON, HALL OF FAME PITCHER

WALK-OFF BALK

The balk[1] is part of that breed of unusual baseball rules that even most baseball players don't completely understand. In its simplest definition, it is when a pitcher comes set with his foot on the pitching rubber and makes any motion that interrupts normal delivery with the intent to deceive the runner or batter—intentional or not. This gets complicated by what is considered "legal."[2] The penalty for "deceiving the runner" is that each runner is awarded a base.

It is the only instance in baseball where runners advance on a ball that never comes into play. Not only that, a run can score.

Since about 1900 there have been 22 walk-off balks. The saddest of these walk-offs is probably a game where the

Rangers and the Dodgers were dueling to a 0 to 0 shutout on June 18, 2015. Rookie Keone Kela was having a good season and was called on to pitch the ninth inning. He was only into the thirtieth inning of his MLB career when he seemed to hit a little hitch in the road.

He was 3 balls and 2 strikes on Yasmani Grandal and issued a walk on the sixth pitch. Enrique Hernandez pinch-ran for Grandal. Hernandez was not really a threat to steal as he'd never stolen a base in his career, but Kela probably didn't know that as Hernandez was a rookie as well. Kela threw a four-pitch walk to Andre Ethier, checking the runner between the first and second pitch with a pick-off throw to first. It was now first and second.

After a pick-off attempt at second trying to keep Hernandez close to the bag, Kela ran the count to 3 and 1 without Alberto Callaspo offering at anything. Callaspo bunted the fifth pitch foul to run the count to 3 and 2.

The bunt was now out of the equation because there were two strikes, Callaspo swung away and grounded the next pitch to the first baseman who started a 3-6-3 double play advancing Hernandez to third. What a relief that must have been to Kela.

Now with two down, all Kela had to worry about was Jimmy Rollins who was hitting .200 on the season. The first ball was a called strike. The second was a swinging strike. One more strike and the game would go into extra innings. He threw a ball and the count advanced to 1 ball and 2 strikes. He still had the advantage. He pounded the strike zone forcing Rollins to foul off the next two pitches.

Let's just frame the moment. A runner on third who is not a speedster, two outs already in the bag. You are ahead in the count to a batter who hits at the Mendoza-line.[3] Then the game stopped without Kela throwing a pitch. He was called on a balk as he appeared to react to Hernandez breaking down the line. One pitch away from continuing the game into extra innings in very favorable odds, Kela made the blunder of worrying about a man who had little chance to steal anything, much less home.

This is the vicious potential consequence of the balk.[4]

People hold records for balking. Hall of Fame pitcher Steve Carlton finished his career in 1988 but not before being called for 90 balks in his twenty-four-year career. No one else even comes close. Bob Welsh is second all-time with 45 —half as many.

Bob Shaw once gave up 5 balks in one game on May 4, 1963. He gave up 2 more balks in his previous start on April 28. Within just two games, he had a total of 7 balks and ended up with a total of just 12 over a career spanning 1,778 innings. Those two days made up 58 percent of the balks he got over a ten-year career. In all, they amounted to remarkably little offensive production. The only run accomplished by balk was in the third inning. After walking Billy Williams leading off, Shaw balked Williams around the bases over the course of several otherwise unproductive outs. In essence, Williams hit a home run just by standing in the batter's box, only he technically never had to take his bat off his shoulder to score. It seems that is a performance that is hard to outdo.

In stepped Jim Gott, August 6, 1988, looking for a challenge.

Relieving in the eighth inning of a game against the Mets with a 3 to 2 lead, Gott threw to pinch-hitter Tim Teufel and walked him on seven pitches. With Dave Magadan at bat, Gott balked sending Teufel to second base, removing the force. Magadan then grounded out on what might have been a double play to the second baseman, but Teufel advanced to third. Darryl Strawberry stepped in and grounded the ball to second. The second baseman threw home and Teufel beat the throw. It was scored a fielder's choice: the run scored and Strawberry ended up at first. It was a run that scored to tie the game all because the balk took away the force for the double play.

Kevin McReynolds ran the count to 2 balls and 0 strikes before taking the third pitch to right-center for a double. It was second and third with just one out. Gary Carter took his turn at the plate and just stood there. Gott didn't even get off a pitch to Carter and balked to score Strawberry. The Mets took a 4 to 3 lead. McReynolds, also awarded a base, went to third. Carter walked on five pitches, actually swinging and fouling off the second pitch. Howard Johnson struck out swinging on just three pitches. Kevin Elster stepped up with two out with runners on first and third, and on a 2 ball 1 strike count just stood there as Gott balked for the third time in the inning. This scored McReynolds and sent Carter to second base. The Mets scored three runs, arguable all because of balks and they led the Pirates 5 to 3. Mackey Sasser pinch-hit for Bob McClure, the Pirates relieved Gott with Jeff Robinson who got Sasser to ground out 6–3 to end what is probably the inning most influenced by balks in the history of baseball. The Pirates went on to lose the game 3 to 5, with Gott taking the loss, having given up 1 hit, 3 walks, 3 balks, and 3 runs in two-thirds of an inning. Gott had 6 balks on the year in 1988, and in 1,170 innings as a big-league player, committed only 15 balks.

Certainly, the 22 walk-off balks were heart-breaking ways to lose games, but not one of those performances balked a man around the bases or scored three runs for the opposing team. They all just brought in a final run when a game was tied and did not contribute to the tying, go-ahead, and insurance runs that a team needed to win a game.

Three balks, one inning, three runs in. That is the ultimate in mechanical despair.

---

1. See the official baseball rules section 6.02(a) for a complete discussion of the definition of a balk.

https://content.mlb.com/documents/2/2/4/305750224/2019_Offi cial_Baseball_Rules_FINAL_.pdf.

2. Until 2013, pitchers were allowed to fake a throw toward third and spin to throw toward first or second, occupied or not.

3. Typically referred to as .200, or 1 in 5 chance of success.

4. The box score shows every step of the event.
   https://www.baseball-reference.com/boxes/LAN/LAN201506180. shtml

SUPER JOE

P layers remembered in baseball lore often remain there because of their antics off the field as much as the achievements on it. A sad and strange corner of baseball is the group of shooting stars who really were great players but often had their careers cut short. The fans of the game are left to wonder "what if..."

In this category, you find players like Mark Fidrych, a phenom in his first year at the age of 21 in 1976. He went 19 and 9 that year not at all depending on striking out batters,[1] instead relying on his relationship with the baseball. Watching him on the mound, it seemed Fidrych was coaxing the ball to do his will by talking to it. He played as if he were a condensed cartoon version of Zack Greinke, apparently doing more to freak out batters than dominate them. Fidrych was named "The Bird" after the goofy, gigantic feathered character named Big Bird on the long-running children's program Sesame Street.[2] Fidrych drew fans by the tens of thousands to ballparks across the league with his on-field dynamic.

Pete Reiser, another unique character, never met a cement or brick wall without serious injury. He played the game with an aggressiveness and skill somewhere between Pete Rose, Shoeless Joe Jackson, and Ty Cobb and is considered by some as one of the greatest baseball players of all time. His downfall was his enthusiasm. Ebbets Field was the first ballpark in the major leagues with padded walls and they were installed because of the insane way Reiser went after fly balls. He was taken off the field on a stretcher a record eleven times. That is a stat that does not make the box score and it is probably ten more times than any other player in MLB history. On June 4, 1947, Reiser was administered last rites after a collision with a wall. He was credited with the catch.[3]

As sensational and yet obscure as these players were, another appeared on the radar for a total of 647 at-bats over 201 games in the early '80s. That's the 1980s. That needs to be clarified because parts of his story seem to be from another era. He was touted as a tough-as-nails type of player who hit for power and average, and did manage to set a record: least games played by a position player after being voted Rookie of the Year.[4] After the 1980 season, he appeared in only seventy more games as his career was derailed by a back injury from which he never fully recovered. Regardless of the brevity of his career, Joe Charboneau managed to make a lasting impression on fans. His first hit, in his first game and second at-bat in the majors, was a home run. Like any true mythical hero, he had a song written about him.[5]

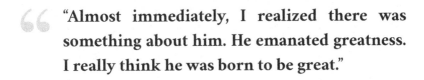

> **"Almost immediately, I realized there was something about him. He emanated greatness. I really think he was born to be great."**
>
> — JOE NOSSEK, AN INDIANS' COACH

As a boy, Joe had trouble sitting still and had trouble not getting into trouble. He likely had undiagnosed ADHD, like Rube Waddell. Eventually, his energy, academic indifference, and other challenges led him to be declared ineligible to play baseball—the one thing he seemed to settle into with some direction and success. This didn't turn out to be an improvement because he found other—less productive—ways to channel his energy. This is how the legend of "Super Joe" Charboneau[6] was born.

During his exile from organized ball at school, Joe sought adventure. He took on odd challenges such as taking part in bare-knuckle boxing matches to earn some extra money. He got $25 for a win and $15 for a loss, but $5 went to the person who set up the match. These were not proper bare-knuckle matches. Everything was legal except for weapons. He lost more than he won, had his nose broken several times, and once tried to fix his wrinkled schnozz with a pair of pliers. He must have been somewhat impervious to pain, as he admitted to pulling his own tooth with a vice grip and cutting off a tattoo he got with a razor when he decided he didn't like it.

Trouble followed Joe into the streets, and he also got into fights with people who were not fighting for money. He claimed to have been stabbed three times in these less lucrative bouts and once closed a wound on his own using fishing line. Later when with the Indians for exhibition games in Mexico City, Joe was approached by a fellow who seemed to be looking for an autograph, pen in hand. The man asked Joe where he was from and when Joe answered, Oscar Martinez —who hated Americans—drove his pen into Joe's side, plunging it in four inches. Martinez was caught and fined 50 pesos. That was the equivalent of about $2.27.

In the days of the minors, he was exposed to other players' antics and took dares like swallowing whole eggs—shell on —which he did once. It lodged in his throat and he began choking when a quick-thinking friend punched him in the egg and it broke up so he could swallow it. He somehow found out that he could drink beer through his repaired nose. He won a $25 bet by eating six lit cigarettes. He bought himself a pet alligator with distinct aspirations, named the gator Chopper, and kept it in his bathtub.[7]

"I was going to train him to wrestle me. He would have grown to be about six feet long, so I would have had the height advantage."

— JOE CHARBONEAU

It became impractical to move Chopper when Joe switched teams, so he left the animal in the care of a teammate. During that time Chopper attempted to escape and fatally injured himself in the process. The alligator is supposedly the reason for a curse that has fallen over the team.

Like many of the pranksters, jokesters, and mythical heroes of the game, Joe's fabled history followed him and people attributed things to his history that were not his own. Some claimed he had his own vaudeville show and said they'd seen him eat lightbulbs and shot glasses. But one thing is certain: he played well enough in minor league ball to be called up in 1980.

 "Making it to the big leagues was the highlight for me. Baseball was good back then. You played for the love of the game and you didn't make a lot of money. There were fewer teams and better pitching. It was harder to make it."

— JOE CHARBONEAU

In Joe's first home game, April 19, Joe went 3 for 3 with a home run, a double, and a walk immediately capturing the attention and imagination of the fans. Later that season, on June 28, Joe hit what is considered to be one of the three longest home runs ever hit in Yankee Stadium achieving what storied Yankee sluggers such as Mantle, the Babe, Gehrig, Maris, and DiMaggio never did.

As the antics and actualities began to mount, Joe became a hero in the city of Cleveland. By mid-season, a song was released featuring Joe and the locals ate up the 45 single. It rose to number four on the charts. Cleveland may not be a big town to win over, but the fanatical fans helped push his fame to greater heights and he ended up on magazine covers and TV shows. Joe found it hard to believe this was happening to him.

When the season came to a close, Charboneau seemed headed for a career with the mega-stars of the sport. But fortunes turned in spring training when Joe injured his back during a head-first slide. He tried to play through it, but his regression at the plate sent him back to the minors. Things did not improve much, and while Joe surfaced a few times over the next few seasons, he was not invited to stay. On June 1, 1982, with his batting average at .214, he left major league baseball for the final time. From there he went to the Buffalo affiliate and was released in 1983.

"Well, maybe this is it. I've had my year and a half in the big leagues. Maybe that's all I've got coming."

— JOE CHARBONEAU TO A REPORTER AS HE
EMPTIED HIS LOCKER

Joe may have no longer had a playing career, but he did have a legend, and that lived on past the end of his career. He made appearances and got to enjoy the power of the myth and legend built around his time in the big leagues.

---

1. Fidrych had only 97 Ks in 250 innings.
2. Sesame Street originally aired in 1969 and still runs on public television as educational programming for young kids.
3. Gene Hermanski admitted much later to putting the ball in Reiser's glove as Reiser lay motionless so he would be credited with the catch.
4. From Bob Bloss's book *Rookies of the Year* (2005). Mark Fidrych only appeared in twenty-seven games after his rookie year, but he was a pitcher.
5. "Go Joe Charboneau" by Section 36. https://youtu.be/S2JV0btxRvQ
6. His name is sometimes misspelled Charbonneau, which is a more common spelling and is confused with a Canadian Archbishop.
7. This is disputed in *Crazy, with the Papers to Prove It,* by Dan Coughlin. He does say Joe acquired the pet, but that he also purchased a $300 aquarium to keep it in.

17

YOU THROW LIKE A GIRL

When I was a kid, I was lucky enough to live next door to a guy who loved baseball. He was a tough construction worker, had a grizzly voice, chain-smoked Lucky Strikes, and spent most of his time in a t-shirt. He and his wife were never able to have children, so Rocco took me and my brothers under his wing to teach us how to play ball. He was no pro, but we learned tons about the game before we were old enough to play it seriously ourselves. He was great at encouraging us. Getting started throwing early made sure I'd never throw like a girl.

Later when I had my first kid, I couldn't wait to have a catch. I probably started way too early, but the result was that she never threw like a girl either. Yeah, she was a girl, but she never threw like one.

Looking back, I'm sure it was because she started at an early age. The mechanics of "throwing like a girl" were really just a myth.[1] The reality is that girls aren't encouraged to throw or play baseball so they don't develop those skills and muscle memory. They don't learn to leverage the torque of their torso and, because of that, their elbow dominates the throw making it look weak rather than throwing from the shoulder.

Now consider growing up next door to a Hall of Fame pitcher, let's say Dazzy Vance, who led the league in strike-outs seven times in a career that spanned twenty years.[2] Imagine he took you under his wing and taught you how to throw his famous "drop pitch." Chances are that even if you were a girl, you wouldn't end up throwing like one.

Joe Engel built Engel Stadium in 1930 to be the home of the Washington Senators' first minor league affiliate, the Chattanooga Lookouts. Over the years that followed, Engel became known as the "Barnum of the Bushes"[3]—the minor league version of Bill Veeck[4] who chose to host baseball games as promotional events to draw in the fans and the sparse dollars of depression-era crowds. He had his players parade onto the field on elephants for opening day,[5] distributed canaries in cages around the park, traded a player for a turkey,[6] reenacted Custer's last stand,[7] raffled off a house to attending fans (cramming more than 25,000 attendees into a stadium that held 12,000), and hired a woman to play pro ball.

 "I don't care what you say about me, as long as you say something."[8]

— JOE ENGEL

Engel was a successful scout who is credited with discovering Babe Ruth and Joe Cronin, amongst other players. On March 25, 1931, Engel scouted and signed Jackie Mitchell, a 17-year-old girl because he saw a promotional opportunity. She was a girl and an incorrigible tomboy whose father started her playing baseball from a young age. Their neighbor, Dazzy Vance, helped to coach her in throwing a ball.

Engel's Chattanooga Lookouts were scheduled for two exhibition games against the New York Yankees, whose lineup still sported both Babe Ruth and Lou Gehrig. The first game, originally scheduled for April 1,[9] was rained out. The next day, Jackie did not start the game, but after the starting pitcher let up a double and a run-scoring single, the coach put Jackie in to face Babe Ruth.

Ruth took the first pitch for a ball. Film of the at-bat shows Ruth swinging and missing on the second and third pitch to make the count 1 ball and 2 strikes.[10] Ruth stepped in and took a called strike on the outside of the plate. He threw his bat down after the call, seemingly in disgust with the umpire.

Gehrig got up and struck out swinging at three straight pitches. Tony Lazzari then walked on five pitches and Mitchell was lifted from the game and replaced with the starting pitcher.

While neither Ruth nor Gehrig ever admitted to the strike-outs being staged, they never fully denied it either. While opinions vary, Engel himself let on that it was a ruse in a letter to the press in 1955.

 "She couldn't pitch hay to a cow."

— JOE ENGEL

Mitchell, either misinformed of the reality of her appearance or refusing to let on that she was in on the gag, insisted until her death in 1987 that the strikeouts were no joke.

 "Why, hell yes, [Ruth and Gehrig] were trying, damn right. Hell, better hitters than them couldn't hit me. Why should they've been any different?"[11]

— JACKIE MITCHELL

Just days after Jackie's appearance, baseball Commissioner, Kenesaw Mountain Landis, voided her contract, essentially banning her from playing baseball. She continued to play in barnstorming games and participated in crowd-pleasing promotional events like riding onto the field on a donkey,[12] but eventually put baseball aside to work at her father's optician's shop.

Jackie's appearance against these great players may have been a burlesque of sorts in the era of vaudeville and the Great Depression, but it should stand as a question as to whether there is really such a thing as "throwing like a girl." A girl can only throw like a girl because they have no other choice. But if that girl can strike out some of the greatest hitters in a game, maybe someday we will see a female player start in the major leagues.

-----

1. This is verified to a great extent in an episode of the MythBusters TV program where they take an in-depth look at what it means to "throw like a girl." https://youtu.be/LD5Xm5u7UDM
2. Vance's career spanned twenty years, but he was injured early on and missed several years before suddenly regaining his form at the age of 31 after having bone chips removed from his shoulder. He then came back gangbusters to lead the league in strikeouts for seven straight years between 1922 and 1928.
3. "Bushes" refers to bush leagues.
4. Veeck was the famous baseball promoter who did many outrageous things, including hiring a little person to pinch hit (Eddie Gaedel); allowing fans to vote on key decisions during a game("Grandstand Manager's Night"); "Disco Demolition Night" where fans were encouraged to bring unwanted disco albums to the stadium to be demolished by explosives (this drew more than baseball fans and forced the forfeiture of the second game of a double-header); and hiring Max Patkin "the Clown Prince of Baseball" to coach, effectively distracting fans and players with his antics from the coaching box.

5. It is not clear from varied accounts whether these elephants were real or papier-mâché, whether there was a parade or an elephant hunt, or whether two different events are merged in accounts of the event(s).

6. Johnny "Binky" Jones whose career MLB stats include 25 hits and 8 walks in sixteen-and-a-third innings while picking up a win.

7. Custer won in Engel's version.

8. "Obituaries," The Sporting News, June 13, 1969: 44.

9. There arises some controversy over whether the whole event was staged as an April Fool's joke because of the original date.

10. https://www.smithsonianmag.com/videos/category/history/the-girl-who-struck-out-babe-ruth/ Skip to 4:42 for the video of Ruth striking out.

11. She said this in an interview with a reporter in 1986 for an article in *Smithsonian Magazine*.

12. Donkey baseball was not really played like this farcical account https://youtu.be/HcNWfcdEJ6E

18

A CATASTROPHIC TIE GAME

How many plays in baseball result in suicide? What does it feel like when you end your career and you have to worry that when you die your gravestone will read: "He was a bonehead"?

Players are sometimes remembered for one career-defining play, and for all the wrong reasons. Bill Buckner had a solid twenty-two-year career and instead of being remembered for his consistency and longevity, he is remembered for a play—a single play—in the 1986 World Series that turned the tide in the favor of the New York Mets. He actually botched more than that one in the series, but at the time he performed the career-defining play, the second botch was no longer critical. It was just bad.

In the top of the tenth in that sixth game with a 3 to 2 lead in wins, the Mets had come from a 3 to 0 deficit to tie in the bottom of the eighth, the Red Sox scored two runs. With a 5 to 3 lead, they looked like they were about to walk off the field as World Champions, dousing the "Curse of the Bambino."[1] With two out in the bottom of the tenth, trailing by two, Met's Hall of Fame catcher, Gary Carter, singled. Kevin Mitchell came in to pinch-hit, and he singled to make it first-and-second. On a 0 and 2 count, the Mets down to their last strike, Ray Knight hit a single scoring Carter and leaving it first and third with two out. Mookie Wilson came up, and in the course of a ten pitch at-bat, he induced a wild pitch to tie the game on the seventh pitch. Three pitches later, he hit one of the most famous ground balls ever. It looked like an easy out to send the game to the eleventh inning, but it went through the wickets of Bill Buckner's legs. Knight was flying with two out and no one could retrieve the ball in time.

Knight Scored the winning and brought them to game 7 where they became world champions. It was a mistake a veteran should not have made, but being on the national stage, his disgrace was broadcast and marked him forever.

Fred Merkle was a 19-year-old kid in 1908 playing in his second season with the New York Giants. In a game on September 23 of that year, he had not yet had one hundred plate appearances and had never started a game until that day, playing backup to the team's starting first baseman, Fred

Tenney.[2] Merkle was called on to start as Tenney woke up with low back pain. He walked once in four plate appearances and then, in the bottom of the ninth inning, Merkle came to bat with two outs, a man on first, and the score tied 1 to 1.

Merkle singled and McCormick advanced to third base. Al Bridwell followed Merkle with another single, scoring McCormick with what should have been the winning run. Fans flooded the field thinking that the game was over because they just saw the winning run cross home plate. But Merkle, possibly confused by the stampede, turned and ran to the Giants' clubhouse without touching second base. He forgot that he was still required to touch second before leaving the field because he was the lead runner in a force play.

Johnny Evers was a shrewd veteran in his seventh year in the big leagues. He noticed Merkle failed to touch second. He retrieved a ball,[3] touched second base, and appealed to the umpire. The ump called Merkle out. As the third out was made, the run did not score and the game remained a tie. With the chaos of thousands of fans on the field and with night coming on, the game was called off and the umpires declared it a tie.

As fate would have it, the Giants and the Cubs ended the season tied for first place. It appeared that the game that they tied had to be replayed to determine who came in first. The Cubs took the makeup game, 4 to 2 ending the season for the

Giants. Then the Cubs went on to win the World Series that year in five games over the Tigers.

Harry Pulliam was the President of the National League at the time of incidents that found the Cubs and Giants in a tie at the end of the season. After "Merkle's Boner,"[4] Pulliam reviewed the decision of the umpires and agreed with them, never expecting that the game would end up being critical to the pennant race. When the tie resulted from regular play, the National League Council held a special meeting to again review the play. They upheld Pulliam's earlier decision, and in a report went on to berate Merkle for his "reckless, careless, inexcusable blunder."[5]

As anyone might expect, Merkle was distraught over his role in the events. When his playing career ended, he moved on from baseball and did not look back for twenty-four years. In 1950 at the age of 62, Merkle accepted an invitation to the Giant's Old-Timers' Day. The kind crowd welcomed him with a standing ovation. Fred died five years later of natural causes. His hometown of Watertown, Wisconsin, has several commemorations raised for Merkle.

While one might expect Merkle to be the one most affected by the events and the weight of his blunder, Harry Pulliam was perhaps more deeply troubled. He took off several months after the end of the season and was noted by acquaintances to have become particularly moody. On September 28, 1909, Pulliam was found shot in his room at the New York Athletic Club. The shooting appeared to have been an attempted suicide, and the damage was great. It did not immediately kill him, though the bullet passed completely through his skull from temple to temple, blinding him. The doctor in attendance asked Pulliam what the reason for the shooting was, and Pulliam answered: "Who is shot? I am not shot." He then became unconscious and never regained consciousness again.

There are many theories about the reason for the suicide that go beyond the idea that Pulliam's state of depression was only due to Merkle's Boner to include the saucy state of affairs in the political battles within the league. Some theories even suggest Pulliam may have been murdered. It is, of course, unlikely that the true story will come to light.

———————————

1. The "curse" had to do with selling Babe Ruth to the New York Yankees. Supposedly, the sale had to do with the owner of the Sox wanting to finance Broadway shows, including *"No, No, Nanette."* To that point (1920) Boston had been a dominant force in baseball. Ruth went for $125,000 dollars ($1,728,681.25 dollars in 2021, see https://www.in2013dollars.com/us/inflation/1920? amount=125000).
2. Merkle's total plate appearances were 91 at the moment of the incident.
3. It is hard to tell if the ball he retrieved was the game ball or not, as accounts differ.
4. The event actually left Merkle with a playing error named after him.
5. "Cubs and Giants to Play Off Tie," *Chicago Tribune*, October 7, 1908.

19

THE SOUND OF SILENT DOMINANCE

Most superstars are remembered for the things they do with a bat or the prowess of their arm. Some are known for aggressive play, foolish antics, personalities, and moments that became larger than life. But there are players who forge long careers in a sort of quiet persistence, not known for anything but their glove. When you are in a game as a rookie and you hit the first home run of your career in the same game that Mickey Mantle hits the 500th of his career, nobody knows your name. Especially when that will be the first of only twenty home runs in an eighteen-year career to go with a lifetime batting average of .228 and slugging percentage of .280. Those are not typos. He holds the dubious honor of being the player who was pinch-hit for the most in history (333).

"There is no such thing as good pitching without good defense."

— SANDY KOUFAX

For a glove-first player to hold real value for a team, they can't just be good at what they do. They have to be the best. These are players who have a fine work ethic and probably nothing short of obsession with the mechanics of playing the field. Their style of play may be sharp and seemingly effortless but it will lack sparkle. In fact, it might be downright dull. Take that player and his eight Gold Gloves and stick him between a third baseman who won sixteen straight Gold Gloves,[1] and two different second basemen who won a total of seven over eight seasons,[2] and there is a defensive dynasty. It is how you come to have four starting pitchers on one team winning twenty games each in the same year. It is hard to believe that situation was just because those players happened to play with one another. It seems more likely that they held each other in esteem, and sometimes held each other up.

 "I never ever saw him blow a routine play. [Blade][3] had wonderful range... He was special out there."

— BOOG POWELL, *100 THINGS ORIOLES FANS SHOULD KNOW & DO BEFORE THEY DIE* BY DAN CONNOLLY

Mark "Blade" Belanger is not a player most people will know unless they are a fan of the Orioles or followed baseball in the '70s. He is also particularly difficult to profile because extensive defensive metrics were not the stats of his day. He ranged in the shadow of probably the greatest fielding third baseman ever to play the game on teams where big bats, great arms, and diving catches grabbed the headlines. Somehow Belanger, although a great athlete, seemed to effortlessly cover the ground he defended and was always just where he needed to be.

> **"Belanger would glide effortlessly after a grounder and welcome it into loving arms; scooping the ball up with a single easy motion, and bringing it to his chest for a moment's caress before making his throw."**
>
> — PAT JORDAN, "YEARS AHEAD OF HIS TIME," *SPORTS ILLUSTRATED*, JULY 29, 1974

The combination of style and smarts gave Belanger some power over the outcome of the game. He shared that as a team player, teaching what he knew to younger guys on the way up seemingly unconcerned that they might be there for his job. He helped create a practically impenetrable wall of defense that made pitchers better at what they did.

> "[Trying to get a hit through the left side of the Baltimore infield is like] trying to throw a hamburger through a brick wall."

— DETROIT TIGERS' MANAGER, MAYO SMITH

One way to see in the mind's eye how Belanger worked is to look at his actions in a complicated play. He was involved in one of the most exotic triple plays in baseball where he let up a run but saved the game. Triple plays are strange enough because you have to have certain conditions. There have to be no outs with two runners on base. That immediately makes it much more rare than a double play. Generally, the ball in a triple play will have the first out made in the infield.

On June 3, 1977, Belanger was playing short in a game against the Royals. It was the often fabled bottom of the ninth inning and the Royals were down 7 to 5. Two innings earlier Belanger sent a fly ball to left field to score an insurance run on a sacrifice fly—which it turns out to be a run the Orioles would need. Al Cowens led off the inning with a double, Dave Nelson walked, and then Freddie Patek hit a single to load the bases. Tippy Martinez who was usually bank for the Orioles just wasn't getting it done. The O's still had a two-run lead, but Kansas City had three outs to inflict some damage with the winning run already on base.

John Wathen pinch-hit with his average at a whopping .417. Wathen hit a fly ball to right field that Pat Kelly caught, but all the runners were tagging up to create some chaos on the base paths. Cowens scored easily after the catch. Kelly threw to Belanger who caught Freddie Patek by feeding the ball to Billy Smith at second who got the ball back to Belanger who tagged out Patek. Dave Nelson skidded off to third base, deciding to try to score seeing the run-down and not expecting it to go so easily. Belanger saw Nelson make the turn and ran at him as he was halfway down the line. Nelson had to choose a direction and headed toward home. Belanger tagged him out ten feet from home plate and the inning was over.

Belanger commandeered the whole mess, masterfully dissecting the play as it unfolded and neatly clearing the base paths for another day. He just didn't do it loudly enough to make the Hall of Fame.

 "The guy had the greatest glove at shortstop I've ever seen. He just didn't have the batting average... Damn right, he's in my Hall of Fame. Blade and Brooksie made me a Hall of Famer."

— JIM PALMER

---

1. Brooks Robinson, 1960 to 1975.
2. Davey Johnson, 1969 to 1971; Bobby Grich, 1973 to 1976.
3. Mark Belanger's nickname.

20

THE SPACEMAN WHO WAS IMPERVIOUS TO BUS FUMES

If Zack Greinke had a forefather in the baseball realm, it was probably Bill Lee. They do look a little alike if you compare them at similar ages. Lee didn't quite dominate in his day like Greinke has but he had his moments and was a competitor. Lee was certainly more outspoken and willing to share his views in a way that is practically opposite to Greinke. The fact that he readily shared his views is exactly what earned him the nickname "Spaceman." He embraced his ideals and accepted uncommon and unpopular world views that may be seen as peculiar by people more conservatively rooted. But if you really consider his words, you have to also consider who is crazy.

"I'm mad at Hank (Aaron) for deciding to play one more season. I threw him his last home run and thought I'd be remembered forever. Now, I'll have to throw him another."[1]

— BILL "SPACEMAN" LEE

It is exactly through these perspectives that you get to know the skewed view of the man and how the skew makes sense. He is not really just some raving lunatic (although he admits to having his moments of tossing garbage pails and breaking chairs), but he does believe in the ideals of enjoying life and revels in history and nostalgia. That really isn't such a crazy thing. if you think about it.

"I love watching the older games and the guys with full windups. These guys are out there and they play baseball. They never pulled muscles. They never had weight machines. They never did stretching. They played pepper, they chewed tobacco, and they went and played baseball. They had a good time [and when] the game was over and they went out had a couple of brews, went home, and did it again."[2]

— BILL LEE

Spaceman was traded from Boston to Montreal after Lee continually had questions with Don Zimmer's handling of the pitching staff. Later, Lee was released from the Expos when he staged a walkout in protest of the Expos releasing Rodney Scott. He was essentially black-balled at that point and couldn't peddle his services to other major league teams. From that vantage, it seemed that Lee became even more comfortable with looking back at his career. One thing was clear, he wasn't very interested in rules.

 "[I cheated] every chance I could get. You couldn't chew slippery elm[3] anymore... a lot of spitballers threw... You put a little pine tar on your thumb to get more friction on the bottom of the ball, then you put slippery elm on the top [of the ball] and then you have a tumbling fastball that [batters] just can't flat out hit. Man! If you can make the ball go down and you can only hit the top half of the ball... you don't need any outfielders you can take them and just put them on the bench... most hitters are dumber than a post, so they'll never make [an] adjustment. I love sinkers. I love spitballs. I love anything will make the ball go downward..."[4]

— BILL LEE

What most people see in Lee's words is not the humor, but the horror of how it grates against their modern reality. His attitude is generally one of loving fun, life, nature, and baseball. It was meant to be a game that you play hard to compete and win, and it turned into a business that broke with the spirit of the game.

 "Baseball is timeless. You play it on beautiful fields when the grass turns green. You don't play when it rains. Baseball is a civilized game without a clock."[5]

— BILL LEE

In 1988, the Spaceman decided to run for president as the Rhino Party candidate. The party's spirit was inspired by an election in Brazil in the 1950s, where dissatisfied citizens nominated and subsequently elected a hippopotamus to a municipal post. Jacques Ferron founded the Rhino Party in 1963 choosing a rhinoceros as a symbol of being thick-skinned, stupid, and myopic while loving to wallow in the mud. One of the more famed platform policies was to lower the boiling point of water to save energy. They believed in bulldozing the Rocky Mountains so Eastern parts of Canada would get more sunlight.

"I don't like working. I like to play. And any day you're not in the sawmill or you're not in the woods cutting trees, and you're on a ball field you live a little longer. So I try to play as much baseball as I can."

— BILL LEE

In the book *The Wrong Stuff*,[6] an oft-maligned pitch about using marijuana suggested to many people that he was a frequent substance abuser. Combined with Lee's interesting perspectives, the idea of being heavily involved in drug culture explained his perspectives and behaviors. Lee never really denies marijuana use. It got him in some trouble with the commissioner, Bowie Kuhn. In an appearance on *Late Night with David Letterman*, Spaceman recalled the phone call he had with Kuhn.

 "The headline said I smoked it. I didn't say I "smoked." I said I "used it"... I [told him I] put it on my pancakes... I'd eat them and run five miles to the ballpark and it makes me impervious to the bus fumes. He says: 'Well I think I could buy that.' And I said: 'Would you like to buy a bridge?'"[7]

— BILL LEE

The curious follow-up was that Letterman asked Lee if he smoked marijuana or used it on his pancakes, Lee quickly denied that. When questioned further as to if he ever tried it, Lee admits to having tried it many times. True to form he creates a smokescreen for the truth where you are left between the dichotomy of his two worlds.

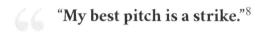 **"My best pitch is a strike."**[8]

— BILL LEE

"People are too hung up on winning. I can get off on a really good helmet throw."[9]

— BILL LEE

Exploring the words and worlds of Bill Lee is one that seems more of a labyrinth of interest and passion for the love of life, living, and baseball than a dive into madness. The craziest ones are those who can't play a game and have fun. This chapter would be misrepresented with anything other than the weight of his own words.

"I want real beer, real hot dogs, real whole wheat buns and that's what baseball is. Baseball is this field of dreams. It's you with your father playing catch... fielding ground balls... [and] never making an error."

— BILL LEE

---

1. On September 14, 1975, Bill Lee did throw Hank Aaron what would have been his final HR if Aaron had retired at the end of the year. Instead Dick Drago owns the badge of having given up Aaron's final homer on June 20, 1976.
2. A great interview on NPR with Bill Lee, *Fresh Air with Dave Davies*, February 28, 2005.
    https://www.npr.org/player/embed/4516268/4516269
3. Slippery elm bark is known to increase saliva and is usually used to help reduce throat irritation.
4. Also from *Fresh Air with Dave Davies*, February 28, 2005.
5. When an interview is good, you use it. *Fresh Air with Dave Davies*, February 28, 2005.
6. The first of four books Lee co-wrote about his adventures.
7. Bill Lee's appearance on Letterman: https://youtu.be/jeKwtn8r0FU?t=746
8. Interview: https://youtu.be/g1Bmr8hoCkg
9. Michael Gershman, *The Baseball Card Engagement Book*, 1990.

YOU ARE BETTER WHEN YOU PITCH A LITTLE HUNGOVER

The title of this chapter is influenced by the subject of the previous chapter. Bill Lee, in talking about the brief part of his career that crisscrossed with Juan Marichal in Boston in 1974, said Marichal suggested to Lee that it was better to pitch a little hungover. The idea was not really that being hungover improved motor skills, but it spurred a competitive advantage because it forced you to concentrate more on what you were doing. You could not simply walk up and use your given skills.

It seems that, just like PEDs, alcohol has those players it favors the fortunes of and those who it takes from the game. Hack Wilson is a tragic case who fell from the height of success hitting 56 HRs, .356, with 191 RBI[1] that year while carousing at the peak of his powers. He carried that behavior into the offseason, reported to camp 20 pounds heavier, and sank into his demise. Later he lamented his downfall and what might have been had he paid more attention to his health.

Paul Waner believed that he was a better player when intoxicated, but that would be hard to prove with any certainty. After all, we all sing better after a few glasses of wine at the karaoke bar. Waner really thought that drinking gave him an advantage and believed that its magic was the key to his success as a hitter.

 "When I walked up there with a half-pint of whiskey fresh in my gut, that ball came in looking like a basketball. But if I hadn't downed my half-pint of 100 proof, that ball came in like an aspirin tablet."

— PAUL WANER

Contemporaries were aware of his tendencies and were only left to tolerate them because they could not disprove the result.

 "Paul Waner had to be a very graceful player because he could slide without breaking the bottle on his hip."

— CASEY STENGEL

"Paul Waner, when he was sober, was the best right fielder the Pirates ever had. The second best right fielder the Pirates ever had was Paul Waner when he was drunk."

— JOE TRONZO, SPORTS EDITOR, *THE NEWS-TRIBUNE*, BEAVER FALLS, PA (1971)

There is one strange and rare achievement that two pitchers have admitted to in modern-day ball that seems to outdo even Dock Ellis' no-no. David Wells, a player never known to shy away from carousing, and Dallas Braden were both able to pitch perfect games while drunk, hungover, or a combination of these. The course of their careers would go in quite different directions.

Wells pitched the perfect game on Sunday, May 17, 1998. Wells was known to hang out with some of the cast of Saturday Night Live[2] in the after-parties when the show was done taping. The season for the show had ended,[3] but part of the group met up anyway. Wells did not make his way home until around 5.30 a.m., and he did not have much time to sleep before getting up to go to his scheduled start on Sunday. He arrived at the ballpark a wreck. He described his condition as still being half-drunk with monster breath and a raging, skull-rattling hangover. It was Beanie Baby Day at the stadium and the promotion attracted a full stadium and a buzz in the crowd.

When Wells went to warm up for the game, he claims he had the worst bullpen session of his career. It was so bad he just stopped throwing.

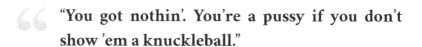

> **"A lot of times when I had good bullpens, I'd feel invincible and try to be too fine, and then don't last two innings. When you get out there and you're too fine, a lot of things can go wrong."**
>
> — DAVID WELLS

Possibly because of something similar to Juan Marichal's logic, Wells got into the game and started mowing down Twins. About halfway through the game, Yankee announcers started doing the unthinkable and mentioning that Wells was pitching a perfect game. His friend and teammate tried to keep Wells in spirits of the non-liquored kind and distracted him from his performance.

> **"You got nothin'. You're a pussy if you don't show 'em a knuckleball."**
>
> — DAVID CONE

Wells didn't throw a knuckleball. But the words from his friend might have been just the thing to get him through the game. About three hours after it started, it was over, and

Wells had pitched only the fifteenth perfect game in baseball history to that date. Wells went on to pitch for another seven solid years before his inning count began to fall. He almost pitched another perfect game that season on September 1, but Jason Giambi broke it up in the seventh inning with a single. He faced only two more batters than the minimum.

Dallas Braden's perfect game hangover came on May 9, 2010. He was not so much casually celebrating like Wells did, as lamenting the loss of his mother some years before on the eve of Mother's Day. The next day, his start was 1 p.m., and his grandmother beat him to the stadium.

> **"There was zero of my usual preparation. Until that day, I had never treated a start or the day before a start the way I did that day. I was [not] telling myself, 'Let's get crushed and tomorrow will be awesome.' It was more like, 'Let's just forget about tomorrow.'"[4]**
>
> **— DALLAS BRADEN**

Braden "got through" his perfect game and went on to pitch another twenty-three games that season to no great success, throwing one other 4-hit shutout and a 1-hit (eight-inning) appearance. But less than a year after his perfect game, he was on his way out of the major leagues.

It is impossible to really know if any of the other perfect games were pitched under the influence or how a player's behavior leading up to a game affected their performance. But there may be something to the sage words of Juan Marichal who seemed to believe that increasing the challenge can enhance focus. It might not be the right medicine for everyone, but apparently, it works for a select few.

 "They say some of my stars drink whiskey. But I have found that the ones who drink milkshakes don't win many ball games."

— FRED MCMANE

---

1. Wilson's numbers were recognized as deserving of MVP, but the financial stresses of the depression were taking their toll on baseball and no official MVP was named in 1930.
2. NBC's Emmy Award-winning, long-running late-night comedy showcase.
3. Many articles get this wrong. The SNL season for the program ended the week before as Marci Klein confirms.
   https://www.complex.com/sports/2017/05/oral-history-hungover-david-wells-unlikely-perfect-game
4. Quoted from:
   https://www.sfchronicle.com/athletics/article/Dallas-Braden-comes-clean-A-s-starter-was-hung-15251241.php

ONE ARM IN THE OUTFIELD

A curious rule change became part of baseball because of a minor league baseball game on June 19, 2008. It was between the Staten Island Yankees and the Brooklyn Cyclones. It was the bottom of the ninth with two out and a runner on first. Staten Island was leading 7 to 2. Ralph Henriquez stepped into the batter's box as a right-hand hitter and Pat Venditte put his glove on his left hand. Henriquez was a switch hitter and moved to the opposite side of the plate to bat left-handed. When he did so, Venditte took off his glove and put it on his right hand to pitch as a lefty. Henriquez stepped to the opposite side of the plate to bat right-handed.

Noticing that this might go on forever and instead of perpetuating the comedy skit, the umpires stepped in to make a decision. After conferring, they decided Henriquez was required to choose a side and remain there. He chose to stand in right-handed. Venditte chose to pitch as a right-hander to leverage the righty-righty match-up and struck out Henriquez on four pitches.

There were rules at the time for similar situations in 8.01(f), 6.06(b), and 6.02(b), but the situation was not fully covered. As such, rule 5.07(f) was added to the official rules.

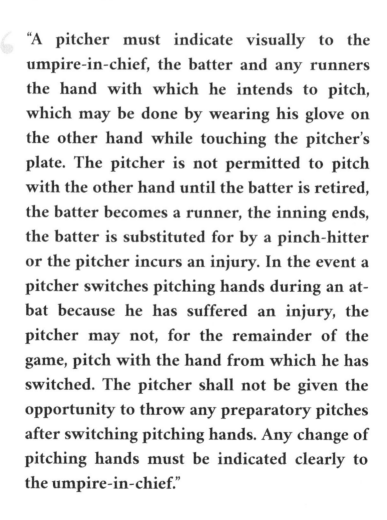

"A pitcher must indicate visually to the umpire-in-chief, the batter and any runners the hand with which he intends to pitch, which may be done by wearing his glove on the other hand while touching the pitcher's plate. The pitcher is not permitted to pitch with the other hand until the batter is retired, the batter becomes a runner, the inning ends, the batter is substituted for by a pinch-hitter or the pitcher incurs an injury. In the event a pitcher switches pitching hands during an at-bat because he has suffered an injury, the pitcher may not, for the remainder of the game, pitch with the hand from which he has switched. The pitcher shall not be given the opportunity to throw any preparatory pitches after switching pitching hands. Any change of pitching hands must be indicated clearly to the umpire-in-chief."

It is interesting that a rather rare physical attribute was not so rare[1] that it could be ignored by the rules and left up to the umpire's discretion.

On almost the opposite side of the coin from Venditte is a player named Pete Gray. Pete played for only a single season in the majors in 1945. In 1923, Pete had an accident that changed his life dramatically. He fell off a wagon when he was only about 7 and got tangled in the spokes of the wagon's wheels.[2] The injury was to his right, dominant arm. When he was brought to the doctor the decision was made to amputate the arm above the elbow. This left Pete to relearn how to do everything as a lefty.

Pete's parents didn't baby him or treat him special because of the loss of his arm. It helped him to adjust and to build his confidence. He saw kids playing ball and started practicing on his own to develop his skills: swatting bottle caps and rocks with sticks. After some time he got up the confidence to ask to join in games. With time he learned to work around his limitations.

Gray's aspirations were like any kid's. He started to dream about playing big-league ball. When he was 17, he claims to have hitched rides to Chicago to see the World Series and said he was there for Ruth's called shot. He was inspired by Ruth's confidence.

He started playing in the church league and then caught on with a semi-pro team. Batting in a left-handed stance, he used a regular bat. Because it weighed 38 ounces, he bulked up his left arm lifting weights. He contributed regularly to the offense and defense and developed deft reflexes, skills, and techniques to compensate for having only one hand.

When the Japanese attacked Pearl Harbor in 1941, Pete wanted to enlist but was rejected because of his missing limb. He stuck to playing ball as people around his age were getting drafted or volunteered and the competition became a little less skilled.

 "If I could teach myself how to play baseball with one arm, I sure as hell could handle a rifle."

— PETE GRAY

He was fast on the base paths and stole 68 bases for the Memphis Chickasaws in 1944—probably his best year in pro ball. He batted .333, hit 5 home runs, and struck out only 12 times in over 500 at-bats. The steals, average, and home runs didn't translate to his upcoming rookie year in the majors, but his performance with the Chickasaws caught the attention of the St. Louis Browns, and they signed him to a major league contract.

Pete did not like to be pitied for his injury because he didn't pity himself—and he let people know. Some of Gray's teammates—particularly pitchers Sig Jakucki and Nelson Potter—

were constantly ragging him. Jakucki once put a dead fish in the pocket of Gray's new sports coat and Gray knocked him down with one punch. Considering that Pete worked his one arm out hard, he probably packed a wallop!

The war came to an end after the 1945 season, and all the talent started filtering back from the war. Pete held his own in the majors, but his .218 average was not enough to keep him in contention for a position and they let him go. He continued to play for years in the semi-pro leagues but never got back to the level of play he had shown promise of in 1944. But in that year, he played in eight games at Yankee Stadium and achieved an almost impossible dream.

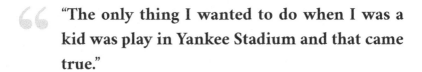

"The only thing I wanted to do when I was a kid was play in Yankee Stadium and that came true."

— PETE GRAY

People all across the US heard about Pete, and he served as inspiration for troops who returned home as amputees. They saw what could be accomplished if they chose a goal and stuck with it. Gray was happy to contribute something to the veterans as he was not able to contribute by serving with them in the war.

"Maybe I wouldn't have done as well [if I had two arms]. I probably wouldn't have been as determined."

— PETE GRAY

---

1. As of this writing, eight pitchers have pitched in the majors who were ambidextrous. The only other in the modern era was Greg Harris who pitched to only two players with his left arm in his fifteen-year career. He did this in his final appearance in the majors.

2. Not only do the accounts of this vary, but what happened isn't clear either.

ESCAPE FROM CUBA

It is rare to think of baseball in the context of international intrigue. When a baseball player's life is tied to human trafficking, bribery, blackmail, kidnapping, imprisonment, and illegally crossing borders, that opens a floodgate to the underworld. A sad reality, when compared to the freedoms that most of the world may enjoy, is the fate of players trapped in their homeland of Cuba.

Players in Cuba play for the love of the game or with the secret desire to someday defect and make a relative fortune overseas. It certainly is not for the meager pay. Under Fidel Castro, players who defected from Cuba and sought asylum in other countries were never able to return. This mostly affected players after 1959, when relations between the US and Cuba became strained during the cold war. The ultimate punishment for defection ended up being that players had to leave behind the world they knew and adopt a completely new way of life.

For defectors, this could mean leaving behind a wife and children, risking their lives or internment if they were captured, and a continued threat to their well-being even if they were successful. Essentially, defection became a dangerous race to escape capture and find sanctuary. The risks do not stop there as players may not have an immediate network of support, money, a contract, or certain success. Even some of the best players were not willing to risk these challenges and potential hardships.

A representative case of those willing to risk the difficulties is Yasiel Puig. A star in his homeland and somewhat reluctant to leave because of the dangers, Puig attempted defection thirteen times, each time putting him at greater potential for more extreme punishments. In his final try, he experienced a harrowing month-long journey to arrive in the USA.[1] Once there in 2012, he soon found himself a multi-millionaire in a very public spotlight.

Within his first five games in the majors, he hit 4 home runs and knocked in 10 RBI. By the end of the season he was batting .319 with 19 home runs in 382 at-bats, and he'd taken fan favor by storm. He was entertaining to watch and often humorous. While Puig got to enjoy his early success, the initial love affair began to wear off and his charm began to tarnish. His work ethic came into question as he did not show up to games on time, failed to give his full effort on the field, and eventually began showing aggression in starting fights.

A lot of this difficulty may simply have been that Puig was not adjusting well to the expectations of his teams, his teammates, and the culture he may have been reluctant to fully adopt. Having the privilege of riches at a young age and being enveloped in extravagance and abundance that had never been a part of his life could also have contributed. He has found himself bounced between teams who do not want the responsibility of handling his behavior.

Age and maturity may have mellowed Puig in time to give him another shot at reviving his career. He made a plea to baseball and the players' union in 2021:

 Latino players do not understand what is expected of us as public figures in the USA. We need to learn English as well as understand American values and social norms. I cannot change the past, but I am determined to become a better person and I want to help other Latino players step into their roles successfully. The media pushed certain narratives about me because it sold more newspapers. They didn't understand my challenges or my culture or how that played an important role in my behavior. I also didn't know how to help them understand.[2]

Puig clearly had trouble with his adjustment, seeing his initial success deflate. If it was due to his inability to integrate with the sport smoothly and adapt to unwritten rules of the game and culture, this can be his opportunity to make a difference.

Should major league baseball accept his challenge to improve and adopt a better global strategy, it could put an end to dangerous trafficking, risky defections, and end the plight of players having to give up their homeland to enjoy their prominence as major league sports figures. Baseball could become a strategic component as a global ambassador not only for the sport but also for international relations. Maybe Puig will have a chance to reset his own compass and lead the way.

---

1. There is no reason to repeat what is well-documented by ESPN :
   http://www.espn.com/espn/feature/story/_/id/10781144/no-one-walks-island-los-angeles-dodgers-yasiel-puig-journey-cuba
2. Paraphrased from Puig's message to MLB.

FIVE-FINGERED DISCOUNT ON THE RUN

For all the glam of powering a home run, in the end it is just numbers changing on the scoreboard. With a home run, the batter swings, the ball goes far, and the player jogs lazily around the bases while the players in the field yawn. So does the crowd. There is not really a strategy except for the normal interaction between the pitcher and batter. A home run can happen in any at-bat. The only people who seem to have fun are the players high-fiving each other in the dugout. An exception to the sleepy ritual of rounding the bases is a bat flip that upsets the other team, but the "unwritten rules" frown on that in an effort to homogenize the showmanship of that bit of fun.

Slick base running, on the other hand, always seems to stir up excitement in a game. There is charm in a smooth move, a bold one, or a brash one. Running the bases is an art of awareness, guile, and baseball savvy. It is a tool distinctly different than the big brawn that is commonly related to substance abuse. Players who use the base paths to make something happen to rally the fans and their team seem to be more inherently interesting. Ty Cobb obviously agrees.

There are a lot of naughty things some players manage in shaking up pitchers and the defense. The apex of that hunt for glory is stealing home. In stealing home, the situation is everything. No one is going to steal home with a ten-run lead or behind by that many. It only happens when runs are critical.

Situations for stealing home happen in two ways: a straight steal or a special play.

Special plays are more theatrics than cunning, although there are some elements of both. This can be when there are less than two out and the offense puts a squeeze play on that the batter tries to bunt and misses. Or, in a situation where it is first and third and there are opportunities to fluster the defense and force a mistake.[1]

A straight steal is when a player is on third or the bases are loaded or it is second and third and there is no sacrifice play on. The idea is, the runner on third is getting no help except for beating the throw from the pitcher to the plate. In this case, the runner at third has to be aware of all his advantages. He must see where the third baseman is and if he is being held. He has to know the pitcher's delivery. He has to be aware of his own skills. He has to know what the competition knows about him. He can use what he knows to his advantage, just as the defense can work against him.

There is a moment when these factors merge into the sublime.[2]

Let's set the stage. A third-string catcher with fewer than one hundred major league at-bats comes to the plate with one out in the bottom of the twelfth in a 4 to 4 tie. He hits a single. Willie McGee follows him with a single, Julio Gonzalez pops out for the second out, and Ozzie Smith hits the third single of the inning to load the bases. Bases loaded. Two out. Scrub catcher as the lead runner at third.

The mighty David Green steps up to the plate. He is batting .339 on that day for that season. It is his rookie year and he already has one hit in the game. The count gets to 1 ball and 2 strikes, but something is playing behind the scenes. With two out and the bases loaded, the Giants are looking for a force play at any base to end the inning. The infielders play back because all they need to do is field a ball cleanly. On a force out, no run will score. A swing and miss or strike looking sends the game into the thirteenth inning with the resolution still up in the air. The odds of seeing the top of the thirteenth inning are very high.

The lefty pitcher is not really paying attention to a catcher on third base.[3] Since when do rookie third-string catchers steal home? Darrell Evans is so far back from the third-base bag he is defending, he is practically playing left field. Glenn Brummer crept down the line with each pitch in the at-bat, testing to see if he could draw a throw. By the time the count was 1 and 2 he was leading a third of the way down the line.

The lefty started his delivery with the same high leg-kick he used on previous pitches, Brummer broke toward the plate. Infielders yelled out that the runner was breaking. Green stepped out of the batter's box. The ump jumped into position to call the play as Milt May, the catcher, stepped up out of the catcher's box before the ball left the pitcher's hand. May caught the ball and tried to put down the tag, but Brummer beat Lavelle's throw to home and the umpire called the runner safe. The Cardinals won the game 5 to 4 with 2 out in the twelfth on Brummer's steal of home. That is how it is in the record book.

No one was right. Everyone botched the play except Brummer.

The steal of home was already something that was already incredibly rare. But there was something unique to this. The third baseman was not paying attention. The pitcher was not paying attention. No one gave the steal sign. The third-string catcher on third running the bases—as slow as catchers are—never should have been going anywhere. And yet he was. Then the defensive catcher stepped out of the catcher's box on a routine pitch before it left the pitcher's hand. The ump stepped out of his position to call the live play, which was technically already dead. He called the sliding runner safe. It appeared he was.

But, wait… was the pitch a ball or a strike? Green didn't swing so if the pitch was a strike the third out was made and the run didn't count. Or was it the case that the ball was in play and the run scored before the pitch needed to be called?

This is messy. The timing of everything was in fractions of a second.

Had the tag been placed on Brummer, he probably should have been called safe because May stepped out of the catcher's box causing a very rare phenomenon known as a catcher's balk, Rule 5.02(a):

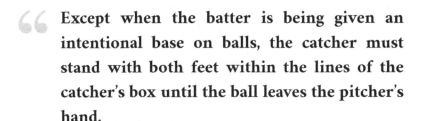

> **Except when the batter is being given an intentional base on balls, the catcher must stand with both feet within the lines of the catcher's box until the ball leaves the pitcher's hand.**

The balk would have advanced all runners and the ball would be dead while scoring the winning run. Had May received the pitch and not caused the balk by stepping out of the catcher's box, the only thing that would have pushed the game into the thirteenth inning was if the pitch was called a strike before Brummer crossed the plate. But, if Brummer crossed the plate before the ball did, he scored the winning run before the pitch even needed to be called. Video shows he touched the plate before anything else mattered.[4]

Brummer had only one other steal that season. It was after he hit a double. He stole third and then scored on a sacrifice bunt. That means he was already flying toward home as the pitcher was releasing the ball, just like on the other steal of home.

This chapter should have been full of ultimate thieves and renegade runners like Jackie Robinson, Ty Cobb, Rickey Henderson, Lou Brock, Oscar Charleston, Tim Raines, Turkey Stearnes, and Cool Papa Bell. Instead, you get a third-string catcher making a moment into the potato of his career on the major league stage. A catcher stealing home that won a game and maybe gave that small incentive to his team to take the division by just three games.

The Cardinals went on to win the World Series in 1982 and Glenn Brummer got a World Series ring. It may have all been on account of his brave swipe of home and one of the ultimate steals in the history of the game.

 "Faster than that."

— BUCK O'NEIL WHEN ASKED HOW FAST COOL
PAPA BELL WAS RUNNING THE BASES

1. There is an example of a failed attempt at this in chapter 4 "Jakey, the Sauerkraut-Faced Boob."
2. To be sure the usage of the word is clear, the definition is "to convert (something inferior) into something of higher worth."—Merriam-Webster dictionary
3. The record for stolen bases by a catcher in post-1900 play is held by Roger Bresnahan. Yes, a relative of the guy who had his number retired in the minor leagues because he threw a potato to the third baseman.
4. A somewhat humorous recounting by Brummer of the event that he gets completely right and wrong at the same time. https://youtu.be/0turz4E5zxU

25

CALLED ON ACCOUNT OF CHAOS

There have been a lot of rare things in the previous twenty-four chapters of this book, including balking in runs, an outfielder with one arm, potatoes being swapped for baseballs, platinum sombreros, base-running gaffs, and a girl in the majors. There is no shortage of stars, personalities, dominance, strange plays, and extremes.

One very famous tale has a defining moment. The funny thing is the defining moment is the only part that gets remembered and the outcome is practically forgotten. The event includes two protests of the same game—made on separate days. A player was effectively traded in the middle of the game, somehow ending up 950 miles away between the second and third out in the top of the ninth inning. Almost 34,000 fans were at the game but only about 1,000 saw the final four outs.

Welcome to the Pine Tar Incident.

On July 24, 1983, the Yankees were playing the Royals in a Sunday afternoon game at Yankee stadium. The Yankees were leading 4 to 3 in the ninth when the Royals came to bat. Dale Murray had been pitching since the top of the sixth and only let up one hit. He got the first two Royals out,[1] then let up a single to U. L. Washington on a 0 and 2 count on a hard ground ball up the middle. Billy Martin, on his third tour as manager of the Bronx Bombers, decided to put in his closer, Goose Gossage, to finish off the game.

George Brett, a feared hitter batting .357 at the time of the game, stepped in and ripped the first pitch into the opposite field stands, but foul. The second pitch was not so lucky. Brett pulled a high fastball into the right-field seats for a home run. That gave the Royals a 5 to 4 lead. At least it seemed to be the apparent outcome at the time. The pitcher pitched, the batter swung and the ball went over the wall in fair territory. Pretty obvious to everyone who was watching. But this is baseball.

Billy Martin came out of the dugout calling the umpire's attention to something. The umpires convened making a fuss about inspecting the bat Brett had just used to hit the home run. Umpire Tim McClelland, a six-foot-six giant of a man walked with the bat and laid it across the width of the plate apparently measuring something. After a brief reconvene with the other umpires, still holding the bat, he took a few steps toward the Royals dugout, pointed to Brett, held up his fist, and called Brett out. So much for that home run. So much for that win. So much for what seemed to have happened just a moment ago.

Pandemonium ensued. Brett broke out of the dugout where he had been sitting calmly a moment before, totally enraged, swinging his arms over his head like a charging gorilla and having to be restrained as he thrashed like a madman in pursuit of McClelland. Gaylord Perry made off with the bat and handed it to someone who fled with it down into the tunnel of the visitor's dugout. The official call on the play was that Brett was using a bat where the pine tar was applied illegally. For that reason, he was called out.

In any case, the call had been made, it was the final out. People began filing out of the stadium because the Yankees had just won 4 to 3. Eventually, things calmed down on the field. Game over. That's where the story usually stops and so does the broadcast of the game. Most people who know the story might still think the Yankees won.

But that's really not exactly what happened. A much more rare and unusual thing occurred.

The Royals put the game under protest. Protests are usually just symbolic. Fans who see a manager protest a game see an umpire make a big "P" in the air and think to themselves "Yeah, right. Much ado about nothing." And it is rightly so because one thing more rare than a perfect game is a protest that affects the outcome of a game.

Four days later, that very rare thing that never really happens in baseball happened: the Royals' protest was upheld. Lee McPhail, the baseball commissioner, determined that the pine tar did not contribute to the home run. The rule had been put in place to keep balls from becoming discolored during play,[2] and as the ball left the ballpark, the pine tar had no effect on the pitch, the swing, the trajectory, or the outcome of the game.

With the call reversed, the game now stood with a score of Royals 5 Yankees 4. As the Royals still had one out left and the Yankees needed to bat in the ninth, the rest of the game had to be rescheduled to play at least the rest of the 4 outs that were still to be had by both teams in the game.

The Yankees and Royals both had days off on August 18 later that season. The Yankees were currently on a homestand and the Royals were scheduled to play in Baltimore the next day of their road trip so the meeting on that date was convenient. After some haggling about fan entrance to the game,[3] play was set to resume in front of what was estimated to be a whopping crowd of more than 1,000 fans.

Billy Martin knew he'd have to score at least one run, so he made a few slick moves in his lineup to get his bats in line and allow some flexibility as to where to slot his pinch-hitters. One issue he also had to cover was that Jerry Mumphrey had been traded to Houston on August 10, so was not able to resume play. He was no longer on the team.

Hal McRae who had been due up to hit twenty-five days earlier stepped in to hit and the pitcher, George Frazier, toed the rubber. Frazier then immediately stepped off. He turned and threw the ball to Ken Griffey who was playing first base in an appeal. The umpire, who had not seen the play, called Brett—who was not even in the stadium—safe.

Griffey threw the ball back to Frazier who again toed the rubber, stepped off, and then threw the ball to Roy Smalley at second base. It was another appeal play, and the second-base umpire, who was also not in the ballpark on the day that the game was played, called Brett and U.L. Washington safe.

This was a shrewd move by Martin, as the umpiring crew was different than the crew who worked the game on July 24. Billy came out of the dugout and questioned the umpires as to how they could possibly make calls on a game they did not even attend. Somehow, they produced paperwork that apparently had an affidavit from the previous crew. Never-theless, Martin put the game under protest again. McRae proceeded to strike out on six pitches to end the seemingly endless inning.

It would be nice if that were the end of the complexity.

Don Mattingly stepped up for the Yankees with a very strange hitting streak on the line. He had hit in fourteen straight games before the game on July 24 and then ten more afterward. The opportunity to come up and bat again and get a hit could connect the two streaks and set a new record for a rookie hitting in consecutive games.

Mattingly flew out to the disappointment of about 900 people—as even the few that were there had started to filter out of the stands—and the streak ended. Smalley got up and flew out. Oscar Gamble pinch-hit and grounded out to second ending the game. Dan Quisenberry, who had come on in relief for the Royals, notched his thirty-third save to lead the league. As it went, the interminable game ended for the fans, players, and announcers twenty-five days after it had begun as Martin's new protest came to nothing.

With the end of that game also came one of the rarest occurrences in baseball. The team that protested an event in a game not only won the protest but won the game as well. Like all mythic adventures of great heroes, the events of those days spawned at least two songs commemorating the days of battling heroes.[4]

---

1. Don Mattingly made a great play to stop an extra-base hit.
2. The most hysterical reason for any rule in baseball. It makes sense. But the next time I am pitching with the game on the line, I am wiping the ball on my face to pick up the eye-black paint so the spin confounds the batter. As far as our research team knows, that is something that never happened in the history of the game and may require a new rule.
3. This is actually funny. Fans who had tickets to the original game wanted to get in for free and the Yankee office wanted to charge $2.50 admission to get fans in the seats. At worst, any fan attending was looking at 4 outs. Never mind how much it took to park a car or travel to the stadium. If you look at the number of fans in the stands, the announcer even jokes

that there are about thirty-two people in attendance. For both announcers it would be the shortest amount of time either one of them spent announcing a live game.

4. "The Ballad of George Brett," by The Barking Geckos (https://youtu.be/uMd5JdDg-Go) and "The Pine-Tarred Bat," by Dennis Reed Jr. (https://youtu.be/NgkXHK9li3c)

PLEASE LEAVE A QUICK REVIEW!

If you have enjoyed these tales and maybe even learned something, let me know. If the book has fulfilled its promise, please put up a review and spread the word to those who will enjoy it. I hope it will be possible to bring more stories to readers.

"I guess my thermometer for my baseball fever is still a goose bump."—Vin Scully

Scan the QR code below to leave a quick review!

mail: lingsterbooks@gmail.com

instagram: @roy_lingster

Facebook: Roy Lingster

EXITING THE EXTREME STADIUM

As every game must see its final out, so we have come to the end of this outing. I hope it leaves readers with a kind of satisfaction and a feeling of richness in exploring the implications of the game.

The mighty depth of baseball lore is often hard to fathom in its complexity, tall tales, truths, and dreams. These stories hopefully helped fans perusing the pages to learn details about other dimensions of the game they did not know while paying homage to stories that are more familiar but of a sort that gets shared by generations of fans. In these stories, and the thousands not told here, baseball creates its own lasting legend through personality, situation, and suspense. The character and passion are more than just a swing or a pitch.

"Baseball is dull only to dull minds."

— RED BARBER

A GAME OF EXTREMES: 25 EXCEPTIONAL BASKETBALL STORIES

ABOUT WHAT HAPPENS ON AND OFF THE COURT

A
GAME
OF EXTREMES
25 EXCEPTIONAL
BASKETBALL
STORIES

ROY LINGSTER

INTRODUCTION

> " "*Not only is there more to life than basketball, there's a lot more to basketball than basketball.*"
>
> — PHIL JACKSON

It's a tale as old as time, and yet, every time it occurs it feels absolutely brand new.

The crowd is dead silent as the sound of footfalls echoes up and down a basketball court. The ball is being dribbled by the best point guard on the team, who looks determined, driven and intense. Sweat drips down his forehead as the clock ticks down. The chance to win the game is slipping away second by second.

The home team is down by two points, so this next shot is essential. If they are able to sink it, the game is tied, and overtime will decide their fate. If they miss, the game is over, and they will walk away dejected and empty-handed.

The clock continues to wind down. The crowd inhales deeply. All eyes are on the point guard. And in a flash of a second, he passes the ball to another guard who has broken free of his defender. In one movement, that guard jumps behind the three-point line, holds the ball, raises his arms, leaps in the air as the defender attempts to block him, and the ball goes sailing to the basket.

It sinks through the net with ease as the buzzer sounds, and the crowd explodes in a chorus of cheers. The game has been one with a last-second three-pointer. The team rallies together, leaping into each other's arms and celebrating. The walls, floor and ceiling of the arena shake in a way that only happens in professional sports.

What a moment. What a play. What a win.

The feeling that fans get from a moment like that is rare. It doesn't happen every day, but it does happen again and again for those who follow sports. Basketball is an especially exciting sport that provides so many wildly exciting buzzer-beaters and memorable events that stick in the mind of fans and are etched into the record books.

Yes, a few sports are really like basketball. The mix of historic backstories, one-of-a-kind athletes, and incredible fans all come together to create countless memories and iconic legends that live on forever.

But even the most devoted basketball fan doesn't know all of the tales in the sport's long history.

That's because there are more than 80 games every season and hundreds of guys playing in them. Even if you pay close attention, you are sure to lose track of everyone and their most stunning moments in the league.

Yet, there is so much to learn. So many wonderful stories and historical events to celebrate. It just can be hard to remember them all.

That's where this book comes into play. In these pages, you will be able to delve even deeper into your basketball fandom by exploring the very best players throughout the history of the league. You will discover their most amazing moments, their unparalleled successes and the stories behind them. You will learn about the strength, the skill, the diversity and perseverance of so many people who have graced the court over the years. What drove them? How did they accomplish some incredible feats? What moments defined them? And how are they remembered to this day?

After years of studying the game and what creates the very best player, I now present to you a culmination of years of examining basketball like no one else can. And I have compiled 25 of the greatest athletes to play the game. In these pages, you will uncover their most stunning moments, their biggest victories, and the personalities, goals and achievements that live on today, years after they retired.

But it's more than just famous moments throughout basketball history that you'll observe here. Instead, you will also gain insight into the minds and personal lives of some of the most brilliant and well-known names to play the game. Along with that, you'll discover the inside scoop on their careers, the highs and the lows, the good and the bad, their home lives and extra-curricular activities that raised or lowered their standings in the league.

There have been very many jaw-dropping moments, people, and stories throughout the history of basketball. And owing to devoted examination, hard work, and in-depth research, you are about to dive into the 25 most exceptional, ground-breaking and memorable basketball stories in history.

1

THE INVENTION OF BASKETBALL

> *"I am sure that no man can derive more pleasure from money or power than I do from seeing a pair of basketball goals in some out of the way place."*
>
> — JAMES NAISMITH

Basketball is a game that finds the players on the court attempting to shoot the ball through the hoop or the basket. That's Basketball 101 and something everyone knows, even those who never watched or played one game before.

The simplicity of basketball's gameplay is one of the things that makes it so unique and special. It's so easy to pick up on how it works and, therefore, easy to get interested in. But where did such a simple—yet complicated—game come from? Whose idea was it, and how did it transform from a game with players lobbing a ball into peach baskets into multimillionaires dunking to crowds of thousands?

To understand basketball, you have to go back to where it all started: Springfield, Massachusetts, in the late 1800s.

When students were compelled to stay inside for days due to a New England storm, James Naismith, a 31-year-old graduate student instructing PE at the International YMCA Training School in Springfield, Massachusetts, had a brilliant idea.

Naismith was a Canadian-American sports coach and innovator looking for new ways to change the lives of the young men he taught and guided through school. He had started working at the YMCA, where he was tasked with the hard job of keeping students engaged and entertained. If you remember your school career well, you will know that this is not a small feat.

It was made even harder because he was teaching in a part of New England known for its nasty winter seasons. Anyone who has experienced a rainy or snowy day at school knows that when the nasty weather rolls around, all school activities come to a halt. How are the students supposed to get outside, be physical and stay active? That's what Naismith was wondering—and when his brilliant idea came to him.

Parade and calisthenics were the typical winter sports that were played when it was too cold and snowy outside, but they weren't nearly as exciting as football or lacrosse played in the warmer months.

Naismith aimed to create a game that was both easy to comprehend and intriguingly challenging. The game needed to support many players at once and be playable inside. The game needed to provide the children with enough exercise while avoiding the brutality of rugby, football, or soccer because such sports pose a greater risk of serious injury when played in a small area.

A light-bulb moment struck his mind, and he was ready to make it a reality. Naismith asked the school janitor for a pair of wood boxes so he could use them as goals. The janitor had two fruit baskets that he dug out of his storage closet. They weren't amazing, but they'd get the job done. The fruit baskets were fastened, one on each side, to the bottom rail of the gymnasium balcony by Naismith. The railing on the lower balcony was 10 feet high. To try to put the ball in their team's basket, the pupils would play in teams. The ball was being picked up from the hoop and placed back into play by a person positioned at each end of the balcony.

Right away, things got a bit heated on the court.

In fact, a full-blown fight broke out during the first basketball match among pupils. It actually turned into a free-for-all in the center of the gym floor as the lads started tackling, slapping, and hitting one another. One youngster suffered a knockout. One of them had a dislocated shoulder, and a few of them had black eyes too.

Naismith didn't come up with all the rules at once; instead, he kept tweaking them until they became the 13 rules still in use in today's contemporary game. Actually, in 2010, Naismith's original game rules brought in $4.3 million at auction.

According to the original regulations, the ball might be launched with one or perhaps both hands in any direction, but never in a fist. A player had to toss the ball from the location where it was received instead of running with it. It was against the rules to push, trip or hit other players. The first infraction was regarded as a foul. A player would be eliminated after a second foul until the subsequent goal was scored. However, if there was proof that a player meant to harm an opponent, that person would be eliminated from the game altogether.

The game's umpires functioned as judges, recorded fouls, and had the authority to eject participants. They controlled the time, determined when the basketball was in play and determined which side the ball went to. Umpires recorded goals and determined when they had been scored.

If a team committed three straight fouls, a goal might be scored by the opposition.

A goal was scored when the ball was hit or thrown into the goal area and remained there. It would be considered a goal if the opponent moved the basket while the ball was on the edges. The person who touched the ball initially threw it back into play when it crossed the line of play. The thrower could only keep the ball for five seconds before it was passed to the opponent. An umpire would fling the ball directly into the field in the event of a disagreement. The umpire would declare a foul on that side if they continued to cause the game to be delayed.

A game consisted of two 15-minute halves with a 5-minute break in between. The winning side was the one that scored the most goals in the allocated period. Once the score was tied, the game might go on until another goal was scored.

The Springfield Republican reported on the first basketball game ever played in public on March 12, 1892, which took place at a YMCA building. The teachers competed with the pupils. A little over 200 people came to learn about this brand-new sport they had never known of or seen before. The students' "science" helped them overcome the professors 5–1, although the narrative published by the Republican gave the teachers credit for "agility."

The sport quickly gained popularity in a matter of weeks. At their local YMCAs, students from different schools promoted the game. The initial regulations were published in a collegiate publication that was sent to YMCAs all around the nation. With the institutions' sizable international student body, the sport was also made popular in a number of other countries. After being introduced in high schools, basketball gained formal recognition as a winter sport in 1905.

The NCAA disputes the existence of the first intercollegiate basketball match between two institutions. Two school newspapers published stories in 1893 detailing various recordings of collegiate basketball games played against rival college teams.

Just 12 months after Naismith invented basketball, women's sports had their first taste of it in 1892—thanks to Smith College gymnastics coach Senda Berenson. In 1896 Stanford University and UC Berkeley played against each other in the first known intercollegiate game, including female athletes.

Professional leagues were forming throughout the country as the sport developed quickly. Basketball supporters supported their new local squads. The National Basketball League (NBL), which had six clubs from the northeast when it was founded in 1898, was the first professional league. Only roughly five years were spent in the league. The league, which had been disbanded in 1904, was revived 33 years later, in 1937, with 13 clubs, a brand-new funding structure, and owners Goodyear, Firestone, and General Electric.

College basketball was a significant staple, even as professional sports leagues attracted national attention. Eight teams competed in the inaugural NCAA tournament, which took place in 1939 at Northwestern University. The University of Oregon was the first national champion in collegiate basketball, and the squad beat Ohio State University.

As you can see, a lot changed in the early, formative years of basketball and, years later, even more had been altered within the rulebook and the way people played.

Already very early on, it had become apparent that James Naismith had created something very special, something that could catch on not only in Massachusetts but across the country and, truly, across the world. It's incredible to think that a game created because of a snow day would later become a billionaire-dollar sport enjoyed by millions of people across the globe. From such small humble beginnings, a revolution in sports was born.

THE SHATTER HEARD AROUND
THE WORLD

" *"When I dunk, I put something on it. I want the ball to hit the floor before I do."*

— DARRYL DAWKINS

If you want to talk about how basketball quickly took over the sports world and impacted young people all over the country, you have to talk about Darryl Dawkins. He may not be a name that everyone knows today, but he was a vital part of the growth of basketball and its lasting appeal. In many ways, his time in the NBA changed the way people thought about being drafted into the sport and also changed the way people thought about the performance aspect of basketball.

When you look at a dunk in today's NBA, it's always a crowd pleaser. People get on their feet, the team's bench falls over itself, and the announcers go wild. A dunk in the NBA is something to behold, something to celebrate and something to watch again and again on the internet as it goes viral.

Honestly, dunks like the ones we witness today simply wouldn't be around if it weren't for the hard work and exceptional athleticism and personality of Darryl Dawkins.

Dawkins was the first player to make the massive jump from high school basketball straight into the NBA back in 1975. Today this is something that often occurs, but back then, it had never been heard of before.

What drove Dawkins to abandon the idea of college and leap into the world of professional sports instead? It was simple, really: he wanted to take care of his family. His siblings, mother and grandmother needed him, and Dawkins felt that a career in the NBA was the best way to really provide for them.

At the time, many players were already making a lifetime's worth of money playing in the league, but Dawkins took that to a whole other level. He signed a contract with the Philadelphia 76ers that was record-breaking at the time, for a sum of $1 million for seven years.

In his first season, he averaged just two points per game while playing off the bench. But throughout the course of his first seven seasons in the league, he gradually increased both his minutes and his output. When he started playing regularly, the Philadelphia home announcer had a little bit of a problem. The NBA, at the time, announced starting players to the fans along with the player's alma mater. However, Dawkins lacked a university background. That was a first for the NBA.

He may have created some complications for the league at the time. Yet, from the start, Dawkins was always able to dunk with such force that it resulted in backboards trembling, seemingly in fear of his power.

It was first evident on November 13, 1979, when the Kansas City Kings' Municipal Auditorium hosted the first of Dawkins' two infamous dunks. In a fierce dunk against Bill Robinzine, Dawkins broke the glass backboard.

In the moments before the big jam, it is rumored that Dawkins said, "Oh man, I gotta get out of here . . . Feet don't fail me now." That's exactly what happened as he sailed through the court and connected with the rim.

Glass fragments flew all over the court. To escape, players dispersed in all directions. The crowd found it hard to believe. At that moment, no one had ever witnessed a dunk performed with such force. Glass fragments were scattered all around the rim that was merely lying on the ground. The arena personnel had to clean up everything and bring in a brand-new basket support, which took more than an hour.

Dawkins also enjoyed giving names to the dunks that stood out to him. Rim Wrecker, Look Out Below, In Your Face Disgrace, and Yo Mama were just a few. Then when he traveled all the way across the court to dunk, they were known as Greyhound Specials.

But on this fateful evening, he had a particular person in mind when he first shattered a backboard. He mentioned the name of the poor athlete he had just dunked on. "Chocolate Thunder Flying, Robinzine Crying, Teeth Shaking, Glass Breaking, Rump Roasting, Bun Toasting, Wham Bam, Glass Breaker, I am Jam" was the name of this one. It was a mouthful, yes, and it meant a lot too.

This was the only topic basketball writers could discuss for weeks. But definitely not the only thing, though. Also ripping up the league at the same time were two rookies who happened to be named Magic Johnson and Larry Bird; they were getting a lot of ink too. Despite that, Dawkins' hard work on the court received a lot of media attention.

At the time, Larry O'Brien served as the league's top dog, the commissioner. The Larry O'Brien Trophy, named in his honor, is the NBA championship trophy. Thus, you may recognize his name. The actual Larry O'Brien, however, did not like Dawkins. He summoned the young player to the NBA offices and made it clear that he was not to break the backboard anymore. If he did, he would face a $5,000 fine and a suspension. In order to stop other players in the NBA from coming up with the same concept, they actually added a rule.

However, Philadelphian supporters begged to see Dawkins do his thing during a home game because Kansas City is where the first dunk was performed, and they felt left out. Dawkins repeated the incredible feat three weeks later when playing the San Antonio Spurs at home. Doug Collins was jogging away before the dunk was even finished when we stepped up for the dunk.

As Dawkins pulled the basketball behind Collins' head, he noticed the expression in his eyes and realized what was about to happen. Then he was up, up, up, and the glass was shattered again.

As a result, the game was again postponed for more than an hour due to the need for the stadium workers to totally rebuild the whole basket support. As suspected, Dawkins was indeed fined, and he was suspended too. But the supporters were insatiable. When they saw the rim lying on the court, they were out of their seats with joy.

Dawkins, regrettably, was unable to remain with the 76ers long enough for them to claim a title. While Dawkins was a member of the squad, they reached the NBA Finals three times. Julius Erving, a.k.a. Dr. J, commanded the group. But the Trail Blazers defeated them in the 1977 Finals. Next, they suffered a defeat to the Lakers in 1980. They fell to the Lakers once more in 1982.

The club then had the chance to improve at the center position. The current League MVP, Moses Malone, was being sought after by Philadelphia, and they were very eager to land him. In order to free up payroll space to pursue Malone, they sent Dawkins away to the Nets. Shortly after that, the 76ers found a triumph in their very first title since Wilt Chamberlain won it in 1967.

Years later, the man sometimes known as the "Man from Planet Lovetron" would pass away, and an outpouring of support and love would be felt from all over the league. He really did make a huge impact on the game—and it went beyond his ability to shatter the backboard. He changed the way players performed, he added personality and style to the NBA and made many high school kids hopeful they could leap straight from school to the big leagues.

Shaquille O'Neal put it best when he said, "Darryl Dawkins is the father of power dunking. I'm just one of his sons." Without Dawkins, the league we see today would be very different and, honestly, very boring.

PELICANS FAN JOIN WARMUP

> "*Heck . . . He may make the starting lineup on the Pelicans this year.*"
>
> — NICK SHULTZ

There are millions of people who want to be part of the NBA. Indeed, even grown men dream of one day suiting up, joining a team, and making some magic on the basketball court.

However, they usually don't do it the way Tony Roberts did.

It was January 29, 2018, in New Orleans, Louisiana. The Pelicans were getting ready to face off against the Houston Rockets. It was going to be an exciting game as both teams

236 | ROY LINGSTER

were struggling to outdo each other in the Western Conference.

For one brief moment, it looked like the Pelicans might have some new talent assisting them.

You may not know the name Tony Roberts, but on that night, he became something of an NBA legend and folk hero to millions of people. That's because he had come up with a plan that got him into the middle of the court. It didn't last long, and it got him into some incredibly hot water, but, in the end, Roberts would say it was worth it.

Roberts was able to create a warm-up outfit that looked exactly like the type the Pelicans wore before each and every game. So he suited up. He threw on his sweats and jacket and made his way to the floor. When he reached the court, he started doing some ridiculous stretches that would set off alarms for anyone paying attention. But apparently, security wasn't paying attention . . . yet.

It is especially important to remember one major thing: Roberts was absolutely, 100% breaking the law by doing this. He knew it was funny and was sure to make some fans, but it could also land his hindquarters in jail.

If you have ever been to a professional basketball game, you know there is security swarming all over the place. In fact, there are guards set up along the courtside and behind either rim to make sure that no one makes it onto the court. Over the last few years, more than a handful of people have been arrested for running onto the court or breaking the rules regarding security. In fact, in June of 2021, a basketball fan was facing criminal charges for racing onto the court at a game between the Philadelphia 76ers and the Brooklyn Nets. Not only was he banned from ever returning to the court again, but he was also thrown in jail for the night.

Joke or no joke, Tony Roberts was going to get himself thrown behind bars if he was caught. He could have been roughed up, thrown to the ground, or even beaten up by security or the players on the floor.

But he stayed on the court, and the joke went on.

Roberts was seemingly not noticed by the powers that be. In fact, one of the warm-up guys for the team actually tossed the young comedian a ball. Roberts, for his part, showed his colors even more when he put up a wildly bad, off-center shot.

Perhaps that shot was what gave Roberts away because shortly after that, the jig was up. He was quickly approached by an officer who grabbed ahold of him and instantly made him understand that his days in the NBA were over before they even started.

Roberts would later say, "All of a sudden, someone grabs my arm, and I turn around, and it's a cop who looks like Moses from the Bible." They meant business, and they were intent on Roberts getting out of there as soon as possible, with force if necessary.

But that wasn't needed because Roberts had lasted longer on the court than he ever imagined, and he knew it was time to throw in the towel and hang up his jersey. Surprisingly, he wasn't banned from the arena or even kicked out. In fact, he was simply escorted back to his seat and given a stern talking-to. They wagged their finger in his face, told him not to do it again, but allowed him to enjoy the game.

Little did Roberts, the Pelicans or the NBA know just how viral the moment would become. The incident quickly started making the rounds online and was soon dominating the blogosphere more than the Pelicans-Rockets game was. People were beside themselves with amusement about Roberts' actions, and they were loving every second of it. With one silly, stupid move, Roberts had lived out the dreams of millions of NBA fans. "We are all @TonyTRoberts fans now," one Twitter user told the world as the video of Tony on the court caught fire online and even made some of the biggest sports shows in the world.

Was it a smart thing to do? Maybe, maybe not. It could have cost him an awful lot, and it could have sent him straight to jail. But Tony Roberts was willing to take a risk. He was willing to do this not just to cause a few laughs and get a few million views. He was also doing this so he could feel the excitement and thrill of being a basketball player in the NBA —even if it was for just a few minutes.

With this one hilarious incident, Tony Roberts turned himself into an inspiration, a punchline, a folk hero, and something of an urban legend too.

4

THE BIGGEST TURNAROUND?

> *"They better not put me in the All-Star Game. I won't shoot, but I'll dominate that easy game. I'll be playing hard defense. I'll be foulin'. I'll be flagrant fouling. Everyone will be like, 'What are you doing?'"*

— METTA WORLD PEACE

He's gone by many names, but his birth name is Ronald William Artest Jr. You probably know him as Metta World Peace and one of the most controversial and wild players in the history of the league. There was a time when he was called a thug and considered downright toxic in the NBA. In fact, there was a time when some thought he would retire from the league early—or even be banned.

But Artest turned it all around, and he transformed into someone who seemed intent on living up to the ideals of his new name, Metta World Peace. During his final years in the NBA, he was a completely different person and player—and that led him to some amazing feats.

The thing about Metta World Peace is that his life before the NBA wasn't easy and that directly influenced how he acted early in his career and definitely led him to making some bone-headed and head-scratching choices. But he grew up over time, got himself together, and eventually became an upstanding member of the league.

Back when he was still known as Ron Artest, he was always referred to as a hot head, someone who could fly off the handle. Worse yet, he was known as someone literally looking for a brawl. And he found quite a few over the years.

Artest didn't grow up in a great environment, and, in many ways, the cards were stacked against him from birth. He was raised in a rough neighborhood among people who didn't hold back and didn't care about rules or the law. In fact, when he was still a kid, he saw a fellow basketball player getting killed right in front of him. That went down during an on-court argument between fellow players. The game grew so competitive and heated that someone broke the leg off of a table and stabbed another named Lloyd Newton, who was just 19 years old.

This was the kind of world that Artest knew far too well when he was young. Then because of a school counselor, he found his great savior: basketball. The school counselor was worried about Artest's temper and was convinced that he'd be able to get control over it if he turned his passion to the game.

Sure enough, Artest really was a natural on the court. And that led him through his high school days and straight into the NBA, where he quickly became known as a powerhouse on both sides of the court. He would get in players' faces; he would talk smack, and he wasn't afraid of getting roughed up. Ron Artest had arrived.

Eventually, Artest would make his way to the Indiana Pacers, and that is where his career took a new, challenging turn. He joined the team at a particularly important juncture because the Pacers had been on the verge of being the best team in the league for a while now, led by the hard work of legendary sharpshooter Reggie Miller.

With the inclusion of Artest and a few other young, up-and-coming players, the Pacers reached a brand-new level. They were racing to the Eastern Conference Finals and likely the NBA Finals too. And throughout all their games, they were ruffling feathers, making opponents upset, getting under the skin of nearly everyone they went against. Artest was a major part of it, and his hot-headed mentality was on full display but used to his advantage.

But it all came crashing down during a certain game against the Detroit Pistons.

It's called the Malice in the Palace now, but back then, it was just another heated game between rivals. Held in Detroit, the game was going to be intense because these two teams had been at each other's throats multiple times throughout the years. But things were different on November 19, 2004. In fact, things were downright violent.

Ben Wallace of Detroit was fouled by Indiana's Ron Artest with about 46 seconds left and Indiana leading 97–82. Wallace then shoved Artest, which prompted guys from both teams as well as coaches to argue on the floor. Artest sat down on the scorers' table to calm himself. For a brief, tense second, it seemed like maybe it was working, cooler heads were prevailing, and all would be well.

Then a supporter flung a beer cup, striking Artest.

A tumultuous situation erupted as Artest and colleague Stephen Jackson dashed toward the throng of crowds. Yes, they ran into the stands and started a huge brawl. All-out madness broke out, and fists, cups, and chairs were flying. Security tried to stop it, and coaches tried to stop it, but soon members from both teams were fighting each other in a wild, intense and chaotic scene.

Just when it seemed like things were cooling off yet again—this time for real—two fans rushed to the floor, and Artest and Jermaine O'Neal of the Pacers swung at them. The fighting seemed like it would never end, and players had to be literally dragged off the floor and into their locker rooms. As for the game, the final 45.9 seconds were never played.

The Malice at the Palace was a gigantic news story that shook the NBA world. Multiple sentences were handed out by the police, both to players and to fans who threw drinks to start the brawl. For his part, Artest was suspended for 86 games, which was the longest non-drug-related suspension ever. He also lost a total of $5 million.

That was the point in Artest's career when it was really hard to see him as anything but a violent and angry thug. He was called that—and worse, by many—even those in the media and the league. It wasn't just that horrible night in Detroit that earned him the reputation. He was also known for breaking Michael Jordan's ribs during a game of pick-up ball.

Artest swears it was just an accident, and he hit him with his elbow too hard. But other people feel this was an example of Artest not being able to control his emotions, even against the greatest basketball player of all time.

Artest knew he needed a change, and that is what he sought. He didn't want to be the same person he once was, so he altered the way people saw him—and what people called him. He changed his name to Metta World Peace, saying, "'I changed my name because I got tired of Ron Artest, he's a [expletive]. And when fans get mad at me, they can't say, 'I hate World Peace.'"

Some people saw the move as a hokey, publicity-grabbing attempt to clear his name. But others saw the man really had changed. He spoke out often about mental health issues, including his own depression and anger issues. He fought for people to be open about their emotional trauma and challenges and was a keynote speaker for many events related to mental health struggles. He has urged millions of young men and women to take their mental health seriously, reach out for help, ignore stigma, and believe in themselves.

Many years have gone by since the Malice in the Palace and the early, ugly days of Ron Artest. He is now retired, much more relaxed and healthy and is still seen commenting on the game that he loves so much. He is a reminder that people really can turn things around. As he said it best, "There's a lot of negativity in the world; I'm trying to be positive."

But the question remains: years from now, will people remember all the good that Metta World Peace has done, or will he still be the player who took to the stands to beat up fans? Are we all as bad as our worst moments, or is change truly possible?

5

PLAYING WITH THE FLU

> *"I didn't wanna give up. No matter how sick I was or how tired I was or how low on energy I was. I felt the obligation to my team, to the city of Chicago, to go out and give that extra effort."*
>
> — MICHAEL JORDAN

We have all been sick to our stomachs before, unfortunately. It's a horrible feeling and can lead to multiple days of truly just feeling like utter trash.

When you have any sort of stomach bug, you can pretty much cancel all your plans and try not to do anything but lay in bed, praying that this awful feeling will soon pass and you'll be feeling more like yourself soon. Can you imagine getting up to do chores, go to the store or do much of anything when you're suffering from this sort of sickness?

Now, can you imagine playing a game of basketball while you feel that way? What about playing a game of basketball and absolutely dominating it? That sounds out of this world unbelievable, right?

For you and me, it *is* unbelievable. But for the greatest basketball player of all time, it's just one of the many things that made him the GOAT and an athlete unlike any other.

It was June 11, 1997, and the NBA season was coming to an end in a way. The stakes couldn't be higher, and the tension couldn't be thicker. This was Michael Jordan and his Bulls attempting to claim unparalleled greatness yet again. He was already being called the greatest of all time, and he was dying to prove it. Remember, while he did have legions of fans back then, and his untouched greatness was uncontested back then, he was still actively playing and, therefore, still had some detractors. The 1997 Finals was a chance to really shut up the critics and build a bigger legacy. It was two titanic teams going against each other: Utah Jazz against the Chicago Bulls. And going into Game 5, the series was tied at 2–2.

Of course, Jordan and his team were considered the favorites to win. Yet, little did they know that just a few bites of the wrong meal would make them underdogs.

Jordan enjoyed a few slices of pizza the previous evening before the pivotal game without giving it any attention. But there was something off about that pizza, and it quickly put the future of Jordan's legacy on the line.

Jordan's trainer, Tim Grover, received a call around two in the morning and went to his room. The top player for the Bulls was wilting away in the fetal position. It was food poisoning, as Grover reasoned. Jordan could hardly stand and passed out multiple times, constantly dizzy, dehydrated, and not looking like himself at all. The man could hardly walk, let alone grip or shoot a basketball. Because of his sad physical state, the team doctors determined that Jordan could not participate.

But this is Michael Jordan we're talking about. That just wasn't going to happen. There was too much on the line, too much to prove.

The next day at a high school in Park City, MJ was hardly able to move while being connected to an IV during shootaround. His readiness for that evening's crucial finals game was in doubt. He slept all day and made it to the Delta Center in the heart of Salt Lake City in time for tip. The idea of Jordan playing was still far-fetched, despite his claims that he could do it. And the idea of him actually doing well in that game and leading the team to another victory was out of the question, even for the most die-hard Jordan fanatics.

Jordan had a drab, damp appearance, but he showed up at the game and said he was going to play. Head coach Phill Jackson knew better than to argue with His Airness. He also recognized that his team needed the seemingly magical abilities of MJ, so he let the man play. He hoped for the best but expected the worst.

Sure enough, he had a difficult first quarter, scoring just four points. In the second quarter, the Jazz jumped out to a 16-point lead thanks to the skillful dominant, one-two punch of Karl Malone and John Stockton.

That's when Jordan did what he always did: he stepped up. Apparently, the world required a reminder of who MJ was, the sort of player he was with or without the flu. With a fever, shaky bones and a body barely hanging to consciousness, Jordan started to play like his usual self. He racked up 17 points during the second quarter, storming back and reducing Utah's advantage to 4 before the half of the game.

As MJ sat on the sidelines in the third, Utah increased their advantage to eight. He answered with 15 points in the fourth, including the winning 3-pointer with 25 seconds left. In the end, he played 44 out of 48 minutes and ended the series with 38 points, 7 rebounds, 5 assists, 3 steals and a single block too. When the buzzer sounded and Bulls fans all over the world cheered the huge victory, Jordan gave out and fell into Scottie Pippen's arms.

Phil Jackson was beside himself with Jordan's work, once again blown away by just what this young man was capable of. "This was a heroic effort, one to add to the collection of efforts that make up his legend," Jackson said after the huge game.

The game immediately became a thing of legend, especially since the Bulls would go on to once again win the Finals. The game in Utah was dubbed "The Flu Game" because everyone thought he had caught a touch of a stomach bug. It would be years before Jordan would admit that it wasn't the flu that had him on his backside; it was a slice of pizza.

Speaking of that pizza, some people actually think Jordan was intentionally poisoned. Remember, the game was in Salt Lake City, and the residents of that city really wanted the Jazz to take a series lead. So is it out of the realm of possibility that a clever pizza delivery driver slipped something into the baking process to make Jordan's stomach upset?

Trainer George Koehler raised the prospect of an inside job again and again, saying, "It's very rare that you get five delivery guys from the pizza place to bring you your pizza."

No matter what caused the illness, this game was truly one of a kind and is still spoken of today when it comes to the drive, passion, and skill of athletes. It's the sort of inspiring story that can be looked at by everyone, even those who have never played a game of basketball in their lives. If Michael

Jordan was able to play in a championship game with such horrible symptoms, can't all of us rise above when we are trying to meet our goals? Once again, MJ showed the rest of the world just how incredible and unparalleled he was.

6

CAGERS

66 *"If I said that the CIAA "cagers" just left town or that March Madness is about to unleash a lot of "cager" excitement; it might be a hint."*

— JESSE BROWN

Not many professional sports are played inside the confines of a metal cage. You see the cage in something like MMA fighting and an occasional WWE match. But aside from that, cages are usually not conducive to the nature of watching sports live.

But that wasn't always the case. In fact, there was a time when certain basketball players—many of them, actually—performed for a whole game inside a cage. For a variety of reasons, the cage was installed to keep players and fans safe and keep the game moving forward.

Did you know that these "cage games," as they were referred to in the newspapers of the time, were actually used in some parts of the country until the 1920s and 30s? What caused this to take place, and did it really get the job done? Were cage games truly necessary as the young game of basketball bloomed and became the beloved sport it is now?

As mentioned before, James Naismith created the game in Massachusetts before the turn of the century. He created basketball as a way to entertain a group of students who were cooped up inside on a snowy winter day. However, what started as a way to occupy bored students soon became a national sensation.

In Trenton, New Jersey, the first recognized professionals played the game just five short years later, in 1896. Their court, located in a local gym hall, was surrounded by a 12-foot-high wire mesh fence installed along the sidelines and behind the baskets of the court.

The cage made logical sense at the time. According to Naismith's original rules, when the ball fell out of bounds, the first player to get to it might toss it back in. Front row fans remained much closer to the action than they are in modern games. Clearly, it would have been awful to enable players to compete for the ball while sitting on the laps of paying customers. The ball never left the cage; hence the rule was irrelevant.

You have to remember that a basketball court looked quite different back then. All courts were different, and it seemed like no two were exactly alike. Plus, the baskets of the time didn't even have backboards. An iron rod hung from the rafters, and it supported the basket. Can you believe that? If you missed the basket, the ball would just sail over it and into the stands. A cage would stop the game from constantly slowing down as people scrambled to get the ball back from out of bounds.

Another reason why the cage was such a smart call was because passions—and tensions—ran high in these early basketball games. Players would often battle it out for possession of the ball. In fact, they would fight, push each other around, and get into intense physical altercations to grab hold of the ball. If the ball weren't allowed to roll or bounce into the stands, no one would be fighting.

Yes, fights were a much more common occurrence in early basketball games. Sometimes it was multiple players duking it out, and sometimes fans pushing back against athletes. It wasn't uncommon for games to be halted as these fisticuffs were solved.

In fact, there were many times when fans would fight their way onto the court to make their angry opinions known. When they didn't like a ref's call, they'd just run onto the hardwood and push them around. If they didn't care for how a certain athlete was performing, they'd physically rush them and give them a piece of their minds.

Yes, things were considerably different back then. It sounds like every single night was a Malice in the Palace. So, the cage around the court was a great way to fix all of that. If the ball couldn't get out of bounds, the game could continue.

However, the cage also presented a lot of problems, and it didn't really take away the ferocious, primal nature some players were indulging in. Back then, players were permitted to push someone into the cage while they were trying to take a shot. That led to even more fights among players. Imagine how hockey players push one another against the side of the ice rink, slamming them against the glass. That's a lot like old-school basketball in a cage.

Players were getting very beat up by the cage. They would end games looking worse for wear, and the number of injuries among athletes skyrocketed.

Old school player Joel S. Gotthoffer really summed it up best when he said, "I played the first few games at Nanticoke in a [rope] cage, and I came home with the cage's markings on me. You could play Tic-Tac-Toe on everybody after a game because the cage marked you up; sometimes you were bleeding and sometimes not. You were like a gladiator, and if you didn't get rid of the ball, you could get killed."

Over time, the rules of the game were changed, and the necessity of a cage slowly faded away. Because of that, in 1902, cages started coming down all over the country, although they were mostly used only in the Northeast of the United States.

By the time the 1920s rolled around, basketball had become far more popular, and cage basketball matches far less so. Yet, a few teams and leagues still played with them deep into the 1930s. As the cages were used less and less, basketball became more recognized throughout the country, although some players felt left out in the cold by the removal of the cages.

"I played in cages up to 1929, when they stopped using them in Trenton. When they eliminated the cages, I never cared for basketball after that," said Albert Cooper Jr., who made his name in cage games. "All of the basketball players in those days enjoyed playing in a cage because there was less chance of injury than there is today. You learned to protect yourself. If you got jammed against the cage, it didn't bother you."

While you will never see an NBA game with a metal cage around the court, some organizations and tournaments still use this unique, historic format when playing games.

Yes, the Michigan Cagers Basketball league still plays with a cage, as does the Sooner Cager Classic, the A-K Valley Cager Classic, and the PH Cagers. Why do they continue to play basketball in such an antiquated way? Well, as you can imagine, it makes the games a bit more exciting. As long as players and fans don't get excited, cager matches can bring a whole new level of intensity to the game.

Basketball has come a long way, and a lot has changed about the game that was started in that Massachusetts gym so many decades ago. Some fads and choices have come and gone, like the cage games of the early 1900s. Yes, although now considered a relic of the past, it still sounds quite exciting. Imagine watching a game during these young, glory days of basketball. It was a wild mixture of both fighting and the NBA. What more could you ask for?

7

THE RIPPLE EFFECT

"I don't care how I got here. In the books, when you look at it 10 or 20 years from now, it's not going to say how he got here, it's going to say he's here and he represented the team."

— VINCE CARTER

He may not be a household name, but Vince Carter has been an incredibly important figure in the NBA over the last 20 years. Since joining the league back in 1999, Carter has earned an average of 16.7 points, 4.3 rebounds, and 3.1 assists a game and has played for multiple different teams.

Carter has done phenomenal work for the then-New Jersey Nets, the Orlando Magic, the Dallas Mavericks, and the Atlanta Hawks, among others.

But it was time with a certain team north of the border that really put Carter on the map and carved a special place for him in the hearts of millions of NBA fans. It was Vince Carter's tenure playing for the Toronto Raptors that really brought him attention and love from the fans and also brought pride to the city and Canada's sole NBA team.

You would think that since the game was created by a Canadian who had moved to the United States, basketball would have a bigger footprint in Canada. Yet, all over the world, the game is seen as a very American sport. In fact, it wasn't until 1923 that the Canadian Amateur Basketball Association was formed in Toronto, years after the sport was already being played by professionals down in the US.

The very first pro basketball game was played up north in 1946, but the team that played it didn't last and folded up just a year later.

After that, a country known for its wet, freezing cold snowstorms was surprisingly dry. Well, dry and devoid of any basketball, that is. There would be a professional team in the country until the year 1995, nearly 50 years since the last.

In 1994, the NBA awarded Canada two franchises: the Toronto Raptors and the Vancouver Grizzlies, who both began playing one season later in 1995. Unfortunately, things got off to a rocky start for the Canadian arm of the NBA. The first selection by the Raptors in their inaugural draft was BJ Armstrong, a player at the prime of his career, one who would work wonders for the team.

The only problem was that Armstrong had absolutely zero interest in playing for a Canadian team and flat-out refused to relocate. In the end, he never even set foot on Canadian soil and instead headed west to the Golden State Warriors.

Yes, Canadian NBA teams were in rough shape for the first few years, but things started turning around for the Raptors when they got ahold of Vince Carter, who was drafted by Toronto in 1998.

Hailing from UNC, Carter was chosen as the fifth pick in the first round of the draft. Because of his talent and the lack of success in Canada, many people thought he'd make a move like Armstrong and demand a trade. But that wasn't how Carter worked, then or now. Instead, he stuck around in Toronto and put the team on the map.

Carter was a superstar in the making from the moment he joined the Raptors, and he achieved 18.3 points, 5.7 rebounds, and 3 assists per game during his rookie year. Fans up north quickly took to Carter, who they called "half man, half amazing." Soon his jersey was flying off the shelves, and he was winning over not just millions of Canadians but Americans too.

To Canadian kids, he was Michael Jordan for a new age. He made basketball immensely more popular throughout the country, and his posters were soon hanging on bedroom walls all over the nation. The "Vince Carter Generation" was born, filled with young kids who didn't care about basketball before but loved it and grew obsessed over it.

He gave the team its first taste of success, taking them to the playoffs in the second year of his tenure. In less than two years, Vince Carter had turned around the fate of the team and made them a force to be reckoned with.

His fame continued to grow, especially when he won the annual NBA slam dunk contest with an amazing, historic dunk—still talked about to this day. The dunk had a lasting impact on the league (it is still played on highlight reels) and also earned him the nickname "Air Canada." If people didn't know before, they knew then: Vince Carter was the real deal, and Canadian basketball was here to stay.

Carter didn't stay in Canada forever and would eventually make his way down to the States to play for a slew of other teams, but it would always be his time north of the border that people remembered most. They still remember it because Carter gave back to his adopted country in so many ways. Through scholarship programs, mentorship work, charity games and more, Carter's impact on Canada went beyond winning games for them. He really and truly cared about the country, the children, and the citizens that were rooting him on.

Many years have passed now, and the landscape of Canadian teams is different: the Grizzlies moved to the US and reside in Memphis, and the Raptors have found great success and even won a championship.

Carter may not have been part of that championship team, but he still remains a vital part of the history of the NBA in Canada. Carlan Gray put it into perspective, summarizing Carter's importance: "When I think about Vince Carter I think about a pioneer in the Canadian basketball landscape," Gray said. "I often joke with people that Vince is one of the reasons why I have the job I have and while it may be a joke on the surface it's probably one of the biggest factors."

Perhaps no greater compliment can be paid than the one by NBA star Tristan Thompson, who reminded people just how important Carter was to young kids growing up in the 1990s: "Vince is the reason I fell in love with basketball . . . it makes you proud to be Canadian."

Many terrific players have called Canada home for their NBA careers now. A few future Hall of Famers spent time playing in the north, but none helped elevate or expand the sport of basketball in Canada more than Vince Carter. Because of that, he will always be a household name to a very grateful country.

8

THE BEST TEAM YOU'VE NEVER HEARD OF

"I think the Rens should be remembered for their perseverance. By constantly being one of the best teams in the game they made the sporting world acknowledge their superior play and the fact that they deserved to be competing against all comers, both Black and White."

— KAREEM ABDUL-JABBAR

J ust because you haven't heard of the New York Rens doesn't mean they aren't one of the most important teams ever to play basketball. Sometimes it's not just about athletes who played for a team or the number of wins they accrued. Sometimes what matters most is the history of the team, what it meant, what it achieved, and how it changed the game and, ultimately, the world.

The New York Rens was a basketball team that existed in an America that honestly didn't want it. In the United States during the first half of the 20th century, Jim Crow laws sought to humiliate and limit African Americans throughout the nation. In most of the country, Black Americans didn't have the same rights as whites. In fact, it wasn't even close.

And while African Americans were permitted to play in sports, they played in a world of athleticism that was completely cut off from the white world. Rarely ever were any games featuring both white and Black players unless organizers were pitting the races against each other in order to drum up ticket sales.

Black athletes existed on one side of the equation, far away from the fame and success that white performers found.

Bob Douglas was a figure who would come to America and attempt to change a lot of that. If he couldn't break down the walls that kept both races separated, he could at least greatly help the Black athletes trying to make names for themselves.

Douglas came to the United States from the Caribbean in 1901 at the age of 19 and found out about basketball just a few years later. He was instantly hooked and automatically in love with the young game that was taking the country by storm.

Douglas immediately got into the game, so to speak. He formed the Spartan Field Club; a location where Black children could compete in amateur sports with others. Shortly after that, he also started the Spartan Braves, which he actually played on until he retired from the sport at the age of 36 so he could focus on managing full time.

The original team started by Douglas consisted of a big five of Clarence Jenkins, Bill Yancey, John Holt, James Ricks, and Eyre Saith. Later on, Charles Cooper and Willie Smith also joined the team.

In 1923, Douglas struck a deal with the Renaissance Ballroom and Casino, finding a home court for his first all-Black basketball team, called the Harlen Rens.

The Rens got off to a good start, winning a number of games against other Black teams in the area. In the 1924–1925 season, they actually won the Colored Basketball World Championship and dominated their league for the next 25 years.

During that era, Black basketball teams were only allowed to play against other Black basketball teams. As for white fans, there weren't nearly as many as there were for other white teams. The Harlen Rens were dominating and were the best Black basketball squad around, but nine out of ten people walking down the street didn't even know one of their players or even who they were. This shows the sort of disconnect and inequality that was a rampant and constant part of not just American sports but the entire American system as a whole at the time.

Years later, in 1939, the first ever World Professional Basketball tournament was held in Chicago. During that time, the Globetrotters were the Chicago team that everyone knew, the fan favorite and hometown squad that had a loyal following. But the Rens changed that when they went against the Globetrotters and beat them in the first semifinals game, 27–23.

There were 12 teams competing in the World Professional Basketball tournament, and the Rens had just taken down the top one. They were making a statement and raising awareness to their greatness.

You have to remember that it was a very different game back then. For example, players got hold of the ball via tip-off after every single point scored. Additionally, they could and would shoot with both hands. Even the creation of the basketball was different back then, and it felt heavy and didn't bounce as well. Therefore, it was harder to dribble and much more difficult to get up the court. Despite all of that, the Rens were experts on the court, weaving past opponents and finding the basket with both ease and pizzaz.

Because they were doing so well in the tournament, the Rens were tasked with playing an all-white team for the final game of the championship. This match-up was sought to attract attention from basketball fans that weren't yet aware of the Rens because of the color of their skin.

In the end, it would be the Rens who won the entire tournament—champions despite so much stacked against them. One of the rewards for their feat was a jacket that said "Colored World Champions" on the back. This didn't sit well with several players on the Rens, who took it upon themselves to actually cut out the word "colored." They weren't just Black champions; they were undeniable, undisputed champions. They had beaten all the other teams—including a white one—so the qualifier on the jacket was just downright wrong and didn't tell the whole picture.

Joe "Wonder Boy" Isaacs put it best when he said, "World champions ain't got no colors."

The Harlem Rens were easily the best all-Black team around back then and were a dominant force in the basketball world during the 1920s and 30s. They ended that era with a record of 2588–539. In fact, at one point, they actually won 88 games straight, a feat that still hasn't been topped to this day.

Because of the history they made and their unparalleled sportsmanship, the Rens were inducted into the Naismith Memorial Basketball Hall of Fame back in 1936, the height of their success.

Today, their bio in the Hall of Fame reads aptly: "One of basketball's first true dynasties . . . The all-black New York Renaissance moved the ball around with such wizardry and deception that the opposition was often rendered helpless . . . The Rens were unsurpassed in passing ability and the fast break left opponents begging for mercy."

There is no denying their talent, their importance, or their success. Yet, to this day, not many people speak of or know of the Harlem Rens. They were an instrumental force in raising awareness of Black players and showing just how impressive, powerful, and remarkable they could be. But they still remain the best team you have never heard of . . . until now.

9

FROM PRISON TO NBA STARDOM

"When he first came into the league, I judged him for his selfishness and swagger. It's taken me a quarter-century to appreciate what I missed: his genius and compassion."

— SKIP BAYLESS

One of the most admired, despised, controversial and well-known players in all of NBA history is Allen Iverson from the Philadelphia 76ers. The opinions of Iverson are divided and always stark. People either love him, or they hate him. There seems to be very little middle ground in the thoughts about this one-of-a-kind player.

Haters of Iverson will claim he was a punk and a criminal. He allegedly introduced a negative reputation to the NBA,

272 | ROY LINGSTER

was obsessed with "hero ball," and failed to lead the Sixers to a title. His critics say he always and only put himself first. And, yes, it is hard to argue that Iverson often saw himself as the best player on his team and wouldn't rely on his fellow peers as often as he should have. Yet, it's hard to blame him because of the talent he had.

Then there is the other side of the equation. Iverson's admirers, however, would claim that he overcame a difficult childhood. Beyond that, they say he was one of the most skilled players in the game's history as well as one of the greatest scorers of all time. They would also claim that nobody played the game with greater fervor. If you're looking for passion, drive, and a determination always to do the best, look no further than Allen Iverson.

But at the end of the day, it's undeniable that Iverson and his teams never won a championship, so is he a crook who just so happened to be talented? Or is he a role model for others who are less fortunate since he treated every game as if it were his last?

That is up to you. But one thing is clear: Iverson, or "The Answer" as he's been called, was a player unlike any other—one who influenced a generation of other players and altered the league forever.

Iverson never had an easy life. He had a 15-year-old single mother when he was born. Iverson didn't have it easy growing up in Hampton, Virginia, where whites and Blacks preferred to hang out with their own kind. His family was struggling, and most of his buddies had been detained several times. Iverson wasn't wealthy, but he did have one thing: a passion for sports. And while he started by playing two sports, it would be one that would find him great fame and fortune and success in his life.

Iverson was the highlight of his high school's basketball and football teams. His greatness was on any field he walked on: both his teams won their state championships under his direction. Friends credit his aggressiveness on the court to his football experience.

During his NBA career, Iverson was classified as 165 pounds, but he was closer to 150 pounds. Yet he used his smaller size to his advantage, ducking and weaving and getting physical when he needed to. Driving to the right into power forwards and centers is one of his favorite court moves, which makes sense.

He was a young player with a lot of potential and the chances of him going far in the NBA were high. He was considered a top prospect among all the rookies in the country.

For Iverson, everything appeared to be going great. It seemed he had discovered his purpose and a means of supporting himself. On February 14, 1993, it was put in total jeopardy.

In his native Hampton, Virginia, Iverson was bowling with a group of pals. Nobody really remembers what occurred after a sizable gathering of white males who were also bowling.

According to other versions, Iverson's buddies approached the white men and made fun of them. According to some versions, the white gang called Iverson and his companion racial slurs and punched them first. But what followed is well known since a full-fledged fight started. It was a fight that would change Iverson's life forever and one that also put the future of his career and his fame thrown in the air.

White and Black teens engaged in a scuffle while using chairs as weapons and hurling them. Four persons were taken into custody after the fight was broken up. They were all Black. However, just one of them was a high school superstar with widespread fame.

Iverson was detained for allegedly using a chair to strike a white woman in the head, knocking her out cold.

Of course, this all eventually led to a trial. Only Black individuals were detained in connection with the event, and the prosecution made use of a legal provision from Virginia dating back to the 1800s called "maiming by mob."

In the end, the sentence was handed down, and it was harsh, something that few people would be able to overcome: Iverson received a 15-year jail term on three felony counts.

He continued to assert his total innocence and affirmed that he left the area as soon as the altercation started. The fact that community service is often required for a crime of this kind in the state of Virginia only served to exacerbate racial tensions in the case.

Iverson ultimately spent a few months in jail before receiving a pardon from the governor due to inadequate proof. Iverson's next piece of news was much better: he had been given a scholarship to play at Georgetown. Years later, Iverson would look back at this time in his life by saying, "You have to go through good times and bad times to get where you're trying to go."

Iverson won the Big East awards for defensive basketball athlete of the year and Rookie of the Year during his first season. He was a standout who scored 23 points on average every game. His crossover dribble as well as his step-back jumper were all learned here.

After his second season, he announced his NBA Draft entry and was regarded as the top prospect in the league—as demonstrated by the Sixers selecting him first overall in the NBA draft in 1996.

He then went on to get Rookie of the Year recognition and quickly made a name for himself as one of the league's top players. The rest ought to have been forgotten. From then, his career should have been straightforward. Iverson was widely expected to play his whole career in Philadelphia, post impressive stats, and take home several titles. There are no happy ever afters with a man like Iverson, though.

Iverson's performance on the court wasn't really an issue. He became perhaps the most imposing scorer since Jordan because of a combination of accurate shooting, smooth dribbling, and persistent effort toward the basket. His four seasons of 30+ points per game and two scoring crowns attest to this.

He may have been the hardest player in the game, pound for pound, while playing through injury during the playoffs. He also received the NBA MVP award during the 2000–2001 campaign. It had been a long time since anyone had seen a player more determined than Iverson. This was a man who lived and breathed basketball and obviously considered the game the most important thing in his life. As he put it, "I'd rather have more heart than talent any day." Luckily, he had plenty of both.

He earned a lot of fans not only because he was great but also because he felt like a true underdog. Because of his past, his size, and the things working against him, many people saw themselves in AI as he burned through the NBA and set the gold standard for MVP.

Around this period, in 2000, Iverson rose to prominence as the most adored and despised basketball player on the globe. The NBA's "new school" of fans adored his enthusiasm. They adored the plays in his highlight reel. They admired how young people were drawn to his swagger.

He was despised by "old school" NBA fans as well as commentators, journalists, and others. From his tattoos to his several nationally broadcast instances of shouting "F*** You!" at referees to his absurdly high number of field goal attempts. No player elicited more wildly divergent opinions when brought up in discussion than Iverson.

Yes, when he left the NBA, many people loved him, and others hated him. But those who really know basketball understand just how special this young player was. Andrew Hanlon once said, "The answer will always be known for his toughness and refusal to back down from any challenge." There is no denying that.

Allen Iverson experienced his fair share of troubles throughout his life, but Hanlon was right when he said AI overcame it all. Through a rocky childhood and a wrongful conviction, he became one of the best NBA players of all time. His story is one of great perseverance, something that any and all basketball fans can appreciate and respect.

A SYMBOL OF INDEPENDENCE

"The 1992 Lithuanian Basketball Team represents what happens in freedom . . . people excel."

— GREG SPEIRS

There is a lot more to professional sports than simply people wanting to cheer on a team. In fact, there have been times throughout history where a group of millions of people finds their identity and national pride in a sports team. There is just something about so many people coming together to root on others for a common goal. It's true that only a few people may be on the field or the court, but they are playing on behalf of so many others, including millions watching from home.

Take a moment to think about the majesty and the importance of the Olympics. Every four years, billions of people all over the world set aside their differences and cheer on their national team. It doesn't matter what's going on in the world, local politics or current events. When the Olympics roll around every few years, it gives entire countries a chance to bring themselves together as one people with one team and one goal: to win.

There are some people who take their democracy and freedoms for granted. Then others know how hard it is to struggle under suffocating regimes that restrict rights and limit peoples' chances and liberties.

And when these people finally do get free and find a team to support, they pour their hearts and souls into it because they are actually cheering on more than a team; they are cheering on a cause and ideals they hold so near and dear to their hearts.

The 1992 Lithuanian basketball team was an example of that. Through their hard work, determination, and skill, they rallied an entire nation that was looking for a solid, truthful win after so many years of persecution and pain.

Lithuania was once a country that celebrated basketball. You might not know it, but it was actually a nation that had a ton of great young basketball players. It was perhaps their most popular national pastime. But when Russia, then the USSR, eventually absorbed Lithuania and made it part of the Soviet

Union, the Lithuanian team had to start playing for a new country.

The USSR held onto Lithuania and its professional sports stars with an iron fist. There were a couple of times when Lithuanian players were set to be drafted by teams in the NBA, but then the powers that be in the USSR shut that offer down and restricted the Lithuanian players from moving to the United States. These people were commanded to play for the USSR and *only* the USSR.

To be fair, the Lithuanians did find great success playing for their new leadership. For eight consecutive years, the Russian team medaled in the Olympics. That's because they had world-class pros on the team and also because the people in charge accepted nothing but the very best from their athletes.

But major changes were coming for the Soviet Union. By the late 1980s, the grand country had run out of money and was falling apart. Shortly after that, the USSR collapsed and was no longer. That meant all the countries owned by the USSR were now free and in a brave new world of freedom and opportunity, including opportunities in sports.

In 1992, Lithuania was independent and ready to take the world by storm. The nation longed to be part of the Olympics on their own behalf but lacked the most important thing: a basketball team.

Professional player Šarūnas Marčiulionis came up with the idea of actually enlisting a team to be in the '92 Olympics, but he lacked the money and organizational skills to put it together. That was when he received help from an astounding and groovy group of supporters.

The jam rock band, the Grateful Dead, were longtime champions of the underdog and people fighting out of their weight class. They heard about the desires of the newly freed Lithuanian people and their longing to be in the Olympics, and they wanted to help. So the band took it upon itself to fund the Lithuanian team and lead them to the Olympics.

Since they were receiving so much money and support from the Grateful Dead, the team wore iconic warm-up uniforms that fit the part: they were all tie-dyes. This one-of-a-kind look instantly put them on the map, and the Lithuanian basketball team was now on the radar of many people, known for their independence, personality and wonderful, inspiring story. Marius Markevicius, a Lithuanian athlete, summed it up neatly, saying, "They looked like the biggest goofballs ever. What they were representing was pure joy."

But they would soon be known for even more: going up against the very country that once owned them. As it would happen, the '92 team would have to face off against Russia in the bronze medal game. As you can imagine, a lot was riding on the results of the game—for both teams. If Lithuania won, it would send a huge message across the world about their power, their skill, and the beautiful idea of democracy. And if Russia won, they would show people that they weren't as weak as people made them out to be. In the early 1990s, Russia was desperate to rebuild itself and once again have some sort of standing in the world. In other words, they wanted to be taken seriously. If they were able to get some kind of success in the Olympics, especially against a country they used to rule, that would help the spirit of the Russian people and would also be a big statement.

With so much riding on the game, both teams came into the bronze medal game with serious intention and determination to win. And they knew they would do literally whatever it took to win at all costs.

Sure enough, the basketball game between Russia and Lithuania was intense and knock-down, drag-out. Early in the game, one player on the Lithuanian team was hit so hard that he bled from his forehead. The blood was spilling on the floor as it poured from the open wound. You would think that would be enough to stop the game or at least delay it. But the Lithuanian team wasn't having any of it and the president of the country urged the athlete and the team to push on, even with the injury.

Lithuanian President Vytautas Landsbergis looked the injured player right in the eyes and said plainly, "Don't worry. You're spilling blood for Lithuania."

Apparently, that was all he needed to hear because the game went on. The team pushed themselves as hard as they could.

During that game, the Lithuanian basketball team wasn't only being cheered on by those in their home country. Instead, they were a testament to fans of democracy all over the globe. People in America, England, Canada, and other nations were rooting on Lithuania and willing them to win.

And win, they did. They ended up taking down Russia in the much-watched game, which was not only a huge feat for the team of athletes but also for the people of the country that were still getting used to the idea of freedom.

When the game was over, the team was so joyful and celebratory that they could be heard singing the Lithuanian national anthem from their locker room. They had come together as a team but, more importantly, as countrymen devoted to their cause.

While the USA Dream Team was the team that won it all in the 1992 Olympics, the Other Dream Team was from the little country of Lithuania. Celebrating democracy and freedom in their tie-dyed uniforms, they defeated the nation that used to own them and sent a message to the rest of the globe while also playing one of the most iconic games in basketball history.

PLAYING AGAINST HATE

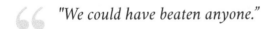 *"We could have beaten anyone."*

— JOHN MCCLENDON

There have been plenty of cases of sports bringing people from different walks of life together for one common cause. But few stories are as inspiring or important as the "secret game" in North Carolina back in 1944. This was a vastly different time when all laws and rules set by the state and the federal government didn't allow people from different races to mix, meet or play against one another.

Sports are so important and can stand for so much beyond just winning a game and scoring goals. So, of course, it would be a sport that brought two distinctly diverse types of people together.

In 1944, it was illegal for Black and white teams to play against one another in the state of North Carolina. There were many Black teams, and there were many white teams, but the Black and white players would never face off against one another, and they certainly would be on the same team at any time.

White teams were given much more media attention and had larger fanbases. Those who played on white teams were the ones who would be drafted by professional teams and would actually find a career in sports. Sadly, Black players were always relegated to the minor leagues and could only play against and with other Black players, never able to crash through the racial boundaries put in place by the laws of the land.

The Eagles basketball team from the North Carolina College for Negroes had only lost one game all season. In other words, they were the best all-Black team in the state and perhaps the country. Few athletes could rival the skill, power, and winning percentage of the Eagles.

While the chances of them actually playing against a white team were still non-existent, the players on the Eagles started going toe to toe against their white peers from Duke at the local YMCA. Even playing friendly games at the Y was dangerous enough and could have gotten all of them into legal trouble, but the Eagles took the idea one step further when they challenged Duke to a game.

Surely Duke would flat out refuse the idea, right? There was no way they could risk so much to play against a Black team. But several players on the Duke team wanted to take on the challenge. So after some hesitation, they accepted the offer, and the terms of the game were set.

Both sides wanted to play but knew they had to be very, very careful. The local politics were intense and heated at the time. Around that time, a Black soldier had been shot and killed for not moving to the back of the bus fast enough. As usual, racial tensions were high, and both those on Duke and the Eagles did not want to add more fuel to that fire.

So they knew they would play a game and formulated a plan to keep it private and hidden from the rest of the world. For starters, they planned to play the game on a Sunday when most people—including police officers and law enforcement officials—were in church and away from the court.

To keep things even more secretive, the Duke team only drove in borrowed cars and took a winding route through town to get to the location of the secret game. No one was there watching the game, and no one said anything to outside parties. This game wasn't about publicity or anything other than a group of young men playing a game they loved, ignoring their races and the world around them.

Most people on both sides of the game expected Duke to win and, sure enough, they started to seem like they were going

288 | ROY LINGSTER

to run away with the victory. But once the Eagles got warmed up, they started scoring on nearly every possession. They were pulling off fast breaks and other plays that Duke had never seen and simply wasn't used to or prepared for.

That is what led the Eagles to pull off a victory and win the game. The final score was 88 to 44, which means the Eagles didn't just win; they absolutely dominated and pulled off a monster triumph.

This was a huge moment for both teams and all the players involved. And it was also an important turning point in the evolution of basketball since multiple guys on both squads learned from one another. So the all-white teams learned new skills and techniques, and the Black players did as well.

In the modern NBA, the league is filled with wildly talented and successful Black players. But back in the day, that simply wasn't how sports worked. Without games and moments like the secret game of 1944, the NBA we know today wouldn't exist.

Scott Ellsworth, who played in the game, summed it up when he said, "It was a part of this generation . . . that really started to lay the groundwork that the civil rights movement was going to thrive on."

It might sound silly because it was a basketball game. But the bravery and perseverance of the North Carolina College for Negroes 1944 basketball team is today celebrated for the lasting impression on the game they loved. They built a bridge to people different from them. And by playing together, they learned that maybe they weren't that different after all.

THE BEST HIGH SCHOOL
BASKETBALL TEAM IN HISTORY

"*From 1981 to 1983, Dunbar High was the most powerful team in high school basketball. Boasting four future NBA players, the Poets took the life out of their opponents and their gyms.*"

— CALVIN FONG

I t's not easy growing up in certain parts of Baltimore, Maryland. That was true decades ago, and it is still true to this day. However, some parts of Baltimore are tougher and harder to live in than others.

Take the area around Paul Laurence Dunbar High School, for example. The school sits in the middle of five different housing projects. That part of town is dangerous and ignored by much of the nation. It's been left to fester in crime and violence for years, yet people still try to live their lives, get through and raise their children, go to their jobs, and try to secure a better future.

Dunbar High School saw a lot of bad things during the 1980s as the crack epidemic was sweeping the nation. Baltimore was being hit harder than many other parts of the United States. In fact, Baltimore was ground zero for much of the deaths, violence, and crimes associated with the crack outbreak.

Partly because of the dangers of drugs, crime, and gangs, basketball became an especially important sport for many young people in the area at the time. But it was more than just a sport; it was an outlet and a way to escape. It was a way of getting out of the life that was gobbling up so many other people and leading them down a dangerous path to death.

Dunbar High students were enthusiastic about playing basketball and were soon taken under the wing of one of the most hardcore, capable and driven coaches in high school basketball history.

When Bob Wade became the head coach for Dunbar High, he had one goal in mind: he was going to shape the young men on his team into professional, respectful and respected athletes. He was going to go about it in a very direct, intimidating way, but he never lost sight of what he wanted to achieve with the high school students coming to him for guidance.

In fact, Wade was so important and influential to the exceptionally young men playing for him that he would someday have the gym named after him in 2015.

What was it about Wade that made him so special? It was his strict style of coaching. For example, he made his players run with bricks during practice, and he would push his students to the limit. He knew he could get the best out of them; he just needed to not go easy on them. He only pushed them because he believed in them.

He may have been harsh on the athletes playing for him, but they took to this style of coaching quite well, and the results were immediate—and they spoke for themselves.

In eleven seasons coaching at Dunbar, Wade went 272–24 with nine Maryland Scholastic Association A Conference titles, four perfect seasons, two national championships, and ten Baltimore City championships too. In the early 1980s, his team had a 59–0 record over two seasons.

Wade led the team during the miraculous 1982–1983 team, still regarded as one of the best high school squads of all time. With that team, the team went 31–0 and was led by some players such as Reggie Williams, Reggie Lewis, and Muggsy Bogues. David Wingate would also play under Coach Wade. As you know, each of these men found varying degrees in the world of professional sports outside of high school. When they did, they all gave much credit to Coach Wade and the ways he inspired and guided them all.

Muggsy Bogues would speak very fondly of Coach Wade years later, saying, "It's beyond basketball. Many of us weren't going to college or be successful, he gave us the tools, the attitude, the willingness, the determination to want to be more than an athlete."

Sure enough, these young men playing for Wade were able to resist the urge to turn to crime, drugs, and gangs swarming all over the city and preying on the weak like vultures. Wade was well aware of that. He knew he could be an inspiring and helpful presence in their lives and did all he needed to ensure they would take a life full of discipline and commitment to the game, not the desire to try drugs and make easy money via crime.

Wade created a team system that acted as a shield against the raging crack epidemic and the dangers lurking beyond the school's walls. This alone was inspiring, but the fact that the team found so much success over the years made it all the more riveting to the locals, sports fans, and of course, the young people playing the game.

Dunbar High stood proudly as a beacon among the many problems exploding in Baltimore. For years, it would be used as an example of a coach and his players fully devoting to a cause, no matter how many distractions were trying to get in the way.

Years later, many books and articles were written about Coach Wade and the Dunbar High School basketball team.

One of those books summed it all up quite well: "The inspirational story of the most talented high-school basketball team ever and the dedicated coach who gave his players a lifetime opportunity by insisting on success."

The team really was something special, as was its unorthodox coach who marched to the beat of his own drum and taught how he wanted and still found great success. It went beyond their amazing win record and the stellar athletes produced there. It was an inspiring and incredible example of sports bringing people together, helping them rise above their situations, and really achieve everything that they can. It goes to show the power of sports can help anyone in any circumstance. What could be more inspiring than that?

13

THE MOST WINS

College basketball is a sport not for the faint of heart. It is challenging, it is cutthroat, and it is always filled with young players who are still figuring themselves out and deciding how they want to play the game.

Therefore, those who find success in college basketball are true athletes and brilliant minds that have mastered a game so few people can. Pat Summitt was one of those people. In fact, throughout her career playing the game and coaching it, she became someone unlike any other.

Today, Summitt is known as the coach with the most wins in college basketball ever, regardless of the era or gender of the athletes. She is not just one of the best—she is *the* best.

Young Pat Summitt grew up playing the game that would bring her such success on her family farm. Perhaps tellingly, she played against her three brothers and always found a way to surpass and beat them, showing that a girl can play the game just as well as a guy.

Summitt was so driven to play the game, in fact, that her family actually moved before her freshman year of high school because the schools in her area didn't have a female basketball team.

Following high school, Pat played the game for Tennessee-Martin, where she dominated the team and any other team that came against her. She would tear through her time in college and eventually become the all-time leading scorer for the school.

In the years following her time playing basketball, Pat became fascinated and driven to become a coach and lead a brand-new generation of ballers. After years of perfecting her approach to teaching and studying the game, she was given the head coach job at the University of Tennessee, Knoxville, where her historic career would really take off.

Summitt was known for her ferocity, and her piercing blue eyes and cold look, which frequently linked with others and bolstered the determination of the athletes on her teams, were a reflection of her competitive fire. On the other hand, she had a mothering tenderness and sense of humor, showing that her criticisms came from a place of genuine concern. They were merely techniques for getting the greatest performance possible from the young girls she was in charge of and prepping them for the hardships of the sport as well as life in general.

Pat became a vital part of the school, its culture, its history, and its success. Summitt coached the Lady Volunteers for 38 seasons, compiling a staggering total record of 1,098–208. She elevated the UT program's reputation and earned it recognition on a global scale.

She received the honor of being named the "Naismith Women's Collegiate Coach of the Century" for the 1900s because of her outstanding body of work in that direction. It was a career-defining accomplishment for a leader who won several awards, including national coach of the year seven times and SEC's selection for the year's top coach eight times.

Summitt was so well respected as a women's collegiate coach that people periodically discussed her as a potential possibility for coaching men. For example, Peyton Manning, an NFL legend in his own right, told Summitt he had always hoped he could have been on one of her teams. He hinted that she possessed the qualities needed to succeed as a football coach as well if she had chosen that career.

However, Summitt had a desire to help young girls become champions, graduates, and productive members of society, and she excelled at it. Her example inspired girls to believe that if they were prepared to put in the effort, they could achieve anything they set their minds to. She has left her mark in many areas, but the development of the sport and the young athletes playing it is just one of them. She wasn't just teaching these young women how to conquer on the court; she was informing them about the rules of life and the way to push through hard times, overcome challenges, and always believe in themselves.

Her win total continues to be the most in NCAA Division I basketball history for either men or women. To this day, no one has surpassed her records. Her career was filled with milestones and high water marks that haven't been toppled by others. She was the first NCAA basketball coach to surpass the 1,000-win mark.

Summitt's teams participated in 22 NCAA or AIAW Final Fours while making a record-breaking 31 straight NCAA Tournament appearances, winning 8 NCAA National Championships and placing second 5 times. UT won the first three consecutive national championships in NCAA Division I women's basketball in 1996, 1997, and 1998, with the third of those teams cruising to a school-record 39–0 record.

Additionally, she led the Big Orange to victories in 16 SEC Tournaments and 16 SEC Regular-Season Championships, including the first-ever SEC Tournament victory in 1980 and her final one as head coach in 2012. During her career, Tennessee dominated SEC opponents, going 458–69 (.869), including 69–17 (.795) in tournament play.

Summitt oversaw 14 UT players that made Olympic Teams. Summitt herself actually claimed silver as a player back during the 1976 Olympics and led the US team to triumph in 1984. She produced 39 All-SEC players as well as 21 WBCA All-Americans. She sent 39 Lady Vols to the WNBA, including 3 first-round picks and 15 first-round picks.

Basketball courts were named in Summitt's honor because of her achievements as one of the game's best teachers. Eight halls of fame, including the Women's Basketball Hall of Fame and the Naismith Memorial Basketball Hall of Fame, inducted her. She has streets named after her in Martin and Knoxville. In 2013, a monument and a plaza were built next to Tennessee's Thompson-Boling Arena.

Summitt encouraged her players to accept and live the qualities of discipline, hard labor, and sacrifice she acquired while helping out on her family's farm as a youngster. Along the process, she also devised a code of behavior she termed her "Definite Dozen."

Respect for oneself and others is one of them. Accept full accountability. Create and exhibit loyalty. Develop your communication skills. Become passionate about your work. Work smarter, not just harder. Prioritize the group over yourself. Make winning a mentality. Become a rival. There must be change. Treat victory with the same respect as failure. These were the principles she taught her athletes, which is why she is still considered one of the greatest coaches ever to play the game, regardless of her gender. "Teamwork is what makes common people capable of uncommon results," Summit once said, highlighting her determination to always bring the team together above all else.

These principles didn't just apply to basketball courts. Summitt was certain they were relevant in school and every other part of a player's life, enabling her to raise educated, independent young women to be leaders in their fields

Summitt was forced to retire from the game she loved so much on April 18, 2012, less than a year after disclosing she had early-onset dementia related to Alzheimer's. Pat Summitt was a living trailblazer who served as a coach, mentor, mother figure, ambassador, pioneer, and role model.

REVIEW A GAME OF EXTREMES: 25 EXCEPTIONAL BASKETBALL STORIES

As a writer it's hard to get reviews, I hope you can help me.

If you have enjoyed these first 13 tales and maybe even learned something, let me know. If the tales has fulfilled its promise, please put up a review and spread the word to those who will enjoy it. I hope it will be possible to bring more stories to readers.

Scan the QR code below to leave a quick review!

14

THE LINEUP THAT CHANGED
THE GAME

> *". . . by becoming the first team to win an NCAA title with five black starters, the Miners weren't just champs on the court: They helped change the rules of the game. They didn't know it at the time, but their contribution to civil rights was as important as any other."*
>
> — PRESIDENT BARACK OBAMA

America during the 1960s was not a kind place for anyone but primarily white males. Minorities across the country weren't just looked down upon but were also legally prohibited from doing many things we take for granted. The differences between Black and white Americans were stark from eating in the same restaurants, drinking from the same fountains, and going to the same businesses.

This was doubly true for the educational system of America. The schools all across the United States were segregated, and white students were given one type of treatment while other students with different skin colors were subjected to a different world—one that was lacking and horrible compared to what their white peers got to enjoy.

Things were even worse in the deep South region of the United States in the 1960s. Jim Crow laws had split the nation apart and created horrendous and cruel living and educational environments for Black people. That had an impact on so many parts of life, including sports. Students in school were not able to talk with each other, learn with each other, or play with each other.

The Civil Rights movement was coming to life during that time, but it had a long way to go before there was anything resembling true equality in the United States. But leave it to college sports to bring people together in ways the laws and the people refused to do.

The NCAA was holding its annual basketball tournament in 1966. But the organization had no idea that the two opponents playing against one another would radically change how people viewed racial strife in America.

The tournament that year came down to two teams: one from El Paso's Texas Western College Miners and the University of Kentucky Wildcats. On paper, that doesn't sound like much of a wild lineup, just two teams that would go against each other every year without any drama or much attention. But these teams and this year were different for the NCAA.

The Miners consisted of seven African-American players: Bobby Joe Hill, Willie Worsley, Nevil Shed, Willie Cager, Orsten Artis, Harry Flournoy, and Davis Lattin. There were four white players as well: Jerry Armstrong, Dick Meyers, Togo Railey, and Louis Boudoin. The team also had one Mexican American, Dave Palacio.

Meanwhile, the Wildcats were full of only white players.

The Miners' head coach, Don Haskins, had selected the best players for his squad, not paying attention to the color of their skin. At the same time, the coach of the Wildcats, Adolph Rupp, admitted that he only chose white players to be on his team.

But now, the two teams were lined up to play against one another, meaning that this tournament would be about more than just basketball. It would be about racial equality, the Civil Rights movement, the laws of America, and the entire country as a whole.

When the Miners showed up in Kentucky for the championship game in March of 1966, most people expected them to be easily beaten by the Wildcats. Most of this was just based on the racial bias of the analysts for the game. The idea of a Black team beating their white opponents just seemed unlikely and, truly, never heard of before.

At first, it did look like Kentucky was ready to win it all, but then the Miners started to come from behind and pushed through the first and second half to finally end the game with a 72–65 win. It was considered a watershed moment, not just for American sports but for the country in general. Never before had there been an event like this. Never before had a group of students written off and held down been able to overcome the odds and the hand that had been dealt.

Coach Don Haskins had a lot to say about his team's triumph: "This is a great, great honor. But our national championship had some social significance that might outweigh anything that would ever happen to me. I didn't know it at the time, but our championship in '66 opened the doors for a lot of Black kids."

Years later, the championship game between the Wildcats and Miners is still seen as one of the most important and stunning victories in all of college sports. It might not have been the most exciting game of all time and might not have ended with a blowout score, triple overtime or anything quite so dramatic. But it was still consequential in ways that just couldn't be correctly summed up at the time. It would only be years, decades really, later that people would see how important and vital that game between the Miners and Wild-cats was.

Winning a title is something to be proud of. But doing so in a history-setting manner is even more impressive.

THE INFAMOUS DUNK OF DEATH

> "I don't want or need to gain respect with what I do off the court. I want respect for what I do on the court."
>
> — VINCE CARTE

It's been called many things—the "Dunk of Death," for example—and has been replayed and studied by millions of NBA fans for years now. But the importance, power, and brilliance of the dunk heard around the world can all be traced back to the man who created it: Vince Carter.

This infamous dunk is still spoken of today. In fact, if there were college courses about the NBA and the showmanship associated with it, this dunk would receive several weeks entirely. There is a lot to discuss about the dunk, what led up to it and why it is still celebrated decades later. But before doing that, you have to understand the dunk in all its physical and functional glory.

It was the 2000 Olympic Games, and the USA Men's Basketball team was, once again, attempting to break some records and bring home a gold trophy. There was little doubt among the rest of the world that the Americans had the best team. For years now, the United States had thrived in the Olympic basketball games, especially since Michael Jordan, Magic Johnson, and the Dream Team led them to glory so many years before.

But it wasn't just enough to win during these games; the Americans wanted to ravage and absolutely destroy their opponents. They wanted to end each and every match-up with an exclamation point, a solid, strong sign that they were the best in all the world and no one was coming close.

But there was more behind the ferocity of the game, especially for Vince Carter.

Carter was already an established basketball player in the United States, having steered the Toronto Raptors from obscurity to greatness in just a few years. Millions wore his jersey, and he had a legion of fans, not just in his home country but up north in Canada too. At that time, he was easily one of the most talked-about players in the league.

So, why did he almost not even make the team for the Olympics?

That's what Carter was wondering. If the Team USA selection committee had its initial way, Carter would have stayed home. In January of 2000, he was bypassed for the final Team USA roster spot in favor of sharpshooter Ray Allen. Allen was a legitimate up-and-coming superstar, but he was young and hadn't proven himself yet. In fact, his biggest claim to fame at that point was that he co-starred in Spike Lee's film, *He Got Game*.

On the other hand, Carter had proven so many haters wrong and made a huge splash for himself and his team with his sheer determination and drive. Didn't he deserve the last spot? Wasn't it owed to him? Wasn't he the summation of all that was great about American athletes?

Apparently, Team USA didn't think so—at least not then.

Fired up about losing that last spot, Carter put up a wild 47 points against Allen's Milwaukee Bucks. But that wasn't the only night when Carter was on fire. For the next few weeks, all the way through the All-Star Game, Vince Carter played every game as if it were his last. He had something to prove; he had something to say. He was trying to show the world—and, yes, the Team USA committee—who he was.

Point made. In March of 2000, Team USA selected Carter as an injury replacement for Tom Gugliotta, who had torn ligaments in his knee previously. This meant Carter was now going to the Olympics alongside Allen, Gary Payton, Jason

Kidd, Tim Hardaway, Steve Smith, Kevin Garnett, Vin Baker, Antonio McDyess, Alonzo Mourning, and more.

You would think that maybe that would ease Carter's attitude and calm him down. But then his Raptors were swept out of the playoffs in the first round by the New York Knicks, firing him up even more. The doubters had been getting to him all year, and now they had proof that he wasn't as good as he said. His team couldn't even make the second round, they said. He really wasn't as impressive as some claimed, they cried.

So by the time the Olympics rolled around, Carter wasn't just intent on making a statement for the committee that originally denied him but also the people back in the States who were snickering behind his back.

The 4–0 US Olympic Basketball Team was facing off against France in its final prelim round game. The United States was, unsurprisingly, doing very well. They were leading the French players by 15 points with just over 16 minutes left in the game.

It was in that moment that everything came bubbling up inside Vince Carter. All that anger, doubt, and smack-talk he had been hearing for months were rushing to his head. He didn't care about his team's lead or the fact that they were well on their way to victory. No, he was ready to make a statement. All he needed was the ball.

Carter made a steal via a French outlet pass and then made his way to the basket with speed. He weaved his way through opponents and lasered in on the bucket. The only thing that stood in his way was another player, France's Frédéric Weis. Weis was no small obstacle; he was seven-foot-two inches tall. He had the size and the power to really get in Carter's way. Actually, he had the size and power to really get in anyone's way.

But Weis had no way to stop Carter, a man with fury and fire in his veins. And little did Weis know that Carter had won the NBA All-Star Slam Dunk contest earlier that year. Even though Carter was smaller than Weis, he set to the sky. He sailed and soared over Weis and slammed the ball into the basket, giving his team a commanding 71–54 lead and silencing critics all over the world.

When you now look at photos from that moment, you can see the emotion and intensity in Carter's face. There could have been anything on either side of the basket in that moment, and it wouldn't have stolen away Carter's attention. He was set on making that dunk; he was set on moving past anyone in his way. Nothing was going to stop him. A tornado ripping the roof off the arena in that very moment probably wouldn't have even caused him to turn his head.

Just seconds after dunking on Weis, Carter screamed triumphantly—and with good reason. He had just committed one of the most memorable, shocking and impressive dunks in the history of the Olympics.

At that point in the international games, no one had dunked on an opponent the way Carter had. It was completely different from anything the fans had seen before, and it felt as though someone had just thrown a giant rock into a small pond: the ripples of emotion were felt throughout the arena. But the reactions didn't just end there. Back home in America, even the most critical of Carter had to admit he was something special and had done something to be proud of. It was a moment that not only changed how the world saw the Olympic games but also had the world see Vince Carter. His career was never the same, and he was forever known as the man who could dunk on, well, just about anything.

As for Weis, he is a little uncomfortable about his association with the dunk. He is no longer a professional basketball player and instead runs a French tobacco shop and is an analyst for French basketball games in his home country. He admits that Carter deserved the praise he got for the dunk but, unfortunately, it had to be at his expense.

But he definitely learned something that day: "I learned people could fly," Weis would later say, only half-jokingly.

You can say what you want about Carter, his career and talent, but you must admit that his impressive man-jumping dunk is one for the history books. The Olympics were never the same, and neither was Carter.

DEREK FISHER'S DAUGHTER

"Derek Fisher had 30 minutes Tuesday morning to decide whether to remove his daughter's left eye."

— LEE JENKINS

Anyone who plays or truly understands basketball will tell you it's about more than just scoring points. Yes, the sport is all about sinking a ball into a basket, but that's just a small portion of what the game stands for. Instead, it's about teamwork, leadership, drive, and determination.

If you look at the greatest to ever play the game—Michael Jordan, Kobe Bryant, Larry Bird, Magic Johnson, LeBron James—you will see these are all men who are driven with a passion that is about far more than dunking on opponents and lighting up the scoreboard. Each of these men is playing for something: sometimes they are playing for their own pride, sometimes they are playing to silence critics, and sometimes—many times, in fact—they are playing on behalf of their family, the people who mean the most to them.

That's who Derek Fisher played for. And one night, he proved that more than anyone would ever expect.

The year was 2007, and Fisher was playing for the Utah Jazz, who were on their way to the NBA playoff semifinals against the Golden State Warriors. But there was a whole lot more weighing on Fisher's mind than the playoffs and his future with the team.

He was thinking of his young daughter Tatum.

Just weeks before, Fisher's wife Candace had suspected something was wrong with the couple's baby when she noted the baby's left eye seemed to glow when looking at the eye from certain angles. The couple decided to get Tatum checked out by a doctor, who handed them horrible news: Tatum had retinoblastoma, a cancer beyond rare. It is so rare, in fact, that only about 300 children in the United States have it every year.

The advice they were given from the medical team was dire: Tatum's eye would have to be removed.

But Candace and Derek sought a second opinion, and a group of doctors at New York Presbyterian Hospital had the experience and expertise to treat Tatum without taking her eye. It wouldn't be easy, and Tatum would lose much of her vision in that eye, but they said removing the cancer was possible.

So the Fisher family decided that was the best approach—but how would Derek attend both the operation and the first game in the semifinals.

In the end, he chose his daughter over the game. He missed the first game of the series as he sat by his daughter's bedside following a successful surgery. The doctors said everything went as well as it could, and Tatum would make a full recovery. They also gave the family permission to fly back to Utah so that Fisher could participate in the second game.

Years later, Derek would reflect on missing the first game of such an important series. It didn't matter to him, not in the slightest: "Just do what's best for my child. How many games I miss in the playoffs is totally irrelevant," he said.

He flew back to Salt Lake City and requested a police escort to the arena so that he could make tip-off. The team, the fans, the analysts—no one knew about the rough days Fisher and his family had just been through. But they were about to find out just how tuned in and dedicated Fisher really was.

Derek only took one shot during the second game of the semifinals against the Warriors, but it was the only shot that really counted. It was the first shot he had taken in more than three days, a clutch shot that led the Jazz to overtaking the Warriors and winning the game. Derek had not only stepped up and fought for his family but also for his team.

But he wasn't done fighting for his family. Just weeks later, Fisher asked to be released from his contract with the Jazz so he could be closer to the medical professionals needed to take care of his daughter. Walking away from such a contract —worth $21 million—is not an easy choice, but for Fisher, it was the clear choice to make. While basketball is the career he had chosen and the passion he loved, it paled compared to his devotion and love for his family.

"I think at this point in my career, and in my life, really, not just as a basketball player but as a man, more than anything —learning how to be a husband and learning how to be a father—those are the sacrifices you make for your family, and you just work it out," Fisher would later say.

Derek Fisher showed how family is bigger than anything. Yes, he was a very important teammate and one of the best basketball players, but he was a father above all else. The choice he made was inspiring to many people. Not a bad word was said about Fisher in the league as he fought for his daughter and his family. People who didn't even care for Derek or his career admired what he had done for his daughter and how he chose her above his own success on the court.

Even the doctors who had worked on young Tatum were impressed and touched by Fisher. Doctor David Abramson, one of the doctors who performed the surgery, spoke highly of Fisher, even though he wasn't even aware of him or much of NBA basketball before the surgery: "I grew up thinking Mickey Mantle was my role model. I think I wished I could hit like him. But this guy really is a role model. This is a husband, a really involved parent—a terrific role model," he later said.

There is no doubt that basketball is a great sport and an important pastime. But at the end of the day, that is exactly what it is: a pastime. It's not real life. It's not the most important thing. Certain causes and situations far outweigh basketball and the success of any team or any game. There is no doubt now that Fisher chose correctly when he selected to aid his daughter instead of winning a game. All these years later, few people really remember the intricacies of the Jazz-Warriors playoff series. Even Fisher himself would probably not be able to recall a lot about it. But the countless memories he has since had with Tatum are worth more than the most beautiful and celebrated trophy in the NBA.

During this challenging, painful event, Derek Fisher made it clear that he values both his family and the game. He chose his family first—and rightfully so—but he also didn't let his team down and showed the world of the NBA why he was such an important player.

THE LEFT-HANDED FREE THROWS

> *"What makes things a little easier for me is that I don't think of Hank as a tragedy anymore. I think of all the good times, and how amazing someone was. He was someone who represented so much happiness and laughter and that usually outweighs the pain of his passing. I chose to celebrate his life."*
>
> — GREG "BO" KIMBLE

There are few things stronger or more steadfast than the bond built between two players on the same team. This is definitely true for basketball players. The way these young men and women grow closer is beautiful, like a family coming together for a common goal.

The people on a team always have one another's backs, and, sure enough, they feel like brothers or sisters together. And when one of them is hurting, they are all hurting. And when one of them is gone, the hole left behind is enormous and terribly painful.

But sports have a way not only of bringing people together but can also help them overcome loss, heartbreak, and rebuild. It can act as the most perfect tribute to those who are no longer with us.

That is what happens back in the late 1980s with Hank Gathers and his close friend and teammate, Greg "Bo" Kimble.

By late 1989, Gathers had finished as the NCAA's leading scorer and rebounder. He was thought of as a future NBA star and a possible first draft pick.

But health issues would not only prevent all of that, but it would also end his life far too soon. Gathers collapsed on December 9, 1989, during a basketball game. Laying on the court floor, it was obvious that something was dreadfully wrong with Gathers, and he immediately sought medical attention.

The doctors told him he had an issue with his heart, but the good news was that medication could greatly increase his chances of surviving. The only thing was that he needed to take the medicine every single day to ensure success with them. Gathers started to take the medication as prescribed, but he quickly found out that he didn't like how it affected him, particularly his performance in the game. He asked his medical team if he could cut back on the medication on game days, which certainly wasn't advised. But Gathers was determined not to sacrifice his basketball skills for anything —even his heart.

There has been speculation that Gathers wasn't just cutting back on his medication but actually skipping out on it altogether on game days. If that's true, what followed next is sadly not surprising at all.

On March 4, 1990, Gathers once again collapsed during a game. He attempted to stand with the help of his teammates but was too weak to do so. He was heard saying, "I don't want to lay down," as the ambulance was called and panic set in on the court.

He stopped breathing shortly after and was pronounced dead at the hospital. Hank Gathers was only 23 years old.

Obviously, the entire NCAA and world of sports were rocked by the loss of Gathers, a talent so young taken way too soon. But no one was more affected by his passing than his teammates and his close friend and peer, Greg "Bo" Kimble.

Kimble was far more than just Gathers' squad mate; he was one of his best friends. The two grew up together and went to Dobbins Technical High School in Philadelphia at the same time. They also moved to California and attended USC

326 | ROY LINGSTER

together. Then they eventually transferred to Loyola Marymount together, where they both made the basketball team and started tearing through the NCAA side by side.

When Gathers passed away, Kimble was rocked to his core. He wasn't sure how he'd go on, and he wasn't sure how he could celebrate his close friend. But he had to do something. As a way to pay tribute to Gathers, Kimble announced that he would shoot his first free throw left-handed in the next game, just like Gathers would have.

When the time came during the next game, a very emotional Kimble stepped to the free throw line. Shooting free throws was not his strong suit, and he regularly had trouble burying the shots. How would he fare doing so with a left hand?

But Kimble obviously had his heart in the tribute and was determined to make it count. He dribbled briefly to compose himself and looked fairly awkward and uncomfortable as he lift the ball with his left hand, something he never did.

With what appeared to be total ease, he shot the ball and watched as it sank seamlessly through the basket. The crowd went wild, erupting with emotion and support as they all understood just what the shot meant for Kimble, the team, and for Gathers' family.

They would go on to win that night's game, and Kimble would also progress forward into the NBA. And even when he was finding success on various teams throughout the association, Kimble never stopped thinking of Gathers. He would always shoot his first free throw with his left hand and made 73% of those shots. The tribute lived on and, because of that, Gathers lived on with it.

Years later, Kimble would comment on the tribute and what it meant to him and the rest of the team:

"At the time, our whole team had come together to turn the tragedy into something positive that we were proud of," he said. "There was bitterness but I only remember the good times. I remember the free throws. None should have returned. But I wanted them to come in even though it wasn't really important. It was really to celebrate the life and memory of Hank."

Kimble and so many others missed Gathers, not just for the talent he took with him (Kimble once said, "We would have won the national championship if Hank were alive") but because of the brotherhood and friendship he provided.

The loss of Hank Gathers is still one of the most tragic and shocking ever to affect the world of basketball and professional sports. But the fact that his brother on his team, Bo Kimble, found a way to respect, honor, and carry on his legacy, speaks multitudes about not just the man that he is but the power of sport and the way a team can come together and never, ever come apart.

61 FOR GRANDPA

> *"Everyone has to die, but I just thought my granddad was one of those people who never would."*
>
> — CHRIS PAUL

C hris Paul has been called a lot of things. He has been called the "Point God" and one of the greatest to ever play in the NBA. He has also been accused of being a cry baby and a sore loser—and winner.

There is no doubt he is a talented player and a centerpiece of every single NBA team he has played for. But Chris Paul is far more than solely a basketball player. At the end of the day, he is also a man. Someone with feelings, a family, and things that matter to him far more than the game.

But there was a time when all of what mattered to him outside of basketball was combined with the game he loves so much. The tragic death of someone incredibly close to him allowed Paul to express his anger, his hurt, and his sadness while also paying tribute in a way that only he could.

Nathaniel Jones was Chris Paul's grandfather and, by all accounts, was a loving, friendly and wonderful man. In his corner of North Carolina, Jones was a celebrated and beloved figure to those close to him.

He was only 61 years old when he died.

Four men attacked Jones in November of 2002. They set upon him outside his Winston-Salem home and tied him up, beat him, robbed him, then left him for dead.

Alone on the sidewalk outside his home, Jones died of a heart attack.

The news blindsided the entire family and especially young Chris Paul, who was an up-and-coming high school basketball star at the time. He was very close to his grandfather and couldn't imagine a world without him. The brutality of his death and the way he was literally stolen from those who loved him were traumatizing and hard to comprehend.

The bond between Paul and his grandpa was unlike any other. They were best of buddies and spent plenty of time together. As Paul took basketball more and more seriously and started to pursue it as a possible career, his grandfather was there rooting him on at every turn. In fact, Jones would shut down the filling station he owned and operated on nights when his grandson was playing basketball. He was his biggest fan and truly one of his best friends.

Following his granddad's death, Paul wasn't sure how he could return to the court or if he ever could. How could it ever be the same without that man who cheered him on the most sitting on the sidelines watching?

It was his aunt who made a touching suggestion: why didn't Paul score 61 points in honor of his grandfather, symbolizing the age he was when he passed away. One point for every year that he brought joy into other peoples' lives.

Paul was a grand basketball player at the time, but the task of scoring 61 points in a single game was daunting even for someone who would eventually have a Hall of Fame career in the NBA. But he wanted to try. He needed to do something for his grandfather, and challenging and pushing himself to do what seemed impossible was perhaps the best way to do so.

Those close to Paul and his team started hearing rumors about his plan. Everyone supported his choice and really wanted him to succeed in doing so. But they also knew that 61 points were no easy task, especially in the competitive and cutthroat world of high school basketball. There was a hushed but energetic excitement and a feeling of support in the air as Paul took the floor and began his game.

He was certainly on fire that night. He was putting up shots and landing nearly everything, and it actually seemed possible that he could achieve his goal of 61 points in the game.

With just two minutes left in the game, Paul had put up a whopping 59 points. But as impressive as that was, it wouldn't mean a thing if he didn't add on those two last points and really pay tribute to his grandfather.

As he has done hundreds of times since then, Paul found a way to make it happen. He weaved through the traffic on the floor, became laser-focused on the basket, and put up a shot.

He was fouled during the attempt, but it didn't matter: the shot dropped. The 61 points were his.

Paul lay on the court floor, overcome with emotions and feeling grateful, heartbroken, and overwhelmed with everything going through his mind. He could have kept playing and scored more, and he would have broken a record because he was just a few points away from claiming a state record for the number of points in a single game.

Paul didn't care. He had scored 61, and that's all that mattered. When he was given the ball for his earned free throw, he threw it directly at the wall, tossing his shot away. His coach immediately took him out and let him sit.

Once he made it to the sidelines, Paul began to sob in his dad's arms. As important as the 61-point tribute was, it didn't take away the immense hurt that was still consuming him. He was an accomplished young athlete who had done something great, but he was also a young man who missed his grandfather.

Of course, since high school, Paul has gone on to have a storied, legendary career in the NBA, playing for teams such as the New Orleans Hornets, Los Angeles Clippers, Houston Rockets, Oklahoma City Thunder, and The Phoenix Suns. He is known as one of the most competitive, driven, and reliable guards in the history of the league.

Paul still thinks of his grandfather often and sees him in a lot of what he does, saying, "His legacy of hard work and service to others is woven through the fabric of my parenting, my community work and how I have approached my basketball career. That high school game where I scored 61 points was a healing moment through basketball."

There are many reasons to like Chris Paul, but the touching and the heartfelt way he memorialized his grandfather following his death is one of the biggest. One thing is for sure: his grandfather is watching down on his grandson with pride and joy about all he has accomplished.

19

J-MAC'S SHOT

> *"I was hotter than a pistol."*

— JASON "J-MAC" MCELWAIN

When people talk about sports, they often speak about how it can make great people and great athletes through hard work, determination, coaching, and persistence. Sure enough, there are countless stories about how people have become the best versions of themselves thanks to the work they put into the sport of their choice.

But sports can also shine a spotlight on the people who don't get to shine enough. When someone plays with passion and enthusiasm and a love of the game, they are able to show their truest self to screaming and adoring fans. They are able to become heroes, even if it's just for a few moments during a game.

It doesn't matter who it is, where they come from, or how they look or act. When someone really puts their heart and soul into a sport, they can be celebrated and crowned as the true hero they are.

Jason McElwain is one of those heroes. And on one very special evening during one very special game, he got to show the rest of the world just how special he really is.

Jason McElwain attended Greece Athena High School and was a well-liked and well-known student. He had high functioning autism and was known for his friendly demeanor, insistence on helping others and unquenchable love of the game of basketball. Greece Athena has one of the best basketball teams in the area, and Jason was their biggest fan. Originally, he requested if he might take on the role of student manager when the basketball tryouts were over, and he learned he wouldn't be making the squad. The coaching staff readily agreed, knowing how lucky they were to have someone who loved the game as much as Jason did.

McElwain, who his students lovingly referred to as "J-Mac" had a relentless work ethic and captivating energy. He didn't do anything unless he did it at 100%. He was all-in on everything, from hyping up the team to staying late after practice to everything in between. He became a fixture of the game, enthusiastically rooting on his guys with pure heart and joy.

Win or lose, thick or thin, rain or shine, Jason was there, and he was ready to make some noise for the guys on the squad. He participated in pregame warm-ups, helped the coach put up the scoreboard, assisted with drills, and gave advice when his friends dribbled and shot. No team knew devotion like Jason's. This was a young man who lived and breathed for the game and specifically for his team.

Athena's coach Jim Johnson promised to make an effort to include McElwain in the Trojans' last home game as a token of appreciation for his services. No one would claim that Jason was a stellar basketball player, but Johnson knew that the young man was a vital part of the team's success, spirit, heart, and soul. He deserved to get on the court, even for a few minutes in the last game of the season.

As soon as word spread that McElwain may play, J-Mac's classmates became his biggest supporters and created placards bearing his name and image. For years, he had been the team's biggest fan, but on that night, he was going to have a legion of his own supporters who were attempting to be louder and wilder than he ever had been. He was going to know just how beloved and supported he really was. With four minutes remaining, McElwain joined the game to the delight of the student section, who had been anticipating his arrival.

He fired an airball as his first shot. He then whiffed on a layup. It wasn't the best start to the game, certainly not what the coaching staff and fans had expected. In fact, Coach

Johnson questioned if he had made a mistake in offering this special occasion to Jason.

McElwain seemed unconcerned, though. When he made a 3-pointer on the Trojans' following possession, the audience, who had been standing in eager anticipation, exploded in jubilation. Then he struck a second. And another. Then another.

McElwain made 7 goals in just 4 minutes of play, including a school-record 6 three-pointers. Shocking everyone in attendance, he scored 20 points in the end. The crowd went wild with every attempt and every made shot. The walls were shaking, and the ground was trembling. The entire gym was in a full-blown explosion of emotion and support for Jason.

The seats emptied as soon as the final buzzer sounded, and parents and kids rushed the court to encircle McElwain. His teammates carried him off the court after lifting him onto their shoulders. The response to his big game was volcanic and amazing. Even players who had been the team's champions just hours before were all celebrating Jason, who was now easily the squad's MVP and triumphant hero.

After the cheers and insanity passed, Jason commented about his game, saying, "I just kept shooting."

Video of his exploits received millions of views on YouTube and was shown on CBS and ESPN programs, and the tale gained national attention. In 2006, McElwain earned an ESPY Award for the Best Sports Moment. He published a book titled *The Game of My Life*. He took part in a Super Bowl advertisement for Gatorade. He became a messenger that it doesn't matter what life throws at you; if you believe in yourself and are a good person, you can achieve what you desire.

"Life is full of dreams—sometimes dreams come true," Jason would later say as he spread his message of acceptance to the rest of the world. He has taught so many people to be fearless and determined and to never, ever stop believing in yourself.

Although that miracle night is long behind Jason and that basketball team, he is still seen as a hero to many, including Coach Johnson, who used J-Mac as an example to his incoming athletes. He is no longer just a fan or a team manager; he is a Hall of Famer.

20

BREAKING A 26-YEAR LOSING STREAK

> *"Tonight's win is a testament to the hard work each member of this team, the alumni and the supporters have put into this program."*
>
> — OLIVER ESLINGER

The California Institute of Technology, or Cal Tech, might be known for many things but having a successful basketball team isn't one of them.

In fact, for many years, they were known as a school that couldn't win a basketball game if their lives depended on it. Indeed, they held a record that no school or team wanted to, and it looked like it might be another lifetime before it was going to be broken.

Back in 2011, Cal Tech was known for many things, such as its stellar science program and its ability to craft future leaders. It was and still is a terrific school. It just so happened that it had one of the worst basketball programs in the entire country. Actually, not *one* of the worst but the actual worst.

Cal Tech's men's basketball team hadn't won a conference game since 1985. To sum it all up, that was a losing streak of 310 games in a row. A record that embarrassingly goes beyond simple bad luck: it shows the sort of institutional issues that cannot be solved without some serious work. It isn't far-fetched to wonder why Cal Tech didn't just retire its basketball program and instead focus on other things. They had been losing longer than the students on the team had been alive!

Coach Eslinger thought that 2011 was going to be the team's year, and he publicly commented again and again about what was coming for them. He even said it wasn't a matter of when the team would win but rather how many games they would conquer. He thought they were going to win a lot.

He was wrong.

As the season started, the Cal Tech team kept up its tradition of losing games. To be fair, they were losing by small margins but were still losing. They even took one game into overtime . . . but still ended up getting beat. It seemed like they had gotten better, and victories were within reach, but they still weren't achieving what they wanted, and the 26-

year-long cure continued without any signs of slowing or stopping.

But then came the game on March 7, 2011, against Occidental College. It was a close game, but even the most devoted Cal Tech fan thought it would end with the Beavers continuing their losing streak. But then senior Ryan Elmquist was tasked with taking two free throws in the final three seconds of the game. He made one of his free throws and put the team up by one single point.

Occidental got possession of the ball and attempted a wild half-court shot, but it didn't land. And that meant one thing: the streak was over, and the curse was broken. Cal Tech had won their first basketball game in years.

As you can expect, the fans went wild. It was just one victory, and it didn't take away the years and years of consistent losses, but it was still a very big deal and cause for celebration. Few people thought that Cal Tech was turning things around in a huge way. No one really expected them to suddenly become the best college basketball team in the country. But it was an encouraging sign that maybe—just maybe—the team had a chance to finally start getting back on track again.

The team still continued a losing streak of sorts. They haven't had a winning season since 1954, and they're still not one of the best teams in the United States. But that one game back in 2011 took away a lot of the sting and pain of constant defeats. Ryan Long put it best when he said, "It's obvious that Cal Tech Team are never going to be one of the greatest basketball teams of all time but they are certainly a very dedicated and passionate side who never gives up."

Yes, the team can teach us all a lot about perseverance. How many times have you felt counted out and like you would never achieve even the smallest of goals? It's easy to feel defeated and like there is no point in even trying. But the Cal Tech team of 2011 proves that you should *always* believe in yourself, even when no one else is believing in you.

CLARA BAER'S RULES

"It was in 1893 that basketball was introduced at Newcomb and into the South. At that time the game had not reached its present development. When Newcomb College first tried basketball in its gymnastic work, there were no published rules for women, none of the fine points of control that characterize the game today. The results were naturally to be expected; its introduction at Newcomb was not entirely satisfactory. Later, a compromise was reached by modifying the game for girls."

— CLARA GREGORY BAER

You might not be very familiar with the name Clara Gregory Baer, but you should be if you are a true basketball fan and historian. Because while she might not be a household name, she is someone who left a sizable and undeniable impact on the game of basketball for years to come. And it all came from a simple misunderstanding.

Back in the last 1800s, Clara Baer was at the forefront of physical education programs in the south of the United States. She spent years perfecting great programs and classes for students of all gender and ages, but she held a particularly soft spot in her heart for young women who were hoping to play sports.

Of course, at the time, the games available for young women were quite limited. There wasn't a whole lot that they could play. But then Baer caught word of a new game making the rounds across the country, originally created by a Canadian man in Massachusetts. Yes, Baer heard all about basketball.

Baer thought it was a game young women would excel at. But the thing was, not many people knew the specifics of the game and its rules. Remember, it was less than a few years old, and there was a lot of mystery and confusion surrounding it. Only one man knew the real rules of the game, James Naismith, the mastermind behind the game. But Baer was willing and eager to reach out and find out the ins and outs of the game. So she wrote to him and asked for all she needed to know. That is how, two years following James Naismith's invention of the sport, basketball made its way to the South in 1893.

Naismith happily sent along the instructions and rules related to the game he created. But it was filled with some complicated writing, diagrams, and other information that could easily be misconstrued or confusing to someone who had never laid eyes on a basketball court or watched the game being played. And you must remember that no one was filming the game or watching highlights back then. It was so profoundly new and different.

So Clara attempted to figure out the rules sent her way and then teach her young female students how to play this new, exciting sport. She became quite enthusiastic about basketball and saw it as a sport that could really grow and become something very special for both young boys and girls. Therefore, after instructing her students in the game, Clara wrote the first book of women's basketball regulations, which was released in 1895.

But Baer was actually changing the game, and she didn't even know it. Since Clara did not apply Naismith's original meaning to the zones set on his court, the rules are subtly but markedly different from what you might anticipate and know as basketball. She had examined the rule book closely and dug into the diagrams sent to her, but she misinterpreted their meaning and direction, and that took basketball in a brand-new direction at such an early phase in its life cycle.

The misreading of the rules created quite a few minor but important changes that would stick with the game for years to come. For example, Clara believed that each woman was limited to one of the seven respective zones. Therefore, in her rulebook, it said that women had to stay in pairs (one for offense and one for defense) in their zones, did not dribble, guard, throw, or shoot the ball with two arms (that being because it compressed the chest). The rules also said that players could not talk and also were prohibited from using call signals. At the time, the basket had no backboard, and the teams switched baskets after each and every goal. Additionally, the points were variable (4, 3, or 2) based on the distance from the goal.

Because of how much her modified rules differed from his, Naismith advised publishing them under a different name. The result was *Newcomb Basquette* or just *Basquette*. The name of the rulebook changed to *Basketball* as her regulations grew more uniform. The men didn't embrace the jump shot and one-handed shooting, two enhancements Clara's rules unintentionally introduced to the game, for another 40 years.

Indeed, the rules Baer had created actually stuck with women's basketball in some parts of the country until the 1960s. And while some people complained about her changes and wrote them off, some of her alterations proved to be downright revolutionary. Take the jump shot and the one-handed shot, for example. Those have evolved over the years into something that is a part of every single basketball game and has made the game faster, more exciting, and just all around so much better.

Clara also made other changes to the game that really advanced women in sports in general. For example, she was able to let the young women wear bloomers instead of dresses during the game, which gave them more flexibility, of course, but also more equality too. And in the years to come, when history was finally able to spread around more equality in the sports among both genders, Clara would be regarded as someone who started much of that movement with her common sense but truly fair changes to the game she loved so much.

When summing up her life, career and the impact on the game, Tulane University praised Clara and her forward-thinking, intelligent approach to basketball, saying, "Ultimately, Clara was a professor of physical education at Newcomb College for 38 years before retiring in 1929. She continued to stay in touch with the college as professor emerita and when she died of a heart attack in 1938, classes were suspended so that students and faculty could attend her funeral services."

Clara Baer was a champion for women in sports and, ultimately, the growth and application of basketball as a pastime. Without her, the game we love today wouldn't exist as we know it.

22

THE LONGEST GAME ON RECORD

Nowadays, it is rare to see an NBA game go into more than one or two overtimes. Is it fun? Yes. Is it exciting? Also yes, but it sure does sound exhausting, doesn't it? Playing basketball is no easy thing to do. You have to pour yourself out and try incredibly hard for every minute of the game. All that running, all that jumping, all that constant moving for the entire game—it sure does add up.

But what if you didn't have to play for the game's regular time but also overtime? And what if it wasn't just one overtime? And not two or three or four or five? What if you had to play six overtime periods? It doesn't happen often. In fact, it has rarely ever occurred. But one night back in 1951, two teams duked it out for six overtime periods, and people are *still* talking about it.

The NBA record for the longest game in history is still the one with six—yes, count them—six overtime periods. How did it come to be? What two teams were subjected to it? And why is it unlikely to ever happen again? Strap in and prepare to learn about the longest basketball game in history.

It was January 6, 1951, and the Olympians and Royals were about to fight it out for supremacy. In the end, both teams would be drained to the point of no return after six overtime periods that left both sides feeling completely deflated and beyond tired. The record they set on that night still stands to this day, but it's unlikely it'll ever happen again. Why? Because of the invention of everyone's favorite time: the shot clock.

The shot clock, a crucial element of the contemporary game, wasn't there in the NBA at the time because it was still in its infancy. Therefore, players were able to hold the ball as long as they wanted. And, honestly, they did that a lot. In fact, since there was no shot clock, most games ended with low scores. In the lowest scoring game in NBA history, the Fort Wayne Pistons defeated the Minneapolis Lakers 19–18 earlier in the season. Without the pressing pressure of the shot clock ticking down, teams would spend all the time they wanted moving around the floor and attempting shots. It didn't make for a very fast-paced game, not by a long shot.

The game was rather straightforward for most of the run time. In the second quarter, the Royals rallied to overtake the Olympians by 23 points.

Going into the supposedly final quarter, the Olympians were up by 5 points, but the Royals gained momentum and kept possession of the ball. The fourth quarter saw the Olympians score just 8 points while the Royals scored 12, tying the score at 65. That led them to their first overtime, which was when the real fun (and, for the players, the real exhaustion) began.

The first few overtimes were not that eventful, and it seemed possible that maybe the game would go on for as many as ten or twelve overtimes. In fact, two of the six extra periods went on without a score by either team. During the second overtime, the Royals actually held the ball the entire time and only attempted one shot—which they promptly missed. Talk about running out the clock!

The third overtime followed the pattern of the first, with baskets scored by both sides and the Royals maintaining possession of the ball. Even though these were overtime periods, neither team was moving with too much speed or determination. In fact, it felt like a normal game to many of the onlookers.

Both sides went scoreless once again in the jaw-dropping fourth overtime, which was a rerun of the second. After the Royals scored immediately in the fifth overtime, the Olympians turned the ball over, allowing the Royals to score once again.

The Olympians had a four-point advantage that appeared insurmountable, but they scored on their next possession, forced their own turnover, and then scored again to level the game at 73. Ralph Beard made a jump shot with a single second on the clock in the remarkable and exhausting sixth and final overtime to give the Olympians the victory. After all that time, the game was finally done. It ended up playing for 78 minutes—78 long, draining, sweat-dripping minutes for both teams.

In all six overtimes, the Olympians managed just 10 points, compared to the Royals' 8 points. For its period, the game actually got off to a pretty rapid start, with the Olympians scoring 20 points in the opening quarter while restricting the Royals to only 10.

Both sides weren't entirely equal during these wild overtime periods. While the Royals fielded eight players, the Olympians only used seven. On both teams, a few players played the full game. For example, the Royals' Red Holzman participated in 76 of the game's 78 minutes.

The game ran so long that it actually caused a huge problem when one team attempted to get back home. The Olympians didn't arrive at the station in time for their train to Chicago due to the duration of the game. Instead, the group rode the train to Detroit, where they booked a private jet to Molina, Illinois.

The Olympians sent their five starting players since the plane could only fit five people. The rest of the squad had to use a bus. But after such a long game, they used that time to rest and get some much-deserved shut-eye.

The game between the Olympians and Royals is still talked about to this day but mostly as a warning. Imagine an NBA that didn't have a shot clock; it would permit games like this one again and again all season long. In fact, most people credit this game with the creation of the shot clock. It showed just how valuable such an invention could be.

Today, NBA players are very grateful for the shot clock. It might be annoying at times and can cause a few headaches, but it really does keep the game moving at a quick, comfortable and fun speed. The shot clock means that a game like this marathon from 1951 will never happen again, thankfully.

23

DEKALB'S MISSED SHOTS

"As a principal, school, school staff, and community, you should all feel immense pride for the remarkable job that the coaching staff is doing in not only coaching these young men but teaching them how to be leaders."

— AARON WOMACK

When someone loses a person very close to them, it's understandable to feel like they can't go on. When you think of your life and someone you love passing away, you certainly recognize the feelings of loss, grief and an uncertainty about what to do next. Some people just emotionally collapse, not sure of which direction to take.

Some people feel like they can never recover and never get back to life as normal.

That's exactly what Johntell Franklin felt when he was in high school. He suffered a devastating loss that is unfathomable and life-changing. Yet he was able to pick himself up and move forward, thanks to his own strength, his love of basketball, and support from his friends and family within his team.

Milwaukee Madison High and DeKalb High out of Illinois competed in the match on February 8, 2009, but it was not a normal competition. It was filled with emotion, grief, and serious love and support for Franklin, who was a senior at the time for Milwaukee Madison. He was actually the captain of the basketball team and was celebrated as an up-and-coming athlete with skill and the ability to lead his team and bring it together. But it was his team who would come together for him on that February night.

It was one of the hardest moments of his life. That's because Franklin had just lost his mother to cancer earlier in the day. He informed his coach that he would not be playing in the game that evening, and everyone 100% understood and supported his choice to sit the game out and grieve the unbearable loss. The game would go on without Franklin, but everyone would be thinking of him, his family, and the tough time he was going through.

But it didn't play out as initially expected. It played out in a much better, much more beautiful way.

While Franklin initially refused to play, later that evening, he thought hard about it and ended up changing his mind and showing up for the game in the second quarter. He wanted to be a part of the team that meant so much to him and play the game that had gotten him through so much. He was feeling overwhelmed by the loss of his mom, but he also felt like playing basketball could help him funnel his emotions and energy into something productive and enjoyable.

And while his team would gladly take him and help him get through the night by playing the game, they didn't expect that. As mentioned, no one thought he was going to play, so Franklin's name was left off the official scorebook by his coach, Aaron Womack Jr., who knew he wouldn't be at the game in advance. In fact, he had spent the day with Franklin and his family at the hospital, so he was well aware of the trauma and pain.

But Franklin *did* show up, and that definitely threw both teams—and the refs—for a loop, even though they were beyond ecstatic to see him. But there was a wrinkle in the rulebook that prevented young Franklin from playing. In order for him to be able to play, his team would be assessed not one but two technical fouls, which would be charged to the bench and the coach, and therefore DeKalb would be awarded two free throws.

This didn't sit right with either team because of the situation Franklin was in. How could they punish someone for wanting to participate with his team and push through such intense pain and hurt? DeKalb coach Dave Rohlman was vehemently against the idea of receiving the fouls, even if it was the right thing to do. He explained the issue to the officials and protested their choice, telling them that although they did not want the violation to be recognized. However, the referees' options were limited, and they were obliged to do so.

If the foul shots had to be taken, they would be taken by someone who cares. They might be on opposite teams, and technically they were playing against each other, but that didn't mean the students on DeKalb wanted to score a few points on Franklin's pain.

DeKalb athlete Darius McNeal came to his coach and told him he would attempt the free throws with everyone knowing he would intentionally miss both of them after conferring with his teammates. This was the best way to technically follow the rules while still showing support for Franklin in his time of need.

McNeal purposefully missed the two free shots, just as he vowed he would. He simply walked to the free throw line, tossed the ball a couple of feet in front of him, and stood still as the crowd erupted in support of his move. He openly admitted to doing it for the man who had lost his mother, saying, "I did it for the guy who lost his mom, it was the right thing to do."

Coach Womack had spent all day in the hospital with Franklin. Therefore, DeKalb High had to wait two hours after traveling two hours on top of that in order for the game to begin. Coach Rohlman even advised that they call the game off entirely. But in the end, it played out in a more beautiful and touching way than anyone could have imagined. When the final buzzer sounded, DeKalb had lost the game, but nobody seemed to care. They all knew they had been a part of something truly special, something that went beyond basketball and sports. Something that is human and downright life-changing.

Showing just how close they had all become, the two groups gathered for a pizza meal after the game. As for Franklin, he touched upon what it all meant to him, his family, and his late mother: "I knew my mom would have wanted me to play. She was always proud of me playing basketball."

Franklin had given her another reason to be proud, even though she was gone.

In a world that can feel so upside and troubled and scary, it is wonderful to know that sportsmanship and caring for our fellow man are still alive and well. It can sometimes show itself in the most unlikely of places, like a high school basketball court.

24

THE CONTRIBUTIONS OF THE HARLEM GLOBETROTTERS

"You must understand as a kid of color in those days, the Harlem Globetrotters were like being movie stars."

— WILT CHAMBERLAIN

If you love basketball, you have likely heard of the Harlem Globetrotters. However, you may be like millions of others who think of the game as just a crew of guys who put up wild shots, have fun on the floor, and delight fans all over the country every year. They're fun; they're lively and like a circus on the basketball court. But nothing more than that.

That's what you might think, but that is far, far, far from the truth. The truth is that the Harlem Globetrotters are a very important contributor to the history of basketball, including the modern NBA that we all love so much.

The Harlem Globetrotters, an African-American basketball team, was founded by its creator, Abe Saperstein, all the way back in 1926 when the entire sport of basketball was still relatively new and not entirely understood. But Saperstein had no idea that on January 7, 1927, when the team took the court for their first away game in Hinckley, Illinois, the transformation of basketball and the possibilities for all Black athletes had just begun. Indeed, the creation of the Harlem Globetrotters was laying the groundwork for a historical change in the way that Black athletes perform and are treated and respected. It took a long time, and it surely didn't happen fast enough. But they were starting something very special that is still felt to this day all these years later.

The Original Harlem Globetrotters were forerunners in popularizing the slam dunk, fast break, point guard positions, and some wild on-court theatrics. They did this by barnstorming around the nation in their early years, like a circus act that would go from town to town. You have to remember that basketball was still a very young sport back then and that people were seeing the game for the first time. And they were also seeing amazing feats of strength and athleticism that were not possible anywhere else.

As they became more well known, they became much more well liked. And they were soon playing on the biggest stages in the country, including some major basketball games in the NBA. The Globetrotters were so well liked in the 1940s that the infant NBA frequently scheduled them as the opening match of a doubleheader in an effort to draw more spectators. Unfortunately, most of the spectators departed once the Globetrotters exited, making the next NBA game poorly attended.

Quickly altering the schedule, the NBA had the Globetrotters play the second game of the doubleheader. In order to get tickets for the Globetrotters' performance, fans then flocked to the NBA game. Obviously, they were connecting with audiences and really attracting some big, devoted crowds.

Despite all of this, many ridiculed the Globetrotters' ability to play against the NBA's then-white squad. Everything was different back in the 1940s. The Globetrotters actually upset the world champion Minneapolis Lakers, headed by Hall of Famer George Mikan, in each of those years in front of standing-room-only crowds at Chicago Stadium, furthering the sport's integration. Yet millions still didn't consider them a real team with real talent.

The very first African-American athlete to sign an NBA contract was actually a Globetrotter named Nathaniel "Sweetwater" Clifton, who joined the New York Knicks in 1950. After then, NBA clubs started selecting Black players far more often. The influence created by the Globetrotters was soon being felt all over the league as Black athletes were

366 | ROY LINGSTER

able to find great success inside the league that was so hesitant to accept them.

It didn't stop there. The Globetrotter's influence is still felt all over the world to this day. In its historic 91-year life span, the team has performed in front of over 144 million spectators in 122 nations across the globe and has visited territories across six continents, frequently shattering social and cultural barriers while giving spectators their first-ever basketball experience.

The American State Department got in touch with Saperstein in 1951 and requested that the Globetrotters play a game in the Allied neighborhood of Berlin to assist in lessening the effects of a sizable communist youth demonstration that had just taken place in what was then East Germany.

On August 22, 1951, the Globetrotters performed alongside Jesse Owens, the Berlin Olympics champion, as a very special guest, in front of 75,000 spectators crammed into Berlin's Olympic Stadium.

The team also broke gender barriers too. For example, Olympic Gold Medalist Lynette Woodard played with the Globetrotters in 1985, becoming the very first woman to ever play with a men's professional basketball team. She didn't know it then—no one did—but that move was paving the way for the WNBA so many years later. The Globetrotters not only broke the color barrier in the NBA, but they also broke the gender barrier in professional basketball.

With all they've accomplished and brought to the game, it's no surprise that those who understand the history of basketball also understand how important the Globetrotters are. And because of that, they are now considered a vital part not just of basketball and the NBA but also of the country's future, race relations and the way Black athletes are respected. In fact, January 7th every year across the United States is now known as Harlem Globetrotter's Day, a sign of respect and a way to honor this team that has done just so much over its 90 years.

TNT Lister, who found enormous success within the Globetrotters organization, once talked about all it has done for him and the sport in general: "The Harlem Globetrotters are a great part of the advancement of today's society. Through laughter, positivity and sports, the Harlem Globetrotters have brought people together of all races and cultures, giving us all a common ground with one another."

He's not wrong. Not even by a little bit.

George Preston Marshall was once quoted as saying, "We'll start signing Negroes when the Harlem Globetrotters start signing whites." If only he could see the world of basketball today.

THE GENEROSITY OF A HIGH SCHOOL BASKETBALL STAR

> *"They were all smart and wanted to pursue their dreams, but were having financial difficulties. I felt it was the right move to help the others, especially when everything else was taking off for me."*
>
> — ALLAN GUEI

It isn't easy to make it to college. It takes a whole lot of hard work, good grades, determination, and so much more. Sometimes a lot of luck is involved too. And that is even more true when you are living in a part of the country that doesn't have a great educational system. There are certain parts of the country where there are more rundown houses than schools and libraries, and it has a way of sucking people into a life of poverty that feels impossible to escape from.

It's not fair. Not even by a little bit. And sometimes, the only thing someone needs is a helping hand, a leg up, a chance to make it out of the environment that will only hold them back. Oftentimes that comes in the form of money for school, like college tuition and fees. It can make all the difference in the world and turn someone who would be sucked into a life of crime and poverty into someone who can have a job, a career, and a future.

That brings us to our last story, perhaps the most important one yet. Throughout this book, you have seen so many examples of people stepping up for one another. Whether it be a team helping out a fan or a teammate helping out another, or the fans helping out the team, basketball has always been a way for people to interact, support each other, and really lift one another up when they need it most.

This last story is all about someone lifting up another, but it's not a typical story about a famous star helping out a needy fan. Instead, it's someone who had yet to make it really helping out someone on their level, a peer who just needed a way forward and an assist.

In March of 2011, eight students at Compton High school were set to compete in a basketball free throw contest. But this wasn't just any free throw contest. This one came with a prize, and it was a doozy. The winner of the contest would be rewarded with $40,000 in college tuition and fees. For many, that amount could be the difference between going to school and staying home. The pressure couldn't be higher because the stakes were out of this world high and important.

Local screenwriter Court Crandall created the contest. Crandall's idea was to hold the contest for any student who had a 3.0 GPA or higher and then film it for a documentary about the negative stereotypes that hold back the city of Compton. Sure enough, people have known of Compton's issues for decades now and, because of them, they have written off the entire city as a dead-end town that will trap anyone growing up in it. But Crandall wanted to show a different side of Compton and, more significantly, the youth of the city.

At the time, more than two-thirds of the high school students in Compton were eligible for subsidized lunches. There was so much poverty and crime throughout the city but so much hope and good-hearted people too. Crandall was hopeful that the documentary could shine a light on the positive sides of Compton.

Of the 80 students who qualified to participate in the contest, 8 were selected randomly to make it truly fair. One of those selected was eighteen-year-old Allan Guei. Guei had an advantage over everyone else in the contest because he was actually the star point guard on the school's varsity basketball team. Therefore, it seemed to make total sense that he would probably go on to easily win the contest, right?

Well, you wouldn't be wrong to put your money on Guei. But you would have no idea as to what would happen after he did.

Sure enough, when the big day came, he was ready for it. Guei easily defeated the first runner-up by making 5 of 10 free throws, winning the match without a shadow of a doubt. Although the other 7 shooters also won some money —$1,000 each—he left with the top prize of $40,000. That was and still is a huge amount and more than enough to start his career in college and point him in the right direction. Guei had made out with a huge cash windfall because of his basketball skills. Or that is how it seemed anyway.

A lot changed within just a few weeks of winning the free throw contest. That's because Guei's future and his pathway to college changed.

The truth was that Guei no longer needed the cash prize for his own tuition and costs after winning a full scholarship at California State University in Northridge shortly after the competition. After he had sunk the important shots in the contest and secured the cash prize, he found out that he was getting a full ride into Northridge, meaning the $40,000 he had earned was going to be just gravy on top. It was going to be a nice little bonus that wasn't even necessary anymore.

Obviously, Guei could have pocketed the full award for himself per NCAA regulations without jeopardizing his scholarship. But that wasn't the type of person the city of Compton had created with Guei. He had a different idea, one that was truly selfless, kind, and beautiful.

Guei decided to distribute his full reward among the seven runners-up instead, giving each of them an additional $5,500 to help pay for their own educational expenses after considering his alternatives with his parents and coach.

Giving the money away changed the lives of those runners-up. For someone, that extra cash was what they needed to make it into college. It could pay for lodging, books, transportation, moving and more. Guei did it because he knew it was right. He felt that everyone deserves the chance to go to college, and he was going to quite literally spread the wealth he was given because of his success in the competition.

"I mean, if I already ate and somebody's starving next to me," Guei later told ESPN after he made his decision, "I'm not going to eat again, right? People I've never met in my life find me and go, 'I'm so proud of you. I'm so proud of what you did. Friend me. Call me.' I've never had that kind of thing in my life."

Here is yet another example of sports and especially basketball being a way for people to connect, help one another, and show the true humanity at the core of the game. It's about far more than shooting baskets and sinking expert shots. And it's about far more than just winning contests.

We could all learn a thing or two from Allan Guei and his kind, open heart.

SHARE YOUR THOUGHTS, REVIEW!

If you have learned a thing or two about the history of basketball and all the game has offered for more than 100 years, it would be amazing if you could review it. Let the world know about all the knowledge, history, and surprising facts in this book and hopefully, together, we can spread the word about just how special this sport is and will be for years to come.

Scan the QR code below to leave a quick review!

CONCLUSION

Hopefully, you have learned a few things through all of these deep, touching, once-in-a-lifetime stories. Hopefully, you have learned that basketball is an extraordinary game. Hopefully, you have found out that the athletes who play the game are beyond professional and talented. They are truly the greatest athletes we have today.

But hopefully, you have learned that the people behind the game are even more extraordinary. Not their technical or athletic skills but their hearts, drives, and souls.

Again and again, we have told stories of people who were willing to sacrifice and give so much. People who have not only fought for their teams and their victories but for the people who mean the world to them. We have seen athletes who have played their hearts out and strive for greatness for their families, their friends, their teammates, their fans, and themselves.

Whether it be the story of Derek Fisher missing a playoff game for his daughter or Chris Paul putting up 61 for his late grandfather, or the 1992 Lithuanian basketball team playing their hearts out on behalf of their newly independent country, there are so many examples of this sport bringing people together and bringing the best out of them.

As you can see, this book isn't just about individual athletic feats. Instead, the stories we have highlighted here are the ones that show that basketball is about more than just a game but a way of life, a way to make people better, stronger, and more open-hearted. The impact of the game is on so much more than just a scoreboard. It can truly bring out the best in people and change lives.

We should all remember the lessons from some of the greatest basketball moments in history. After all, there are many things we can learn from the selfless and courageous acts of others. When we see them rise above merely trying to score points and instead actually affect other people and live a good life through the game, we see that basketball can truly heal and help others.

We should think about how much the game has changed since it was created on that cold winter day in Massachusetts more than 100 years ago. Be thankful for all the advances the game has undergone. For example, how much better is the game today, thanks to things like the invention of the shot clock? Imagine all the overtimes you'd have to sit through if that wasn't invented. Or imagine how intense the game would be if it were still played in cages as it often was back in the early 1900s. Yes, basketball has changed—and changed for the better.

Basketball is more than a sport. It's more than just people tossing the ball into the basket. Now that you have traveled through the history of the game and discovered so many amazing stories about it, hopefully, your love of the game has only grown.

SOURCES

▶ **Chapter 1**

Original thirteen rules (*compare them to the rules used now and how they have changed over the years*)

https://www.usab.com/history/dr-james-naismiths-original-13-rules-of-basketball.aspx

"Be strong in body, clean in mind, lofty in ideals." –James Naismith

https://www.worldofbasketball.org/famous-basketball-quotes.htm

▶ **Chapter 2**

Even so, he sat on the bench the first few years

https://www.blackpast.org/african-american-history/dawkins-darryl-1957-2015/

https://www.sportscasting.com/the-tragic-death-of-former-nba-star-darryl-dawkins-the-backboard-breaker/

Responsible for the NBA going to breakaway rims after shattering two backboards in three weeks

https://www.sportscasting.com/the-tragic-death-of-former-nba-star-darryl-dawkins-the-backboard-breaker/

▶ **Chapter 3**

Security noticed him and escorted him back to his seat, giving him a stern finger-wagging

https://clutchpoints.com/pelicans-video-new-orleans-fan-sneaks-warmup-players-caught/

Roberts' interview about the incident

https://www.espn.com/nba/story/_/id/22922431/a-tiny-oral-history-comedian-tony-roberts-sneaking-court-new-orleans-pelicans-warmups

▶ **Chapter 4**

Accustomed to playing rough–even witnessing a fellow player get killed on the court

https://www.allamericanspeakers.com/celebritytalentbios/Ron+Artest/388439

▶ Chapter 5

His personal trainer and personal assistant think he may have been intentionally poisoned

https://www.espn.com/nba/story/_/id/31606593/the-truth-michael-jordan-infamous-nba-finals-flu-game

"It's very rare that you get five delivery guys from the pizza place to bring you your pizza." –George Koehler

https://www.usatoday.com/story/sports/nba/2021/06/11/michael-jordan-flu-game-24th-anniversary/7652703002/

▶ Chapter 6

Most cages were eliminated from games by the 1920s, though a few still played with them until the 1930s

https://jessebrowns.com/2016/03/know-term-cager-refers/

▶ Chapter 7

He never even set foot on Canadian soil and was traded to the Golden State Warriors

https://raptorsrapture.com/2018/09/02/toronto-raptors-history-expansion-draft/

▶ Chapter 8

He struck up a deal with the owner of the Renaissance Ballroom and Casino, thus creating the Harlem Rens

https://www.blackfives.org/new-york-rens/

▶ Chapter 9

Iverson was granted clemency after spending 4 months in prison, and his conviction was later overturned due to lack of evidence

https://www.npr.org/2010/04/13/125870182/a-town-divided-allen-iverson-and-hampton-va

To complete the best comeback after a rocky start due to being wrongfully convicted, he won Rookie of the Year

https://bleacherreport.com/articles/804030-nba-the-rise-fall-and-eventual-disappearance-of-allen-iverson

▶ **Chapter 10**

The Soviet Union dominated basketball, medaling in 8 consecutive Olympic games

https://www.thesmartset.com/article03101402/

https://sportshistoryweekly.com/stories/lithuania-basketball-olympics-nba-grateful-dead,622

▶ **Chapter 11**

The Eagles challenged Duke to a game, and after some hesitation, Duke agreed

https://nccueaglepride.com/sports/2011/3/8/MBB_0308110905.aspx

▶ **Chapter 12**

In Baltimore, Calvert Hall Catholic School, which had a mostly white population, was known as the best team around, even though this was likely untrue

https://medium.com/@uarkpress/the-greatest-high-school-basketball-team-ever-4445533123a7

Led the team to a 59-0 record over two season in the early 1980s

https://howtheyplay.com/team-sports/EAST-BALTIMORE-POETS-The-Greatest-High-School-Basketball-Team-Ever

▶ **Chapter 13**

She went on to be the all-time leading scorer for the University of Tennessee-Martin

https://tnmuseum.org/Stories/posts/pat-summitt-early-life?locale=en_us

▶ **Chapter 14**

Cover the game and the coach's decision to start with five black players against an all white team and how this shaped the landscape of basketball

https://www.blackpast.org/african-american-history/texas-western-miners-1966/

▶ **Chapter 15**

It is said to be the greatest dunk of all time

https://www.espn.com/espn/feature/story/_/id/13713188/after-15-years-saw-vince-carter-leap-frederic-weis-sydney-believe-witnessed

"I learned people could fly." –Frederic Weis (the defender he jumped over)

https://www.espn.com/espn/feature/story/_/id/13713188/after-15-years-saw-vince-carter-leap-frederic-weis-sydney-believe-witnessed

▶ **Chapter 16**

In that moment, he became a role model for all parents

https://www.nytimes.com/2007/05/11/sports/basketball/11utah.html

https://www.today.com/news/nba-star-risks-everything-daughters-health-1C9015537

▶ **Chapter 17**

He then went onto the NBA and shot his first free throw with his left hand every time, making 73% of them

https://bettergolfzone.com/bo-kimble-the-left-hand-tribute/

▶ **Chapter 18**

He died of a heart attack

https://www.12news.com/article/news/local/arizona/men-convicted-of-murdering-suns-player-chris-pauls-grandfather-will-remain-in-jail/75-9ed7e672-ffab-46ba-a8d2-ef008536dfac

Paul went onto have a lucrative NBA career

https://abcnews.go.com/GMA/story?id=125484&page=1

▶ **Chapter 19**

He still works with kids playing basketball, and he is a role model to many

https://www.karmatube.org/videos.php?id=320

▶ **Chapter 20**

And while they haven't had a winning season since 1954, they are making more gains each year

https://news.uga.edu/caltech-basketball-wins-first-conference-game-in-26-years/

"It's obvious that Caltech Team are never going to be one of the greatest basketball teams of all time but they are certainly a very dedicated and passionate side who never gives up." –Ryan Long

https://fadeawayworld.net/entertainment/the-basketball-team-didnt-win-a-game-for-26-years

▶ **Chapter 21**

She also was able to get women allowed to wear bloomers instead of dresses during athletic play, gaining them one more step toward equality

https://peoplepill.com/people/clara-gregory-baer

▶ **Chapter 22**

The game ran 78 minutes

https://nbahoopsonline.com/Articles/History/6Overtimegame.html

https://www.guinnessworldrecords.com/world-records/428821-longest-
nba-basketball-game

▶ **Chapter 23**

The two teams went out to pizza together after
https://www.mlive.com/news/grand-rapids/2009/02/
playing_fair_with_fouls_sign_o.html

▶ **Chapter 24**

You must understand as a kid of color in those days, the Harlem Globetrotters
were like being movie stars." –Wilt Chamberlain
https://www.azquotes.com/quotes/topics/globetrotters.html
They have their own day now
https://www.harlemglobetrotters.com/about/

▶ **Chapter 25**

Even though he was allowed to keep the money, after he won, he split the
money amongst the 7 other students, stating they also deserved the chance
to go to college
https://www.momsteam.com/empathy/youth-sports-hero-month-allan-
guei-compton-calif

A GAME OF EXTREMES: 25 EXCEPTIONAL FOOTBALL STORIES

ABOUT WHAT HAPPENED ON AND OFF THE FIELD

A
GAME
OF EXTREMES
25 EXCEPTIONAL
FOOTBALL
STORIES

ROY LINGSTER

INTRODUCTION

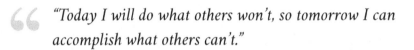 *"Today I will do what others won't, so tomorrow I can accomplish what others can't."*

— JERRY RICE

While many people refer to baseball as America's pastime, there is no doubt that football can easily rival that sport for the title.

There is just something so American about watching football. From the energy of the game, the determination and grit to win, and the devotion of the players and fans, the game simply feels like something that is tailor-made for the United States.

Almost every American knows at least *something* about the sport too. That just goes to show how absolutely ubiquitous it is. Even if you don't really like football, you at least know some of the players and team names, where they reside and who they represent.

Of course, some people take football very, very seriously. In fact, some fans are downright devoted to the game and live and breathe football. When Sunday rolls around, these people put away anything that can distract them, and they tune into the game and only the game. Football has a hold over them. It has some sort of mystical power that makes them want to do nothing else *but* watch football.

These people—these avid followers—are the ones that go above and beyond. They are not merely casual followers of the game of football; they are disciples, they are die-hard true believers.

No matter how devoted and committed they are to the game, certain things summarize every type of fan. A fan is someone who shows up at the game again and again. They want to watch every play and know each athlete's story, strengths, and weaknesses. They want to truly understand the game better than a casual person who only sometimes tunes into the game.

But there is more to a fan than just that. A devoted and true fan wants to know everything about the game, the ups and downs, the intricate details, and every minute subject that can be studied about football.

These people all have favorite teams, but their love of football goes beyond the team they root on. In a way, they support every crew and squad because they just *love* football that much. They don't just cheer on their favorite players and teams, but they cheer on the entire idea of the sport.

Their adoration of football is so deep and ingrained in them that they love the idea of the game, not just the people playing it. Their love of football goes beyond just who wins the game and who claims the latest Super Bowl title. Their love is about supporting every aspect of football.

Maybe that's you. Maybe you are one of those people who has a favorite team and favorite player. Yet, at the end of the day, what you really love above everything else is football, the game, the concept and the feelings it gives you. And if that does sum you up, then you are probably sick and tired of hearing the same old stories and learning the same old things about football.

You probably want to know the inside scoop of what goes on behind the scenes in the world of football. You want to hear the things that most people don't usually hear about. And you want all the details—accurate and laid out plainly. You want to learn more about the game, and you want to know more about its history and the people who shaped it, led it, changed it, and made it into the phenomenal sport it is today.

That's why you've come to our book. Now you will get a collection of stories featuring the heroes and legends of the game. They might not always be the most well-known people, but they all had a hand in changing football into a hobby and a game that was mostly just played on high school and college fields into a worldwide sensation that garners billions of viewers and fans every single year.

This book is for many different types of people. It's for those who love and adore football and are eager to dive even deeper into the legendary tales that don't always fill the history books. But it's also for the people who don't know an awful lot about football. Maybe they're curious, casual fans who are intrigued by football but want to know more than just the Xs and Os and the regulations and rules that make the game what it is today. To really understand something and give it the respect and attention it deserves, you need to learn more than the surface-level facts. You need to dive into the deep end of the pool.

Football was started as a mix of the English sports of soccer and rugby. It started in the 19th century and would eventually transform from its humble beginnings to a behemoth of sport that generates billions of dollars every single year. It started as a rather simple mash-up of both soccer and rugby but was advanced and changed and taken to the next level by a man named Walter Camp, who is considered one of the most important people in the development and evolution of football to what it is today.

After a few tweaks to the rules and changes in how it was played, Camp's new iteration of the game found fans nearly immediately. More changes would come over the years, and the game would progress in leaps and bounds in terms of popularity. A long list of football heroes would come and change the game, people like Vince Lombardi, Joe Montana, Reggie Bush, Joe Namath, Eli Manning, Tom Brady, Brett Farve, Jim Brown, and so many more.

You will learn about those people, but you will learn so much more within the pages of this book. You will not just learn about the players, though. You will learn about their back stories, triumphs, challenges, and desires to always be better and push the game forward.

I have spent years studying the game of football. During my years as a military sports instructor with the love for all things athletic, I have never been satisfied with just knowing the bare minimum about anything. I have found a strong interest in all sorts of sports and a wide range of games that have shaped me as a person, a fan, and a professional.

All of my education, my desire and my devotion to football—and all sports—have been poured into this book. For anyone who wants to deeply understand, respect, and adore the game that has made so many of us happy for so long, this book is perfect for you. So many terrific stories revolve around this wonderful sport, and it's time for us to celebrate them and share them all.

1984 – THE RECORD-BREAKING SEASON

Make no mistake, the game of football has been popular in America for decades now. But the fact of the matter is this: the game has been more popular in certain years and decades and less popular in others.

The 1980s was a different, complicated time—not just for football but for the entire country and world. But football was specifically in a very weird place in the early 80s, and more, the press revolving around the sport was mostly incredibly negative.

Perhaps the most explicit summation of how rough the NFL had things in the 1980s was the NFL Players Association strike in the early 80s. In 1982, the NFL Players Association went on strike. Because of the contract disputes, both sides couldn't see eye to eye, and a strike threw a huge monkey wrench into the billion-dollar industry. Due to that, owners of the teams lost millions of dollars, and only a few were actually breaking even financially. In total, the strike lasted eight weeks and shortened that season to just nine games per team.

That strike, financial difficulties, and trouble within the free agency of the NFL put a damper on the early years of the 80s. Baseball was supremely popular, and basketball had never had so much success. Because of that and the problems plaguing the NFL, some people actually wondered out loud if maybe—just maybe—football in America was losing its footing and could possibly become a relic of the past.

But then 1984 came along, and it changed everything. During that NFL season, a select few players and teams injected a lot more energy and enthusiasm back into the game, and it reminded people that, yes, Americans still loved the game of football and had plenty of reasons to.

Walter Payton's miracle season was one of the biggest NFL stories of the year, as he broke the rushing yard record for the Chicago Bears on October 7, grabbing the attention of dormant NFL fans and riling up the fanbase of his team.

But Payton wasn't alone in setting records and wowing the crowds. Future Hall of Famer Dan Marino set a new single-season passing yards record with a jaw-dropping 5,084 yards.[1] Then, the San Diego Chargers' receiver Charlie Joiner became the leader in career receptions.

The Seattle Seahawks broke their own record, setting NFL milestones for interception returns and defensive takeaways too.

At the end of the season, the surging San Francisco 49ers won the Super Bowl and became the first team to win fifteen games in a regular season—and eighteen in the entire season.[2]

1984 was a major moment for the game and the young, athletic men who played it. Salaries for the pro players began to increase, and some of them grew by as much as 50%, which showed a large shift in dynamics between the owners of teams and their players.

Because of the excitement and broken records, people turned their TVs back on and started filling arenas again. Ratings began to increase once again, and American football was saved. But it wasn't some clever advertising, inventive sales techniques, or the work of team owners that brought the people back to watching football by the millions. Instead, it was the talented players who saved the sport they loved so much. They poured their hearts into the game once again, showed people what they were missing, and anew found a place in the hearts of millions.

---

1. Marino also set the record for most passes completed in a season in 1984
2. The San Francisco 49ers, along with the New York Giants, Washington Redskins, and Chicago Bears, were all part of the dominant NFC in 11 straight Super Bowls from 1981 to 1992.

THE MAN WHO LET DOWN THE NFL WHEN THE NATION WAS MOURNING

S ports have always been used as a way to bring people together. No matter their religion, their political beliefs, and their employment, folks from all walks of life are able to be joined by their love of sports. From basketball to baseball and especially to football, athletics have bound people and groups from all different walks of life.

Sports can bring people together in the best of times but can also bring people together in the worst of times too. In fact, the worst of times can be sports[1] shiniest moments and the time they can work the most magic and create a soothing balm on an entire nation.

But sometimes sports *do* have to stop. Some events are so big, shattering, and shocking that they require the world of professional sports to take a few days to observe moments of silence. And when that doesn't happen, it can create serious tension and discomfort for literally everyone involved, including the players on the field.

The year was 1963, and it was a very different America than the one we know and love today. The president, John F. Kennedy, was youthful and incredibly unique. When he was elected back in 1960, he set a tone and an attitude about the country that was hopeful and exciting. After generations of leaders who felt ancient and stuck in a different era, Kennedy was forward-thinking and felt like a major step in the right direction to millions of Americans. Despite political differences, people from all parts of the country felt proud that the nation had selected such a significant leader.

The entire country was shattered on November 22, 1963, when President Kennedy was assassinated as he drove in a motorcade, waving to fans in Dallas, Texas. The generation that had voted for Kennedy had never known a trauma like that, and it literally left people in tears on the street.

The entire country came to a screeching halt. School was canceled, people were sent home from work, and people from coast to coast just shut down as America reeled from such a loss.

There were sporting events throughout the US that were promptly canceled following Kennedy's murder. But the NFL, which had a slew of games lined up just a couple of days after the 22nd, actually did *not* cancel their games.

Pete Rozelle was the man in charge of the NFL at the time, and he would live to regret this error for the rest of his life. Being the commissioner of the National Football League from 1960 to 1989, Rozelle had seen a whole bunch of major world events that could complicate the world of professional sports. But Rozelle had never experienced anything like the Kennedy assassination. Immediately after the shooting, there were calls from every direction telling Rozelle to cancel the weekend's games. Some people even called on Rozelle to end the season early. No one wanted to think about football, people said. Meanwhile, the AFL, still a separate entity at the time, had already cleaned its slate of games.

But when Rozelle spoke with Pierre Salinger, President Kennedy's press secretary, he decided the games would go on. Salinger encouraged Rozelle to keep the games playing on the weekend.[2] And JFK's brother, Robert F. Kennedy, also said he wished the games would be played.

So that decided it: football would be on that weekend.

Ironically, one of the teams set to play just days after Kennedy's death was the Dallas Cowboys. This was painful for multiple reasons, but most specifically because the word "Dallas" felt cursed in the days after Kennedy's death. How would the team fare when they were representing a city that had just taken away the country's leader?

Well, they didn't fare well. When the Cowboys arrived in Cleveland to play the Browns, the players noticed they were not being welcomed with open arms. That wasn't true by a long shot, in fact. Many people blamed Dallas and anyone associated with it for the death of the president. The people working in the hotel turned their backs on the Cowboys. People stared them down and kept their distance; the team even ate in small, disconnected groups in the evening as to not draw attention to themselves and who they were.[3]

And the day of the game was awkward and uncomfortable. The stands, sparsely populated as the nation mourned, had a few people who yelled at the Cowboys during warm-up, telling them to go back home.[4] The owners of the Browns, Art Modell, hired a group of off-duty policemen to protect the players, and he ordered them to never utter the word "Dallas."

It quickly became apparent that no one—not the players, the coaches, the refs, or the audience—wanted to really watch football on that day. But that is what they did. The players performed like zombies and seemed completely tuned out from the opening snap until the very last play. When it was all over, the Browns won 27–17, but no one seemed to really care.

The entire situation was so completely unique in the worst and most painful ways. The members of the Cowboys dreaded being in Cleveland and receiving such a cold reception, but they also couldn't stomach the thought of returning to Dallas and feeling the horrible heartache of being there. The situation was made even more complicated by the fact that some of the people on the team actually knew Jack Ruby, the local Dallas business owner who had just shot and killed Kennedy assassin Lee Harvey Oswald. It felt like the country was on a dreadful roller coaster that everyone wanted to stop.

Years later, Rozelle would admit that he made the wrong call. He would later say he should have canceled the games and joined the rest of the world of professional sports in quiet solidarity and mourning. The lessons that Rozelle failed to learn would later be accepted and followed by Paul Tagliabue, who took over for Rozelle years later. He saw over the NFL in 2001, when the nation suffered another unfathomable tragedy on September 11, 2001. But Tagliabue, remembering what Rozelle had told him, canceled all games following the attacks of 9/11.

John F. Kennedy once said, "Politics is like football; if you see daylight, go through the hole." His association with the game was something that many people held close to their hearts. He brought the worlds of politics and sports together, which made his loss even more painful for fans across the country.

The tough decision to play after the assassination of JFK shook the world and the players involved in the league. In the end, it would be recognized as a bad mistake, but it would hold a special place in the history books, not only of America but also of the NFL. Forever shrouded in regret and pain, the games played after Kennedy's death will never be forgotten.

1. Aside from the AFL, college and high school games were also canceled. Additionally, all but four games in the Big Ten were rescheduled.
2. The story was summarized in the book *Clouds over the Goalpost.*
3. The players were forced to carry their own bags to their hotel rooms as the bellhops working at the hotel would not pick them up for them.
4. "We were [viewed as] killers, we had killed the president," Cowboys star Pettis Norman would later say. "It was amazing. I just could not believe that."

THE GAME FOREVER KNOWN AS ONE YARD SHORT

I t isn't easy playing in the Super Bowl; anyone who has been there before can tell you that.

The pressure is off the charts high. The anxiety and expectations are also unparalleled. No matter how many games you have played and how many experiences on the football field you have had, nothing will prepare you for the Super Bowl. Even the most seasoned and successful football superstars will tell that to you again and again. Nothing can prepare you for a game at the level of importance.

Think about how much is riding on that one game. First of all, literally, billions of people are watching. Secondly, the winner of the game is declared the winner not just of that match-up but of the entire season. The winner of the Super

408 | ROY LINGSTER

Bowl is literally the best team in the NFL and will be considered such until the next year's Super Bowl.

It's win or go home. You either beat the rival and claim the trophy, or you walk away in second place. But in this case, being the second-best team in the league is little comfort. In fact, it's usually worse than not even going to the Super Bowl at all.

With thousands of people in the stands and literally billions watching all over the globe, two teams go head-to-head in the Super Bowl and leave it all on the floor.[1] They pour it all out on the field and walk away completely drained and either victorious or utterly drained and defeated.

Imagine if your team lost and you were the one that so many people blamed for the defeat. Or imagine your team won and everyone considered you the reason why. As you can imagine, those are two wildly different fates that rarely ever happen.

But it did happen back in 2000 when one single tackle changed the outcome of the day and is still talked about to this day.

Super Bowl XXXIV was held on January 30, 2000, at the Georgia Dome in Atlanta. The two teams set to face off in the league's biggest game were the St. Louis Rams and the Tennessee Titans. Both teams entered the Super Bowl with a record of 13–3. It hadn't been an easy season for either squad, but they had fought, scratched, and clawed their way to the top of their respective conferences. And at the end of January, they were ready to square off.

The game started off strong, with both teams having intense defensive strategies that dominated the first half of the game. But by the time halftime rolled around, the Rams had a small but substantial 9–0 lead over the Titans.

At the end of the game, as the fourth quarter came to an end, the Titans were down by just 1 touchdown. The game sat at 23–16, and the Titans were just yards away from scoring, evening the score and sending the Super Bowl into overtime.

Frank Wycheck, a tight end, was to be used as a ruse in Tennessee's strategy. To distract linebacker Mike Jones from receiver Kevin Dyson, Wycheck would sprint directly down the field on the right side. Then Dyson would veer left and travel through the center of the field. The quarterback, Steve McNair, would toss the ball to Dyson, who was going to be open from around five yards out to run in for the touchdown while Wycheck occupied Jones.

Mike Jones, a linebacker with the Rams, served as the defensive signal-caller. A combined coverage, dependent on where the offensive lines up, was the 77 Blast he had called. After they had lined up, Rams safety Billy Jenkins ordered a match-up coverage in which three Rams players, Jones, cornerback Dexter McCleon, and Wycheck and Dyson would each have a zone coverage.

Everything seemed to go according to plan as the play started. At the start of the play, Wycheck and Jones ran together up the field. Jones, who was standing at the goal line, peered over his left shoulder as the pass was being made to Dyson, though, and saw an open Dyson receiving the ball. Jones turned around and sprinted in the direction of the Titans' receiver. With roughly two and a half yards remaining, Dyson made a direct run for the end zone, but Jones caught his legs.

Dyson still had a chance to reach for the end zone while getting the ball over the goal line, even though he was being tackled by the legs. Dyson extended his hand with the football forward toward the goal line in an effort to score the touchdown, and both players started rolling. Even though the ball was only a few inches from the end zone and within his grasp, it was still not quite enough to score. Jones was now standing on top of Dyson's legs as the rolling motion came to a stop, and as his shoulder made contact with the ground, Dyson was knocked to the ground.

The Titans had a couple of seconds left on the clock at this moment, but they were unable to run another play since they had used up all of their timeouts. As a result, the game was finished. It would have been the first Super Bowl to ever go into overtime if Dyson had scored and the extra point had been made.

The final play of the game was so monumental and important that it was forever known as "The Tackle" or "One Yard

Short." Within moments, it was recognized as one of the most important moments in football history and one of the greatest Super Bowl moments ever.[2] It was the first Super Bowl win the Rams had since 1951, and it was one of the most talked-about sports moments of the generation, still spoken of to this day.

For his part, Jones is now forever known as the man who made The Tackle. In the world of sports, he was considered something of a one-hit wonder. But he doesn't get too hard on himself about being known for only that. In fact, he has since made money for charity based on that play, that tackle, and the fame that came from it.[3]

American politician Ross Perot once said, "Most people give up just when they're about to achieve success. They quit on the one-yard line. They give up at the last minute of the game, one foot from winning a touchdown." This wasn't the case for Mike Jones.

---

1. At the game were 76,625 fans in attendance
2. ESPN.com ranked it as the 35th greatest moment of the past 25 years in sports (in 2007).
3. Jones would later say, "Everyone asks, 'Does it bother you that you're known for making one play?' It could be a whole lot worse. I could be known for missing the tackle. It's great. It brought some notoriety and helped my foundation to raise money for different things."

4

THE GAME DESCRIBED AS SWIFT AND CUNNING

"There are no traffic jams along the extra mile."

— ROGER STAUBACH

The Washington Redskins and Dallas Cowboys have one of the biggest, greatest, most intense rivalries in all of football history. It's been seen time and time again, and even to this day, fans consider the other team the enemy.

But there were few games that summarized this strong rivalry as much as one back in 1979.[1] During this one game, one player would make history for his team before retiring and leaving the world of professional football behind.

Let's go back to December 16, 1979, and a game between the Redskins and Cowboys that will never be forgotten. Before the game, both teams had 10–5 records, but because of the complicated tiebreaker rules in the NFL, the Cowboys were guaranteed a berth in the playoffs no matter the outcome, while Washington would secure the NFC East championship with a win but may be refused a spot in the playoffs with a loss. This made the stakes even higher and made the tension between both teams even thicker. Heading into the game, things felt at a fever pitch between both sides of the match.

Just before the start of the season, the Cowboys' defense behind head coach Tom Landry had lost three key players: DT Jethro Pugh, Ed "Too Tall" Jones, and Charlie Waters, who was taken out because of a knee injury in the preseason. Still, DT Randy White and DE were left. The offense, led by Roger Staubach, Tony Dorsett, Harvey Martin, MLB Bob Breunig, and Cliff Harris, was strong. Tony Hill and Drew Pearson were the wide receivers. Altogether, the Cowboys had a strong team, but would it be enough to get the job done over the Redskins?

The offense, led by Roger Staubach, Tony Dorsett, Harvey Martin, MLB Bob Breunig, and Cliff Harris, was strong. Tony Hill and Drew Pearson were the wide receivers. With this ragtag group of tough fighters, Dallas started off strong with a 7–1 record. However, after that, they dropped four of five games in a turbulent stretch that saw Landry bench Thomas Henderson for lack of effort.

Enter John Riggins. Riggins was the focal point of Jack Pardee's attack for Washington, which also featured a strong passing game with Joe Theismann, the NFL's second-best thrower. The defensive backfield, which included cornerbacks Lamar Parrish and Joe Lavender, Mark Murphy, Ken Houston, and teammates Brad Dusek, Lamar Parrish, and Neal Olkewicz, was among the greatest of its time.

The Cowboys were furious with the Redskins after they lost a game to them in Washington just four weeks earlier. Coach Pardee stated that it was because there was a chance that point difference may affect a playoff spot. But many Dallas players regarded it as the Redskins slapping them in the face for the defeat.

When the Redskins gained a 17–0 lead in the second quarter, aided along by Dallas turnovers, it appeared as though Washington was well on its way to a division championship. After a fumble by Cowboys RB Ron Springs in the first quarter, Mark Moseley kicked a 24-yard field goal. Theismann connected with Danny Buggs on a 39-yard pass play after Robert Newhouse's fumble was recovered by Dusek, and three plays later, he raced around the end for a one-yard score. During the second quarter, Theismann finished off a seven-play drive with a 55-yard touchdown throw to running back Benny Malone.

The Cowboys, however, rallied back as Springs first scored from a yard out. With fewer than ten seconds left in the half and facing a 3rd-and-20, Staubach completed a 26-yard touchdown pass to running back Preston Pearson to finish an 85-yard drive. At halftime, Washington's lead had shrunk to 17–14.

Dallas scored a 2-yard touchdown on their opening drive of the third quarter to take the lead. But in the fourth quarter, Washington appeared to seize control decisively. Riggins then scored 2 touchdowns, one from 1 yard out and the other on a 66-yard run, after Moseley made another 24-yard field goal. The Redskins maintained a commanding 34–21 lead with little under seven minutes remaining. The clock was ticking, and time was running out.

When Washington running back Clarence Harmon fumbled, only four minutes were left on the clock. Randy White recovered the ball. The Dallas offense erupted as a result of Staubach's three consecutive completions, covering distances of 14 yards to Butch Johnson, 19 yards to Tony Hill, and 26 yards and a score to Springs.

On their subsequent drive, the Redskins attempted to stall the time, but on a key third-and-two play at their own 32, DE Larry Cole dropped Riggins for a 2-yard loss. With 1:46 remaining in the game and two timeouts, Washington was forced to punt, and the Cowboys took over at their own 25.

The pressure was on, and the options were limited. But it was in this moment that the players stepped up in a way that would live on forever. Staubach, a well-known expert at mounting comebacks, completed passes of 20 yards to Hill to get to the Washington 8-yard line. With 45 seconds left,

Staubach had planned to pass to TE Billy Joe Dupree, but in response to a full-fledged blitz by the Redskins, he instead lofted a high, arching pass that Hill miraculously intercepted in the corner of the end zone. Dallas had gained a one-point advantage after the successful extra point attempt.

Washington still had one more chance, but it was blocked by Dallas' 42-yard line in the last 39 seconds. The Cowboys triumphed astonishingly, 35–34.

Despite turning the ball over three times to one for Washington, the Cowboys outgained the Redskins. Using 24 of his 42 attempts, Roger Staubach completed throws for 336 yards, 3 touchdowns, and just 1 interception. Preston Pearson came in second place with 5 receptions out of the backfield for more than 100 yards and a score, closely followed by Tony Hill, who grabbed 8 passes for 113 yards and a touchdown. In Tony Dorsett's stead, Ron Springs gained 79 yards on the ground on 20 attempts.

The leading rusher was John Riggins, who made 22 attempts for 151 yards and 2 touchdowns. Joe Theismann attempted 23 passes in the air, completing 12 of them for 200 yards and a score while avoiding any interceptions. Benny Malone had the most yards receiving on passes with 55 on his single catch, which led to a touchdown, while Danny Buggs was just behind him with 46 on his 2 catches.

Dallas now led the division with an 11–5 record thanks to the victory. Due to having a worse conference record than

Dallas, Philadelphia, who was also 11–5, took second place and the first wild card position. Washington finished third with a record of 10-6 but missed out on being the second wild card club because the Chicago Bears, who finished with a record of 10–6 as well, defeated the Cardinals 42–6, defeating the Redskins on the basis of point differential.

The Redskins gave it their all, so it's unfortunate that they had to lose, but that was the way this intense game worked out. The Redskins performed well enough to get to the post-season. They merited a better outcome. Staubach said that the game was "the most exciting I've ever played in," which was undoubtedly high praise in his situation. Other people on the team were feeling heartbroken, dejected, and a bit hopeless. But they also knew they had to shake hands with the competitors, move forward, and put the loss behind them.[2]

The fact that it was Roger Staubach's final regular-season game before his summer retirement was unknown at the time. He had the highest passing rating in the NFL in his final season, tossing for 3,586 yards and 27 touchdowns, which was right behind the league co-leaders. The Hall of Fame would be his next trip.

Tony Hill and Drew Pearson each amassed more than 1,000 receiving yards, and Hill was chosen for the Pro Bowl. In his third season, Hill caught 60 catches for 1,062 yards and a career-high 10 touchdowns in his second as the starting wide receiver. In his sixth season, Pearson caught 55 passes for 1,026 yards and 8 touchdowns. Preston Pearson had 26 receptions for 333 yards and a touchdown against the Redskins. His 108 yards against Washington were the second most of his 14-year career, and he was praised for his ability to grab passes out of the backfield.

Beyond the statistics, beyond the numbers, beyond the final score, this game between the Redskins and Cowboys would be remembered for decades to come because of how close it was, how intense it became, and how it ended up being Staubach's last regular-season game.

Few people are able to leave their professional careers in the way that he did during that game in 1979. It is still talked of today—and with very good reason.

---

1. Coach Jack Pardee would later say, "The Lord giveth, and He can take it away in a hurry; that's the only way to understand what took place here."
2. "We thought we had the title," linebacker Neal Olkewicz said. "Then to have this happen. When we had the ball with a 34–21 lead, I thought we were in."

5

THE 2012 GAME WON IN 52 SECONDS

> "*Mental toughness is doing the right thing for the team when it's not the best thing for you.*"
>
> — PATRIOTS COACH, BILL BELICHICK

There have been very few football teams in history better than the 2012 New England Patriots. The records they broke, the success they found, and the way they played are still spoken of to this day and will be for a very long time. It's been just over ten years since that team stormed through the entire NFL, and people still speak of it as a legendary, unstoppable crew with the wind at its back and wasn't slowing down or stopping for anyone.

2012 was one heck of a year for the Patriots. It wasn't just one thing that set that season apart from so many others that came before it. Firstly, this was the year the team hit 557 points, the second time in team history and the third in NFL history.

You have to think about what that means and how impressive that is. A football team usually scores maybe about 20 to 30 points in a game. They are able to do that if they're lucky and very talented. So now imagine nearly 600 points across the entire season. There are not many games in an NFL season, so that achievement is remarkable and really unheard of. The fact that the Patriots did it made them a clear favorite and a truly competitive and frightening opponent to any other team in the league.

But the Pats did more than just that in 2012. Their offense set an NFL record for the most first downs in a season with a total of 444. The previous record was a stunning 416, set by New Orleans just a year before in 2011.

New England would score 67 touchdowns in the 2012 season, the second most in team history and tied for the fourth most in the entire history of the NFL.

Those are all impressive stats and some wonderful numbers to respect, but it was one game in 2012 that really summed up the power of the Patriots and, specifically, three players on the squad. For this game, it wasn't Tom Brady who was getting the most attention and sitting firmly in the spotlight. Instead, it was Shane Vereen, Steven Gregory, and Julian

Edelman who got the most attention and created the most headlines following the game on November 23, 2012.

The Patriots were playing against the New York Jets. To one player, in particular, it was personal. Steve Gregory was a New York native, and he was looking to make an impact and leave a mark on his hometown team.[1] And, sure enough, Gregory put on a show for everyone watching, including the New York natives who were rooting him on even though he played for the competition.

In the opening of the game, Gregory had a first quarter interception. He then continued his good work in the second quarter with a fumble recovery and then capped it off with his first career touchdown as the Patriots led 21–0.

Gregory's most impressive moment in the game—and the most impressive moment for the entire Patriot's lineup—was the 52-second span in which the team scored not one or two but *3* touchdowns.

Gregory was a vital part of this incredible stretch of the game. He recovered the fumble by Jets running back Shonn Greene at the Patriot's 31-yard line. This then led to an 83-yard touchdown pass from Brady to Shane Vereen. Boom, a huge victory in and of itself.

Then, Vince Wilfork of the Jets pushed his way through New York guard Brandon Moore into quarterback Mark Sanchez, who tossed up the ball when slamming into Moore's backside. Gregory was there, swooping in and taking the ball 32 yards to score his first touchdown.

After the ensuing kickoff, Julian Edelman picked up yet another fumble and then went for a 22-yard touchdown, just moments after the last one. It was the first time in Patriots history that the team returned to two fumbles for touchdowns in the same game.

"That was a lot of points in a short period of time. I think that really set the momentum for the game; that really turned things into kind of a lop-sided deal there," said Gregory after the game.[2]

The reaction to the game and the Jets' utter collapse was major and instant. The newspapers didn't go easy on them, and the fans themselves were also very disappointed and heartbroken by what they saw. It's so rare to see 3 touchdowns in less than a minute in-game. If someone had decided to take out the trash or make a quick snack during that time, they would have come back to their TVs looking at a radically different game than the one they left. It was shocking, and it was rare. It just never really happened like that in the NFL.

But this was a period in the history of the Patriots when they were coming into their own in a huge, impressive way. This was a time when the team was really figuring out what it was, who was leading it, and the power inside. There had been multiple complaints about the Patriots in the months before, but they were really getting things together. And they were becoming stronger, more competitive, and nearly unstoppable at times.

Of course, we all know that this was just one of many incredible games for the Patriots. 2012 marked the beginning of the team's era of ruling the NFL, an era that wouldn't slow down or end for years to come. That one game in 2012 against the New York Jets was just a prime example of all the Patriots had in store for their fans in the seasons ahead.

---

1. Gregory would say that he wanted to do well because the game was a chance to "play in his backyard."
2. Gregory didn't even really understand what happened until after the game when he was able to watch a replay of those exciting 52 seconds.

6

201 YARDS, 4 TOUCHDOWNS AND A FANTASY FOOTBALL DREAM

"Do you know what my favorite part of the game is? The opportunity to play."

— MIKE SINGLETARY

The story and life and career of Jonas Gray are not ordinary.

What Gray has been through and what he accomplished—no matter how brief—is really impressive and stunning and something to be proud of. And the fact that he did it all in the ways that he did only makes Gray's story even more impressive and remarkable.

Just like every other sport, the NFL loves finding someone who is down on their luck and counted out and then making them a hero, even for just a short amount of time. But make no mistake: those selected from obscurity and given the chance to really shine still have to do the work. They are not given everything handed to them. They must have natural skill and talent and drive. They must capitalize on the opportunity given to them and make something of it. The NFL isn't easy, and it's not going to hand anything to anyone.

Jonas Gray knew that. But he had those required desires as well as the belief in himself. He just needed a chance to prove himself.

As a young man, Gray was well on his way to the NFL. No one who knew Gray and has seen him play could deny that he was a very talented young football player and would have a bright, successful future in the professional league. Growing up in Michigan, Gray was an absolute unit on his high school football team, leading to an appearance at the state championship with his Detroit Country Day team. In the state semifinal, he rushed for 305 yards on 29 carries and scored 4 touchdowns.

He was considered the fourth best running back prospect of his class as his time in high school came to an end. He then attended the University of Notre Dame from 2008 to 2011 but mostly played as a backup to other players. He had some impressive games and did some wonderful things on the field, but it was all cut short when he tore not only his ACL but also his MCL and LCL during a game against Boston College.

Gray's future in the NFL was definitely thrown in the air and turned on its head after that severe injury. Despite that, he was signed by the Miami Dolphins as an undrafted free agent. But he never played for the team. Still mending his injured knee, he was cut from the team just weeks after being signed. It was then that he was acquired by the Baltimore Ravens but finally found his long-term home in the NFL with the incredible New England Patriots. And it would be here when he would show off his impressive skills, wow the fans, and also make a lot of money for a few fantasy football fanatics.

Despite what most people think, you can still be broke while technically being an official NFL player. If you aren't playing often and being tossed around the league from team to team, as Gray was during that time, the money isn't really flowing. Gray was finding a hard time making ends meet. He lived in a one-bedroom apartment and took odd jobs to pay the bills, including attempting to be a stand-up comic. When he was signed by the Patriots, Gray knew that his chances were running out. If he wasn't able to make a big impact on the team, he might as well give up his dreams of playing football for a living.

Gray's time with the Patriots wasn't a huge hit right from the beginning. In fact, he was initially signed to the practice squad after signing a future/reserve contract with the team in January of 2014. Then, months later, on October 16, he was signed to the active roster of the team as they pushed through the regular season with an eye on the postseason.

Just a few weeks later, it was Gray who stole the show in a game versus the Indianapolis Colts. Heading into that game, Gray had never scored a touchdown in an NFL game. And he certainly also never was on SportsCenter or never went viral online among fans. He was a nearly unknown player on a team full of multiple superstars. Yet, during that game, it was going to be Gray's time to shine.

In just one game, Gray rushed for 201 yards and set a franchise record fifth 4 touchdowns on 37 carries.[1] This not only led the Patriots to a great 42–20 victory over the Colts, but it also put his name on the map—even if it was just for a short while. Gray was the first NFL running back since 1921 to score 4 rushing touchdowns in a game after entering the match with zero career touchdowns before that. He was also the first running back in the Super Bowl era to account for more than 25% of rushing touchdowns in a week with at least 10 games.

All in all, Gray scored 24 points in the game, tied with Marshawn Lynch for the most by any player in a single game in the 2014 season.[2]

Obviously, it had been such a long time since anyone had seen a performance like the one from Gray, and the results were astonishing to those who were paying attention and believing in the young player. Before the game, ESPN estimated that Gray only appeared in 1.3% of fantasy leagues. That means that he was completely overlooked, ignored even.

In the following weeks, he was in nearly 80% of all fantasy leagues. People had seen what Gray had done in just one game, and they were completely sold on him. This young player, who had spent most of his career on practice squads of injured reserves, was now the star of the biggest team in the entire NFL.

For his efforts and his strong showing in that game, Gray made the front cover of Sports Illustrated.[3] He also became a fantasy football hero. That's because anyone who bet on Gray before his big game experienced a huge payout thanks to his impressive showing due to that game. Two of the people who received the biggest reward for selecting Gray in their fantasy leagues were his own brothers, who made large sums of money for betting on their kin and his skills.

Gray would never reach the same heights as he did during that single game in November of 2014. Instead, he would bounce around to a few more teams within the league before leaving the NFL in 2016.

For many people, Gray is a footnote during the era of the New England Patriots. However, he is a very impressive footnote, one best summed up as a powerful, driven, dedicated sign of someone who always believed in himself and never gave up hope that he could have an impact on the game, even if just for one game.

---

1. This was the best performance by any running back during the season.
2. Patriots owner Robert Kraft actually pulled Gray aside to tell him he was set to have a big game before it began.
3. The headline on Sports Illustrated read, "Jonas Gray . . . Because of Course."

7

FOOTBALL'S EPIC BLOWOUTS

 "Nobody who ever gave his best regretted it."

— GEORGE HALAS

N o one likes losing a game, but we all know that it's going to happen.

No matter what sport you are playing and how good you are, it's just inevitable that you're going to lose a game at times. It's a natural part of playing any game. You might train all you can, and you might have the best team, coach, and fanbase, but there will come a time when a loss is going to hit you hard in the face. It's just something that is impossible to avoid. So few teams ever have perfect seasons. And that's okay because even the best teams will lose once in a while.

Again, it's part of the game. It's part of being competitive. Competition means losing every once in a while.

But while you are going to lose at times when competing against others, most everyone avoids being blown out. No one wants to get dominated in a game. Because while a loss is impossible to avoid, a blowout loss is not. Getting beat by 20 or 30 points is something that all competitors attempt to avoid like the plague. That is because few things are as embarrassing as being decimated by someone in a game. Whether it be a single player or a whole team, people go to great lengths to avoid losing by many points.

But it happens! It might not happen too often because trained professionals are quite good at the sports they play, but blowout losses do occur. And when they do, it is very hard for people to forget them. Fans talk about huge losses for weeks, months, and even sometimes years. People will bring it up again and again as an embarrassing note that will tarnish even the best records.

Some of the biggest blowout defeats have been lost to the passing of time, but they are still worth noting. In the most recent history, one of the most startling losses was when the New England Patriots took down the Tennessee Titans 59–0 on October 18, 2009. This came after the Titans posted the league's best record in 2008. But when they got to 2009, the team had a lot of issues and actually lost five consecutive games.

But the Patriots absolutely dominated the Titans during that October game. New England scored 6 touchdowns in the first half, including 5 through the air from Tom Brady in the second quarter of the game. That was actually an NFL record and only made the Titans' loss all the more embarrassing and painful.

There was another record the Patriots set during that game, and it was even worse. They had the largest lead at halftime in NFL history when they went up 45–0 in the middle of the game. Ouch!

When the Los Angeles Rams overcame the Atlanta Falcons on December 4, 1976, 59-0 was also the final score. During that blowout, the Rams held the Falcons to just 81 total yards, featuring just 22 passing yards.[1] They also forced 4 turnovers. Thankfully, the Falcons would find great success in later seasons because things couldn't get a lot worse than the 59–0 drubbing from the Rams.

If we are talking about the biggest blowout in playoff history during the Super Bowl era, you have to mention the Jacksonville Jaguars' defeat of the Miami Dolphins in 2000.

In addition to being the largest rout in NFL playoff history, this 2000 AFC Divisional Round game also served as the final contest of Hall of Fame quarterback Dan Marino's storied playing career for the Dolphins.

This loss was downright awful and painful from the beginning. The Jaguars, who were the AFC's top seed at the time, scored 24 points in the opening round, highlighted by Fred Taylor's 90-yard touchdown run. Before Marino completed his first throw of the game, Jacksonville had already scored 38 points and started their backup quarterback, Jay Fiedler. A jaw-dropping 7 turnovers were made by the Dolphins, including 4 by Marino himself. Miami just gained 21 rushing yards compared to Jacksonville's 257. The Tennessee Titans defeated the Jaguars 33–14 in the AFC Championship Game, preventing them from winning the Super Bowl.

Of course, some teams have been taken down resoundingly during the biggest game of the year. The Super Bowl has been home to just a few blowouts, but few of them more embarrassing than when the San Francisco 49ers destroyed the Denver Broncos, 55–10, during Super Bowl XXIV on January 28, 1990.

At its height, the NFC dominated. As overwhelming favorites (-12), the 49ers performed admirably. You may also be familiar with Joe Montana and Jerry Rice, who hooked up seven times for 148 yards and 3 touchdowns.

Montana recorded the second-highest passing rating in the history of the Super Bowl with a total of 297 yards and 5 touchdowns via the air. Additionally, Denver's defense was the best in the league in 1989, allowing the least amount of yards and points per game in the league. John Elway, a legendary Bronco, was unable to save his group. [2]But, later, Elway stopped the NFC's Super Bowl winning run in 1997.

However, the biggest and most embarrassing and startling blowout in the history of the league goes way, way back to the year 1940. December 8, 1940, was when the Chicago Bears absolutely destroyed Washington in a 73–0 explosion of embarrassment and pain.

The game was still the most lopsided in NFL/AFL history by a margin of 73 points. The Bears scored a touchdown in each of the first, third, and fourth quarters despite both teams having identical 9–3 records going into the game.

At least 40-yard touchdown runs were made by three different players. Three separate Chicago defenders, including one each from Bulldog Turner and Hampton Pool, returned interceptions for scores in the third quarter. The Bears' defense recorded 9 takeaways, including those 3 interceptions. Additionally, they gained 381 yards on the ground while averaging 7.2 yards per run. Chicago won four championships in that decade, with coach George Halas leading the club to three of those triumphs, solidifying the Bears as one of the league's finest team-coach combinations.

It was during this game that Halas used his patented leadership style to help the team propel to the huge, lopsided victory. Additionally, his T-formation offense, along with the incredible skills of Sid Luckman, was able to help the Bears earn such a coveted, historic blowout win.

All these years later, people *still* talk about that game and how it showed the true grit, determination, and skill of the

Chicago Bears. A lot has changed in the time since that game. In fact, football is like a completely different world and sport in the modern day compared to how it was back in the 40s. But one thing remains the same: the explosive victory the Bears had back in 1940 is still a wildly impressive feat of sportsmanship unlike any we have seen since.

You don't see as many blowouts in the modern NFL because teams have gotten so good, and coaches have learned the best ways to train and prepare their teams for the competition. But when one happens, it is worth noting and talking about. However, there will never be a blowout that is as shocking as the one unsuspecting football fans experienced back in 1940 when the Bears took down Washington in such a stunning way.

---

1. The game featured Rams running back Lawrence McCutcheon, who was selected for his fourth Pro Bowl in 1976.
2. Elway earned the third worst passing rating in Super Bowl history at 19.4.

8

THE FALL OF A LEGEND

I magine participating in the Olympics on behalf of the United States. What an honor. What a pleasure. What pressure and what a call to greatness to make your country proud.

Those athletes who go to the Olympics to play for their nation are doing something both for themselves but also for their people too. It's such an incredible, awe-inspiring, awesome moment for anyone.

So, imagine you are feeling all of that and are called to such a task. Now imagine that your shoes are stolen just hours before you are set to compete. How would that feel? What would that do to your heart, your mind, your soul, and your desire to achieve so much for your country?

That's what Jim Thorpe had to go through. Although Thorpe played for America, he wasn't treated like most Americans. While millions adored him, many others poked fun at him or ridiculed him because of his background and the color of his skin. Despite such adversity, he earned a gold medal and won millions of fellow Americans over. However, his accomplishments weren't written about much in the history books due to some rough times later in life and the way his story ended.

Thorpe's story is an important one, and it deserves to be told, not just to sports fans across the country but to anyone who is proud to be an American.

Thorpe was the first Native American to win an Olympic gold medal for the United States. In fact, he actually won two of them—although one was stripped from him. He also played professional baseball, basketball, and football, which made him one of the most famous athletes of his time. Yes, he was supremely popular and well known all over, but many people today aren't aware of his name or accomplishments.

Thorpe was one amazing athlete. What's more, he was able to run the 100-yard dash in 10 seconds flat and the 200 in just 21.8 seconds. He was also noted as running an entire mile in only 4 minutes and 35 seconds.

But he could do more than run—he could jump too. He was able to long jump 23 feet 6 inches and could pole vault up to 11 feet too.

When the 1912 Olympics came around, Thorpe decided to participate not only in the decathlon and pentathlon but also in the long jump and high jump too. He won a whopping four out of the five events and then placed third in the javelin.[1]

Thorpe's final event was the decathlon, which was his first and actually only attempt at the sport. He ended up winning in that event and was able to finish in the top four in all ten events, and his Olympic record of 8,413 points stood for more than two decades.

Perhaps even more remarkable—and troubling—was the fact that Thorpe did all of this while facing serious disdain from others simply because he was Native American. As mentioned, someone stole his shoes before he was able to compete in the decathlon, which would have seemingly ended his chances of running. Instead, Thorpe located a mismatched pair of replacements, one of which was found in the trash, and he won the gold medal wearing them.

Thorpe came back home as a victor and was seen as a national celebrity and prized athlete.[2] In truth, he was treated to a ticker-tape parade when he made it back to the United States.

In 1916, 1917, and 1919, Thorpe played for the Carton Bull-dogs and helped them become unofficial world champions. When the NFL was formed, Thorpe was actually nominated president. He did a whole lot for the perception of sports and football and how people saw it and followed it.

However, Thorpe struggled after his days of being a professional athlete. He struggled to find regular jobs, and he also found great strife and challenges during the Great Depression of the 1930s.

Thorpe found himself deep in the throes of addiction, and his alcoholism led to a lack of jobs, a lack of money, and declining health. Because of that, he passed away in 1953.[3]

Additionally, strict amateurism rules for the Olympics back then prohibited athletes from receiving money prizes for competitions. When it was discovered that Thorpe had played professional baseball before the Olympics, he would later be stripped of his Olympic titles, medals, and awards.

Thorpe was mostly lost to the halls of history, and not many people spoke about him as football—the sport he loved—rose through the ranks of popularity in the United States. However, Thorpe's legacy would eventually rise again, and he would soon be held in the high regard he deserves. Ten years after his death, Thorpe entered the hall of fame, and his gold medals were restored 70 years after his passing.

Thorpe was a hero but also sadly negatively affected by his times. He wasn't not viewed as a regular American athlete because of his race, and he was always held back a bit because of that. Additionally, strict rules impaired his legacy and attempted to overrule it completely. However, in the end, the wrongs would be righted, and Thorpe would be looked upon as a trailblazer with versatile skill and ability.

It is also important to note that while Thorpe did experience racism even after being so hugely successful, millions of Americans didn't judge Thorpe because of how he looked and where he came from. In fact, they weren't bothered at all with the thought of rooting on a Native American athlete. When Thorpe was being stripped of his medals, the majority of Americans thought it was wrong and cheered for Thorpe's accomplishments. Therefore, he didn't just change the world of professional sports but he also changed the world in general.

1. He actually had never participated in the javelin before the 1912 games.
2. He would later be quoted as saying, "I heard people yelling my name, and I couldn't realize how one fellow could have so many friends."
3. His wife struck a financial deal for his remains to be sent to a town in Pennsylvania rather than to rest with his family members in Oklahoma. Following that, a legal battle started that went on for decades.

9

WHEN PLAYING TWO-WAY WAS THE NORM

> *"No man played more for the Giants but needed to be coached less than Mel Hein."*
>
> — STEVE OWEN

Have you heard much about football legend Mel Hein? Oh, you haven't? You might not even know his name, even though if you were watching football during its early years in the 1930s, you definitely knew of him.

Hein was an MVP, a team leader, an incredible athlete, and a force on the field. Powerful, fast, and brutal, he was also a gentleman off of the field and known for his kind demeanor and care for others.

Hein was also the sort of player who could be a true menace to the opponents on both offense and defense. This made him the centerpiece of the New York Giants and one of the greatest NFL players alive for ten seasons. Yet, he has been forgotten by far too many, and that needs to change. A look back on his career and his skill is necessary to highlight and celebrate Mel Hein and his important place in football history.

He had a huge, successful, important career in the NFL, but his life as a football star didn't start as smoothly as some expected. In 1930, Hein received All-American recognition at Washington State, but professional football was uninterested.[1] Hein took the initiative and actually wrote letters to four NFL clubs to let them know he was ready to play as time passed and no team got in touch with him.

Finally, an offer came his way. The Providence Steam Roller made him a low-key offer that was far below what he expected or wanted for himself, but he knew he didn't have a choice. Therefore, Mel reluctantly put his signature on the document and mailed it. A greater offer, totaling about $150 per game, was presented to him a short time later by Ray Flaherty, a coach with the Giants.[2] In a mad dash, Hein hurried over to a local post office, and a helpful postmaster assisted them in getting his mail from Providence. And that was how Mel Hein joined New York.

Hein never looked back on the trade, and neither did the Giants. Hein was the first center to be inducted into the Pro

Football Hall of Fame when it initially opened in 1963. Hein was perhaps the finest two-way center to ever play in the NFL. That meant he could play incredible defense and tackle like an animal let out of a cage but could also run up the field, score and catch like a man with magnets on his fingertips.

He blocked like a beast on offense, and the Giants were able to go from a complicated setup where any one of three back-field players may receive the snap.

He was renowned on defense for his savage tackles and ability to defend pass catchers. He was also a team leader on top of all that and was the go-to guy when it came to pushing the team upfield and to the end zone.

Ultimately, Hein spent fifteen years with the Giants, playing for them in seven Eastern Division titles and two league championships.[3] From 1933 through 1940, Mel received this honor eight times in a row as the center for the All-NFL team.

He was named the NFL's Most Valuable Player in 1938, an amazing distinction for an interior player. He intercepted a Packer pass during a crucial late-season victory over Green Bay and sprinted 50 yards to record his sole NFL touchdown.

Hein was incredibly resilient. He never missed a single game in more than 200 regular, championship, plus exhibition games, generally playing the entire game. And it's not like he wasn't roughed up in some painful ways that would make you and I visit the emergency room. Do you want to know how tough Hein was? Well, consider this: he allegedly only ever requested a time out for a broken nose. But he wasn't some scary, intense man. He was known to be gentle and caring off the field and was considered one of the nicest men in the league. He could lay a player out flat on the field, but he would never even hurt a fly.

Hein might not be spoken of with the likes of Tom Brady, Joe Montano, Jim Brown, or others, but he was at the forefront of the advancement and evolution of the NFL and football. He was a true force of nature in every aspect and angle of the game and a truly wonderful man too. While it was common for players to play both the offense and defense in those days of football, few did it as well as Hein—and few since then have even come close to his skill and ability.

1. He led Washington State to a Rose Bowl bid in the year 1930.
2. Providence's offer was $135 a game.
3. Hein played with the Giant from 1931 to 1945, a feat still not surpassed by most modern NFL players, especially those who were as physical as him.

10

THE LONGEST PLAY FROM SCRIMMAGE

"To succeed, you need to find something to hold on to, something to motivate you, something to inspire you."

— TONY DORSETT

1982 was not a very easy year for fans of football. In the end, everything would work out as it was supposed to, and there would be plenty of great games and terrific memories. But it got off to a very rocky start that left many things in question and the future of the league and all of football in question.

The season started out like any other . . . but there was a huge shadow hanging over what was ahead. Just one week into the new season, on Tuesday, September 21, an NFL players' strike began. In the end, the strike would last for 57 days, which is a long time by football season standards.

What was it that the players were asking for? The union was demanding that a wage scale based on percentage gross revenues be implemented. Essentially, the NFLPA wanted the percentage to be 55%, which was the main sticking point that dominated all negotiations and kept the league's future in doubt.

The NFL canceled all games until the strike was settled and both sides came to terms. This meant that football fans sat at home with no games to watch, although the NFLPA promoted two "AFC-NFC all-star games," which would feature the biggest names in the games outside of the restraints and the confines of the NFL.

Weeks later, the strike would officially come to an end, and the games would start up again, pleasing NFL fans, coaches, and players. This meant that many games had been canned, and the team was near the end of their season before it ever really began. A particular game between the Vikings and Cowboys became one for the record books, one that is still spoken of to this day because of an amazing play from Tony Dorsett.

It was during this game on January 3, 1983, that Dorsett scored the only 99-yard rushing touchdown in NFL history. It was a thing of beauty, something that needs to be seen to be believed, and truly a feat of beauty that hasn't been surpassed in the time since.

It was made even more amazing by the fact that Dorsett did it on a play where the Cowboys only had ten players on the field.

Dorsett's record-breaking run actually happened by accident, making it even more wild and impressive. You see, fullback for the Cowboys, Ron Springs, actually misunderstood a play call and ran off the field, which left the Cowboys with only ten players, putting them at a huge disadvantage that was rare and incredibly challenging for Dallas.

It all went down like this: Dorsett took the ball at the Cowboy's first-yard line. Rather than passing it off to another player, he took the ball, and he ran. And when he started moving, there was no slowing him down. His feet lifted, he sped like the wind, he sailed across the field and reached the end zone in what felt like the blink of an eye.[1]

His 99-yard run was incredible and unlike anything that had come before it. He took a place in history, but just barely. The previous record was 97 yards, set by Andy Uram back in 1939.[2] But even if he didn't break a record during that run, it still would have been remarkable to see.

There is nothing like watching a long, furious run by a player in an NFL game. It's something so exciting and unparalleled in terms of the elation that it creates, both in the fans and the guys on the field. Watching a highlight reel of Dorsett's run, you can practically feel the electricity flowing through the crowd, and the way that Dorsett was running, like his life depended on it. Even someone who had never watched a game of football could understand just how special it was.

There are many ways to score a touchdown in football, but Tony Dorsett did it unlike anyone else and set a remarkable record back in 1982. Watching him achieve this feat was like watching a magician perform a trick. It's really something you rarely ever see, and it's a moment in football history that every fan should be aware—and in awe—of.

The 1982 NFL season really was one unlike any other, with good moments and bad. However, when talking about the good that came out of 1982, no one can forget the miracle run that Tony Dorsett went on on that cold January day.

1. After the game, Dorsett said, "I just saw a lot of green" before he started his marathon sprint down the field.
2. Uram played for the Green Bay Packers. In 1949, Bob Gage would match this record when playing for the Pittsburgh Steelers.

11

BEHIND THE SCENES OF THE XLVII SUPER BOWL

"Beyonce must have been good. She took all the power with her when she left the stage."

— TORREY SMITH

E ven if you don't know a thing about football or the NFL, you do know that the Super Bowl is easily the biggest game of the year. And it's not just the biggest football game of the year; it's the largest annual sports event in America—from baseball to basketball and beyond.

Hundreds of millions watch the Super Bowl every single year. It is a wildly popular event that is considered a national holiday to some people. That was definitely true for the 2013 Super Bowl, Super Bowl XLVII.

458 | ROY LINGSTER

Many factors contributed to so much attention being paid to the game set for February 3, 2013. Firstly, it was taking place in New Orleans, which was still considered hallowed ground to many because of the lives lost just ten years before in Hurricane Katrina.[1] Therefore, many people saw the game as a chance for them to celebrate, commemorate, and honor the lives lost and the city that was so special to so many.

But there was more: it was also going to be the final game in a Hall of Fame career for Ravens linebacker Ray Lewis. That would have garnered a lot of attention under any circumstances.[2]

Finally, a wild, unheard-of family element was part of Super Bowl XLVII. For the first time, the game was going to be coached by two brothers: John Harbaugh would be in charge of the Ravens while Jim Harbaugh would lead the San Francisco 49ers. Two brothers had never faced off like that before, and it was something that created many headlines and news stories.

Finally, Beyonce was set to perform during the halftime show. She was—and is—one of the biggest acts in the music business and was guaranteed to bring in huge ratings.

All of these things made so many people fascinated, anxious, and ready for Super Bowl XLVII. But in the end, it wasn't those bright stories and stars that people would remember about that game—it was the darkness that swept in.

The game was off to a great start, and Beyonce had performed brilliantly. As the second half of the game opened, the Ravens had a 28–6 lead. But shortly after Jacoby Jones of the Ravens helped his team build upon their lead and inch closer to total victory, the lights went out.

Yes, some backup lighting remained, and most of the arena went pitch black. The giant screens went off, the elevators stopped where they were with people trapped inside, and business and security were threatened by the total darkness of the shocking blackout.

Officials from the local power company would later say the outage occurred when sensing equipment detected what it considered an "abnormality" in the system. A piece of equipment monitoring the electrical load in the arena sensed this abnormality and opened a breaker, which partially cut power. Backup generators then kicked in before full power could be restored.

This all happened despite an awful lot of work put into the Louisiana Superdome. Just years before, the arena was used as a shelter for those escaping the horrors of Hurricane Katrina. It needed some serious and extensive renovations following that due to damage done to the building and the roof being ripped off.

More than $500,000 was spent on the rebuilding needed in preparation for the Super Bowl. $4.5 million was also spent on new cables and switch gears, showing just how seriously the NFL and the city of New Orleans were taking this event. Despite all of that, it wasn't enough to stop the blackout, even though it was described as a minor issue. It might have been a minor issue, but it certainly put a complete stop to the game.

Sure enough, the Super Bowl was halted for a full 34 minutes, thanks to the blackout. Fans stood in the stands, nervous and anxious about what was going on. Local authorities swarmed through the arena to ensure everyone was safe, and this wasn't the result of some horrible criminal plot or terrorist plan. Back in 2013, the thought of someone attacking the Super Bowl was still a very pressing, terrifying thought. But the FBI was quick to note that the blackout had nothing to do with that and that no one was at risk. Still, it led to a very awkward, uncomfortable, and uneasy half hour as everyone—players, coaches, fans, and vendors - quite literally stood in the dark.

Thankfully, the lights were turned back on, the players took to the field again and, in the end, the Ravens were able to overcome the 49ers, although they didn't win by the largest margin. John Harbaugh's Ravens claimed a 34–31 victory over his brother Jim. They shook hands, hugged, and made nice following the game, both of them knowing just how wild an experience they had been through.

Many things can hold or delay a football game, but it'll always eventually go on. It is rare, however, to see such a major halt to the biggest sporting event of the year. For 34 minutes, players in Super Bowl XLVII stood around, stretched, drank water, threw passes, and waited around for news—any news at all.[3] It was a moment that football fans would always remember. There really hasn't been a Super Bowl like 2013's Blackout Bowl.

---

1. New Orleans actually used to be a normal part of the Super Bowl rotation, and the hope was that the game would make it part of the regular lineup of cities holding the Super Bowl.
2. It was also the coming out game for Baltimore's Joe Flacco.
3. Fans were spotted doing the wave and playing games in the stands while the players rested.

12

THE SCABSKINS OF 1987

> *"Treat a person as he is, and he will remain as he is. Treat him as what he could be, and he will become what he should be."*

> — JIMMY JOHNSON

S trikes are never easy on anyone. When a group of employees decides they are going to refuse to work, they are only doing so because the demands they have are so important that they are willing to really shake things up and cause serious disarray—to their businesses and their own lives. A group of employees not working will face pay cuts, jeopardizing their own lives. Meanwhile, the companies they work for will also lose money, and tensions will rise. That's why going on strike is seen as such a drastic move and is best avoided, both by the hard work and compromise of both employees and employers.

The world of football doesn't see too many strikes, thankfully. However, they do occur. And they usually do when the league is growing in some new, huge ways and the players and their union feel they need to be better represented and compensated.

There was already one strike of players during the 1980s. The 1982 strike greatly shortened the season and disappointed millions of fans all over the world. During the strike, games weren't played in the NFL and essentially the world of football was halted.

But that wasn't the case in 1987. In 1987, the strike resulted in some major differences and a few teams that will always be remembered, even if few of the players on them ever became household names. They featured employees from 7-Eleven, gym teachers, the unemployed, and even a convict.[1]

The important individuals in the 1987 strike were actually fill-in players, referred to as "scabs" because they were working when the union refused to. They were the solution that the Redskins figured would put pressure on regular players and put an end to the strike. In many ways, they were right.

The 1987 strike led to a very unique, bizarre, and somewhat uncomfortable new reality: teams presented impromptu lineups made up primarily of unsigned rookies and NFL rejects after the real players were on strike two games into the season.

And because of these players, life in the NFL sort of went on like normal. Well, mostly normal. The major athletes of the time were not on the "scab" teams, but some new heroes were born in the strike season. The unconventional stretch was used to the Washington Redskins' advantage. They were one of just three teams to actually triumph in all three of their make-up contests, and at the conclusion of the season, they were 4–1 and in first position in the NFC East.

After that, they won seven of their next ten contests to finish with a strong 11–4 record and win the division. The Redskins then defeated the Bears and Vikings in the playoffs before thrashing the Broncos 42–10 in Super Bowl XXII. Thanks to the hard work of some unlikely players, the Redskins were able to go all the way.

This certainly wasn't the first NFL players' strike to throw the league into disarray. The first time occurred in 1982 when NFL players staged the league's first ever walkout in an effort to increase their share of broadcast income, among other demands. There wouldn't be any NFL football games for 62 days, which few could have predicted at the time. Games from eight weeks were dropped.

In 1987, speculation of a potential strike grew throughout the playing season. Dissatisfied with the CBA's provisions, the National Football League Players Union established a strike deadline for September 22, immediately following the second week of competition. In the event of a strike, the owners decided to play with anybody who broke the picket line.

According to John Kent Cooke, the Redskins' executive vice president at the time, "We decided to have replacement squads just to show the regular players they were not the game, but an integral part of the game, and that the league would go on no matter who the players were."

The season started out well, and there was hope that the strike wouldn't happen, and the regular NFL games could continue. That's what Washington was hoping for because the Redskins won against the Eagles but lost to the Falcons in their first two games, splitting the series.

After the second week of play, the professional NFL players kept their promise and quit their jobs in protest of low pay and an unfriendly type of free agency. The strike was on, and that put the rest of the season in question. Would the NFL just shut down games as they did in 1982, or was there a plan in place to keep things moving, albeit unconventionally?

It was then that the owners of teams put into action their plan to substitute players for contests that would count toward the standings, as opposed to the 1982 strike when play had just ceased. The games would go on, but who would play?

Management for the Redskins was ready. While a week of the normal schedule was canceled, Bobby Beathard, GM of the team, and the front office oversaw attempts to find and sign substitute players.

The Redskins were abruptly represented by strange names. They included Derrick Shepard, a punt returner, wide receiver Anthony Allen, Lionel Vital, Wayne Wilson, Craig McEwen, defensive linemen Dan Benish and Steve Martin, and tight end Craig McEwen.[2] In the future, players like Allen, McEwen, Caravello, and Shepard made the regular roster, but many of the others would never make it in the NFL again, only known as members of the "Scabskins" or 1987.

The Redskins' substitutes swept their first two games, 38–12 against the New York Giants and 28–21 over St. Louis, when Allen set a club record with 255 receiving yards.

The league's disgruntled union players then made the decision that enough was enough. After a 24-day strike without having any of their requests satisfied, they decided to return to work.[3]

The experiment to replace well-known players with unknowns or "scabs" was mostly seen as a success by the Redskins' management. Of course, the players union was supremely unhappy with how it all went down, and they were frustrated that team owners chose to replace the talent instead of working with it and coming to a solution.

As for the "Scabskins," most of them never saw glory again in the NFL. Sadly, it would take thirty more years before they were awarded their Super Bowl rings.[4] No matter what you think of their participation in that wild 1987 season, no one can deny that they tried hard, played their hearts out, and left it all on the field. Thankfully, they were finally able to show off their rings and reminisce about a time when they were actual, legitimate football stars—even for just a brief moment.

---

1. This would later inspire a Hollywood film titled *The Replacement*, starring Gene Hackman and Keanu Reeves, which was released in the year 2000.
2. One player, Tony Robinson, a Heisman Trophy candidate when playing for Tennessee, was on a work furlough from prison after a cocaine conviction.
3. Other teams featured a few regular players who crossed the picket line, including running back Tony Dorsett and defensive tackle Randy White. The Redskins were actually the only NFL team not to feature any players crossing the picket line.
4. The team earned more attention and fame years later thanks to an ESPN 30 for 30 documentary titled *Year of the Scab*.

REVIEW A GAME OF EXTREMES: 25 EXCEPTIONAL FOOTBALL STORIES

If you are enjoying this book and want to help spread the message and the stories of football, the NFL, and all the amazing legends involved in it, why not leave us a review? Writing a review for this book will help others find it, and that's the best way to really celebrate football! Spread the word and let the world know about all the incredible figures who have made football such a special sport.

Scan the QR code below to leave a quick review!

13

THE SIGNIFICANCE OF PATCHES AND FLAGS

"If you don't perform at a standard higher than everyone else, I will terminate you. No one will ever say, 'He was a Big Ten official because his old man is the boss.'"

— DAVE PARRY, TALKING TO HIS SON, FELLOW
REFEREE JOHN PARRY

Sometimes people forget that the people who participate in a football game—at every level—are more than just officials and athletes who make good money to perform on such a huge stage and let millions of people watch them every single game. Sometimes people forget that underneath the uniforms and beyond the spotlight, fame, and hefty paychecks, these are just ordinary men and women who live normal lives, have regular feelings, and share the same sort of values and dreams and aspirations that we all do.

The story of NFL referee John Parry is a great example of that. His story is in so many ways like the same ones you would hear from your friends or family. In fact, his story might sound a lot like one you have experienced because Parry's story is filled with relatable emotion and hopes and dreams, as well as painful loss and grief and the desire to carry on the memory of someone close to you long after they are gone.

You can imagine that many NFL players and officials get nervous about big games, but you cannot truly understand the pressure and emotions that come with such a major event. Week in and week out, these people participate in something that is seen by millions, sometimes billions, of people. And they do it all while still maintaining composure, staying professional, and also being regular human beings with feelings and personal lives.

John Parry followed in the footsteps of his father. His dad, Dave Parry, officiated many games during his career in the league, and his son was going to do the same. In fact, his father worked his way up, starting small and then eventually being a side judge during the 1983 Super Bowl, a massive honor that he would never forget.

As John came into his own career, he spoke with his father a lot and relied on him for advice and just general support from someone who would totally understand the position he was in. Both father and son Parry would speak twice every weekend of the season, once to go over the game and get advice and then another time to just have a pep talk and feel inspired. It was always a touching, moving, beautiful moment before a dad and his boy.

And then it all changed in 2007, when Dave passed away, leaving a major void in the life of the entire Parry family and especially in John, who was tasked with moving on and carrying his job without the biggest cheerleader and supporter he had ever known. He felt an ache in his heart when he thought of returning to his job and officiating again. But then he thought of ways to keep his dad with him during the game they both loved. His solution to both honor and remember and keep his dad with him was unique and different and led to some touching—and historic—moments for the NFL. It involved patches and flags, and it's a story that doesn't get told enough. But it perfectly sums up the love of a son and his father and their shared value of the game that was so important to them.

A Super Bowl's first points have never come on a safety in more than 40 years, and intentional grounding has never been called in the game, either.

Over the course of the following three hours, Parry called the Giants for holding, only to have Patriots nose tackle Vince Wilfork tell him there had been no infraction; he checked the engine to make sure that New York's Mario

Manningham had both feet inbounds during one catch. Also, he watched the ball elude Wes Welker late in a 17–14 Giants victory.

Parry had a sense of protection, guidance, and assistance throughout the process as he presided over the largest competition of his life.

14

THE FOOTBALLERS BREAKING CURFEW

Max McGee was one of the first NFL heroes to touch the hearts of fans all over the country. Today, not many people know his name, but back in the early days of the NFL, McGee was someone who was a perfect mix of athletic and devilish, someone who was going to do whatever he wanted no matter what he was told but, when push came to shove, would step up for his team and do what was needed.

Here's a fun fact you might not know: Max McGee scored the first ever touchdown in a first ever Super Bowl. That's an amazing feat in and of itself. But the way he did it and the circumstances around it make it even more interesting and exciting.

In Overton, Texas, on July 16, 1932, William Max McGee was born to a family of promising athletic stars. Max was just one of six children—five boys and one girl—and he was the youngest. Growing up in this small neck of the woods in Texas, the McGee boys all ended up being active athletes who participated in football at the local White Oak High School. In the middle to the late 1940s, Coy, Max's older brother, played under coach Frank Leahy at Notre Dame.[1]

For the 1946 Fighting Irish squad, Coy McGee played half-back. At the same time, back at White Oak, Max carried on the McGee heritage of excellent football.[2]

Max ended up being the first high school football star to run for more than 3,000 yards in a single season. In total, young Max gained 3,048 yards by running over as well as through his rivals during his senior year in 1946.

At White Oak, McGee lettered for four years and twice received the All-Texas honor. His outstanding performance throughout his senior year of high school earned him much notice. Sure enough, Max chose Tulane University in New Orleans to pursue his playing career and enhance his skills.

When graduating, McGee had 1,401 career running yards for Tulane, enough for fourth place all-time.[3]

The Packers have experienced financial difficulties despite their early franchise success. McGee was selected with the 51st overall choice in the 1954 draft, and Green Bay was in the midst of a losing skid at the time. Since the Packers claimed the NFL championship in 1944, no season had seen them win more than six games.

1954 was a poor year for McGee as a rookie.

Green Bay struggled to a 4–8 record in his debut season as head coach. One of the few high points that season was McGee. McGee was the NFL's leader in punting yards while also serving as the team's offensive receiver. Additionally, he hauled in 36 passes for 614 yards and 9 touchdowns.

McGee went on a leave of absence from the club prior to the 1955 season to join the Air Force as a pilot. He participated in the military throughout the seasons of 1955 and 1956. The Packers eventually welcomed McGee back in 1957, albeit he didn't quite carry on where he left off.

He caught 17 receptions for 273 yards and a score during the season. McGee continued to do his punting responsibilities while also carrying the ball five times for 40 yards.

Around this time, the Packers decided that something needed to change. The team was tired of losing, and to stop that, they needed to shake things up at the top. That brought them to hiring a new coach: Vince Lombardi, who would, of course, go on to be one of the best and most well-known coaches in the history of the league.

Lombardi wasn't messing around and immediately went to work changing the team, shaping the players, and turning them into the squad they could be. And progress was soon seen: the Packers were able to achieve a 7–5 record in the first season under Lombardi.

Playing for Lombardi was advantageous for McGee as well; a career-high 51 receptions for 883 yards and 7 touchdowns in 1961 after a total of 38 grabs in 1960. With those numbers, McGee was selected for his first and only Pro Bowl.

1962 saw 49 additional receptions for 820 yards and 3 further touchdowns. Despite not scoring in either championship game, McGee led the Packers in catches and receiving yards in both championship seasons.

It was clear to his teammates and coaches at that stage in his career that McGee was a highly skilled player. However, McGee's status on the Packers' roster in his eleventh season was primarily due to his experience. McGee did not make a single start that season due to old age and injury.

Throughout the year, he only managed to catch 4 receptions for 91 yards and a touchdown. During that season, McGee was primarily recognized for his wild behavior with a few of his teammates. And it would be this type of lifestyle that would lead to the most fabled story about McGee, one that would be both humorous and oddly inspiring.

It was January 1967, and football fans were about to experience their first Super Bowl. Nowadays, the Super Bowl is the biggest event of the year and an annual occasion that gets all football fans on their feet and beyond excited. But back in the late 1950s, the idea was certainly exciting but also new and very different. Honestly, people weren't entirely sure *what* to think about the Super Bowl.

Max McGee wasn't sure what to think of it either—and he was playing in the big game! At the time, McGee was an 11-year veteran in the league, and his Packers were about to hopefully win at the very first Super Bowl. But even the biggest game in the season wasn't enough to make McGee stop his wild and crazy and fun ways.

The 34-year-old star didn't get a lot of sleep the night before the game. In fact, some say he didn't get any sleep at all. Instead of staying in his hotel room and getting a good night's rest, McGee was spending the night out with a couple of flight attendants he had met. He was out on the town, enjoying himself in all sorts of surely sordid ways. He knew that he was going to be fined for his activities. Back then, the fine for breaking curfew was $5,000. By today's standards, that would be approximately $48,000. That still didn't stop McGee. Like a kid breaking out of his parent's house after being commanded not to, McGee was going out, and no one was going to stop him.

When his night was done, it was morning. In fact, McGee was spotted entering the hotel lobby at 6:30 in the morning, just hours before the Super Bowl was set to begin.[4]

McGee curled up in bed so he could catch just a little shut-eye, and he was honestly not too worried about being tired because he didn't expect to play much in the game. At that point in his career, McGee expected to be sitting on the bench for the majority of the game, if not the whole thing.

But that wasn't what fate had in mind.

Hours after getting just an hour-long nap, McGee was called upon by Lombardi in the Super Bowl because starting wideout Boyd Dowler re-injured his right shoulder in only the third snap of the game. McGee, the aged and sleepy vet, needed to step up and help his team win.

That's exactly what he did. He would go on to score the first touchdown in Super Bowl history and would catch six more passes for a grand total of 138 yards. His terrific performance helped the Packers win, 35–10, claiming the very first Super Bowl victory in history.

McGee's story is fascinating and fun for several reasons. It's relatable too. While we haven't all experienced all-night benders with flight attendants, all of us *have* shown up for a day of work feeling a bit drained and not prepared for what's ahead. At the end of the day, that's what was going on with McGee, yet he still made the best of it! He was able to step up, dust himself off, achieve his greatness, and help lead his team. That's admirable, and it's no surprise this story has become something of NFL legend.

1. Coy's 1946 Notre Dame team is still considered one of the greatest college football teams of all time.
2. The 3,000-yard mark has since been reached and surpassed 87 times.
3. In that season, Max led the SEC with 125 rushing yards per game.
4. McGee actually passed quarterback Bart Starr in the lobby as Starr was preparing to start his busy, historic day.

THE RISE OF FEMALE AMERICAN FOOTBALL

T he NFL is filled with all sorts of powerful, impressive, athletic men who are constantly battling to reign supreme over the competition. And since its inception, women have sadly not been a huge part of the league.

Yes, there are millions of female NFL fans, but that's really where most of their interaction with the league ends. But that's not to say there aren't so many capable female athletes who would really be able to go toe-to-toe with some of the best men in the league. But for various reasons, the NFL has never integrated and allowed women to play alongside men.

But this doesn't mean that women haven't been playing football. And it also doesn't mean that many of them haven't become masterful with their skills, knowledge, and expertise of the game that so many people love. Yes, women *have* been

484 | ROY LINGSTER

a major part of football; they just aren't as celebrated as they should be.

The truth is that women have been making an impressive mark on the field, going so far as to leading England to win the Euro Championships recently. In fact, across the Atlantic Ocean, women have been trying to enter the world of American football for nearly a century. While they haven't ultimately achieved that goal, their efforts have not gone unnoticed by some of the most important and knowledgeable football fans.

The earliest example of a woman playing professional football would be Patricia Palinkas, who made her debut on August 15, 1970. It was all bad luck—and good fortune—that allowed Palinkas to play the game. She was actually acting as a holder for her husband on the Orlando Panthers in the minor league Atlantic Coast Football League. In total, she played two games in the preseason but then left after her husband Steve was ultimately cut from the team.

If we are talking about the first woman to score points in a men's football game, we have to talk about Abby Vestal. Vestal kicked 3 out of 4 extra points on April 23, 2007, for the Kansas Koyotes, part of the indoor American Professional Football League, as a high school senior. Vestal's feat attracted a lot of attention in the media, even getting stories on ESPN and other sports networks and websites. She would later attempt to find success playing football in college, but she was cut from her team after just the fourth game at university. But it doesn't matter because she would later go on to try her hand at football for the women's tackle team, the Kansas City Storm, and then she would later find great success playing rugby.

Katie Hnida was a placekicker for the Fort Wayne Fire-Hawks in 2010 and played three games.[1] Julie Harshbarger was the first woman to score a field goal in a men's professional football game when she played for the Chicago Cardinals in 2010. Jennifer Welter, meanwhile, was the first female to play in a non-kicking or skill position when she was running back for the Texas Revolution of the Indoor Football League in 2014.[2] She would also go on to become the first female NFL coach as an intern with the Arizona Cardinals.

As you can see, plenty of women have broken the glass ceiling when it comes to playing on the field alongside other men in football. But they have yet to break that ultimate top and play in the NFL. But with so many women making such giant leaps and bounds, it feels like it's only a matter of time before a woman is in the NFL, even if for just a brief amount of time.

There were other women throughout the history of the game that had a huge impact on what would come later. For example, let's talk about Susan Tose Spencer.

Tose Spencer wasn't someone who played football, but she ultimately changed it forever. In 1983, she was hired as the

Eagles' general manager and was tasked with the major goal of rebuilding a franchise just three years after its first Super Bowl appearance.

The Eagles were gaining an awful lot of attention when Tose Spencer was hired due to the acquisition of Randall Cunningham, a younger player who was dubbed "The Ultimate Weapon." Tose Spencer knew that a lot was riding on Cunningham and, therefore, the entire team. This player had the ability to turn around the direction of the team and make it one of the best in the entire NFL.

Susan's father, Leonard Tose, was one of the most popular owners in the history of the Eagles. Not only did he help the team achieve new greatness, but Tose was also a member of the Philadelphia community and helped the city in many ways, including contributing a lot of money to the Ronald McDonald House.

When Susan took over, she was in charge of negotiating contracts with players like Cunningham and Ron Jaworski. She also oversaw the NFL Draft for three seasons with her team and focused on recruiting brand-new rookies who could beef up the team and the bench. Not only was her hiring a historic moment in the history of the NFL, but it also worked wonders for the team, who found great success with some of the new players she signed

Yes, some women have played football, and some have even run teams, but did you know that females have also officiated games too? And, honestly, there might not be a more important job than being a ref. The fate of teams and entire seasons ride on the shoulders of referees.

Sarah Thomas was the first female to officiate a college football game as part of the Memphis-Jacksonville crew.[3] After that, in 2013, Thomas was among twenty-one finalists in the NFL's officiating development program. Then in 2015, she became the first female hired as a full-time official for the NFL. Flash forward to 2019, and Thomas became the first female on-field official in playoff history during the Divisional Round game between the Chargers and the Patriots. And in 2021, she was the first woman to officiate a Super Bowl.

Of course, Thomas was honored by all this, but it was made even more special by the fact that her family had accompanied her to the big game. After Super Bowl 55, Thomas said, "I often say being the first in any of this is not what I set out to do, but being a mom first is what I am to do. So having them there and to share this with me, it was just unbelievable."

There was a time when women were only brought into football games as halftime entertainment.[4] They were never seen as possible players or people who could do more than make the audience dance, clap, and have fun. But the truth is that women have been an important part of the game for decades now. In 1999, the Women's Professional Football League was founded, and in the last few decades, female players have found fame and fortune in football leagues all over the world, specifically in the UK. It is a shame that women have not been able to really make their way into the NFL, but they are impacting the game in so many other ways. The glass ceiling has been broken, and there is no doubt that it will be broken again and again.

1. Hnida later played for the Colorado Cobras and the KC Mustangs.
2. Welter would coach inside linebackers at training camp and during the preseason.
3. Thomas got her start officiating grade school football games, followed by high school games after that.
4. This was first noted during the Frankford Yellow Jackets games back in 1926 when the team hired women to perform during the halftime show.

FROM GROCERY STORE WORKER TO MVP

> *"If you're willing to put yourself and your dreams on the line, at the very least you'll discover an inner strength you may not have known existed."*
>
> — KURT WARNER

No one starts at the top. No matter if you're talking about football players, basketball players, actors, musicians, tech billionaires, or high-end chefs—no one begins their career at the peak of their abilities and success.

Now, it is true that some people don't have to fight as hard as others. Some are born into families that already have proven success, some people know the right connections, and others just have wonderful luck and seemingly sail through life. Then others have to struggle, fight, scratch and claw to make it. And even after years of battling and putting their all into their efforts, they still sometimes don't make it.

But sometimes they do. Sometimes the people who never give up and never lose faith and never stop rooting themselves on are the ones who make the biggest splash, find the biggest success, and inspire the most people. When that happens, it doesn't matter which team you root for or which sport you watch; you'll still be excited to see them achieve so much and make their dreams come true.

One person who was able to do more than most people ever imagined was Kurt Warner. He started out small, without a lot of faith and belief from the powers that be and was able to turn his enthusiasm and faith into success in the NFL. And his success wasn't small or brief; it was truly unparalleled for many reasons.

Warner was the sort of young man who had loved football from an early age. Ever since he was a kid, he was someone who was devoted to the sport, followed it religiously, and saw himself one day playing it professionally. But he was a realist and understood that achieving that goal wouldn't come easy. He'd have to fight for it. He'd have to pour his heart into it.

Luckily for Kurt Warner, heart was something he had a lot of.

Although he loved the game and played it constantly, certain people didn't see Warner as the next big thing. When he tried out for college ball, he wasn't awarded a scholarship, and he didn't even become a starter for his team until his final year of school.[1]

Following his five years in university, Warner tried out for the Green Bay Packers in 1994, but that audition didn't go well, and he wasn't given a spot on the team. Instead of playing in the NFL, Warner signed with the Arena Football League and put his time and energy into the Iowa Barnstormers from 1995 to 1997.

During this time, Warner had trouble making ends meet, but he didn't want to give up on his dream of playing professional football. He sucked up his pride and took a job being a grocery store bagger, earning $5.50 an hour. It wasn't the most glamorous work, and it would be a low point in the life of many. But Warner never gave up on his belief in himself. Instead of sinking into despair and losing faith, Warner just spent his time wisely: he would work at the grocery store to earn an income and then hit the gym often, perfect his game, and continue to push himself and build a future in the NFL.

He would eventually strike a deal with the NFL, but not in the way he imagined. He signed with the St. Louis Rams in 1997 but was instead shipped off to play for the Amsterdam Admirals as part of NFL Europe.

Although he wasn't playing in the American league, Warner didn't let this time go to waste. It was then that he started to prove what he was really worth and what he was capable of.

While playing for the Admirals, Warner started in all ten games and led the league in passing with 2,101 yards.

This was enough to finally get the recognition and notice he had been fighting for, and the NFL finally came knocking at his door as he had always wanted. In the 1998 NFL season, Warner was called up by St. Louis and spent the year serving as the team's backup quarterback, appearing in only one game during the 4–12 campaign. He was eager for more, ready to prove himself and wanting to really have an impact on his team. He would get it; he just had to wait for one more season.

In the 1999 preseason, when starting quarterback Trent Green suffered a knee injury, Warner took over as the team's starter and guided the Rams to an improbable comeback. With the leadership of Warner, the Rams won thirteen games that season, the second-highest single-season victory increase in league history. Warner was a force to be reckoned with straight out of the gate, topping the NFL in pass completion percent, touchdowns thrown and passing rating.

The Rams progressed to a spot in the Super Bowl the following January, and Warner was awarded the NFL's MVP. There, the Rams defeated the Tennessee Titans 23–16 to win the franchise's first Super Bowl championship, And Warner, who just a few years before was working in a store, was voted the game's MVP after throwing for a Super Bowl record 414 yards.

This was the sort of underdog story that everyone loves but also one that few people ever really see. Even the best Hollywood writer would have assumed a tale like this couldn't be believed. But it *was* real, and Warner *was* doing it. Even if he never experienced success like that ever again, he had created a story that was improbable and truly astonishing.

Sure enough, the road ahead for Warner was complicated, to put it gently. In the year 2000, Warner took the Rams back to the playoffs, but they were eliminated in the first round this time. The 14–2 Rams entered Super Bowl XXXVI as heavy favorites but were upset by the 14-point underdog New England Patriots. Warner won his second MVP award that year after leading the NFL in all significant throwing statistics.

Then, things got a little tough for Warner, and he was unproductive during his little time on the field in 2002 due to an injury that kept him out of all but seven games. Warner was demoted to a backup position for the rest of the season in 2003 after a dismal opening game in which he fumbled six times. He played with the New York Giants for one forgettable season after being dismissed by the Rams at the end of the year.

It seemed as if his career was coming to an end, but Warner had a few more tricks up his sleeves. In 2005, he signed with the Arizona Cardinals, and his career surged back to life. In 2008, he started in all sixteen games for Arizona and was named to his fourth career Pro Bowl.[2] He even led his Cardinals to the Super Bowl, although the team was beaten in a close loss to the Pittsburgh Steelers.[3]

In the following year, Warner decided to retire from professional sports, and he was able to look back at his career with pride and true awe at all he had achieved. He had really risen from blue collar to NFL champion in a matter of years. And while many people helped him get there via their support, it was all Warner's doing that got him to that point.

For his efforts and skill, Warner was inducted into the Pro Football Hall of Fame in 2017. To this day, people speak of Warner as an example of how hard work, skill, and determination can pay off. Kurt Warner never stopped believing in himself, leading him to the highest ranks of the NFL.

---

1. Warner was unable to get a scholarship to a Division I-A school.
2. He at first started just over half the team's games in his first three seasons in Arizona.
3. In 2008, Warner threw for more than 4,000 yards for the first time since 2001.

17

THE ONLY NFL PLAYER TO RECOVER FROM THREE ACL INJURIES

You might have heard of athletes suffering from a "torn ACL," but you might not know what exactly that condition means or why it's so damaging, painful, and dangerous.

Indeed, if you hear that your favorite athlete has torn his or her ACL, you should be very concerned. Because it won't just end a season, it can end an entire career.

The ACL is really a set of tendons and ligaments that help stabilize and support the knee joint with every single movement and step taken. Everyone who walks uses the ACL. Just walking up the stairs requires the ACL, as do driving a car or walking around the block. Of course, athletes need the ACL more than anyone else. Figure skaters, tennis players, basketball stars, baseball icons, and, of course, football players need the ACL to function.

People experience an ACL tear when the anterior cruciate ligament becomes partially or completely ruptured. What makes an ACL tear so terrifying is the fact that once torn, an ACL cannot regrow or heal on its own. Surgery and serious rehabilitation are needed for the person to recover fully.

Now, some well-known athletes have been able to overcome an ACL injury. Rob Gronkowski, Adrian Peterson, and even Tom Brady have felt the pain and heartbreak of an ACL tear but have still returned to the field and have experienced great success. But the truth is that half of all people never come back and never play as they once did. NFL star Teddy Bridgewater comes to mind. After he suffered from his ACL tear, he was never the same, and his career ultimately ended because of it.

The treatment for an ACL tear is long, painful, and not always effective. It requires an in-depth, complex surgery, followed by months—if not years—of recovery. During that time, the athlete needs a lot of rest and healing. That means they cannot practice; they cannot work on their game or return to the court or field to even practice jogging or move-ment beyond a slow walk.

When they *do* get back to playing—if they ever do—they will usually not be able to achieve the same amount of speed, drive and power. To make matters even worse, athletes who suffer ACL tears often experience them again. But it's not often that someone experiences not one, not two, but *three* ACL injuries.

That is exactly what happened to Thomas Davis, if you can believe it. The former football star suffered a fate feared by so many athletes three different times, but he came back every single time, not content to giving up on his dreams.

Right from the beginning of his life, Thomas wanted to play. Davis always had a natural affinity for sports and all different kinds of them. He excelled in baseball, basketball, running, and football by the time he reached high school. His skills were getting noticed, and he received some media notice on a national scale before graduating, with scouts praising his commitment to strenuous exercise. However, because of how tiny his Georgia school was, he was unable to draw too many people's attention to himself. As a result, he only received one Division I offer.

But he was ready for that challenge and ready to prove himself. He accepted the offer, joining the Georgia Bulldogs in 2002. He made himself at home here as a rushing line-backer. In his three seasons, he made 272 tackles. Since the NFL was already aware of Davis' skills at this point, he made the decision to forego his senior year and enter the 2005 NFL Draft instead. It was a wise decision. He was selected by the Panthers in the first round.[1]

Davis began training camp as a safety but immediately switched back to linebacker. He rapidly made a name for himself by collecting significant tackles and sacks, including one of Tom Brady. Above all, he maintained his health. But in 2009, that all changed in a heartbreaking way.

The first tear was the most sudden and surprising. Davis tore his ACL during a losing effort versus the New Orleans Saints. Understandably, he was finished for the year after just seven starts as all of his attention needed to be focused on rehabilitation. Davis' recuperation was indeed his life now, as it often is after an injury. It went well . . . at least for a while. When he returned to training camp in 2010, it appeared as though he was a player who never missed a beat. But then bad fortune struck again, and a second injury emerged. He had another ACL injury in June and was out for the whole 2010 campaign.

Most stars wouldn't get another chance at a career in the big leagues after two ACL injuries. But Thomas Davis wasn't like most stars. The Panthers' management knew what Davis was capable of for the 2011 season. They were certain he would work hard as long as he appeared healthy. He successfully completed training camp and the first week of play with no problems. He then suffered his third ACL tear after falling into a group of teammates during his second start.

At this time, a lot of clubs would let a player go. But Davis demonstrated that he was just a different sort of player with his attitude and on-field performance. He had all the opportunities he required. Despite these three terrible wounds, his body survived.

According to ESPN, Davis now has a patchwork of surgically rearranged tendons from his hamstring and other knee tissue where his ACL should be. He attends routine acupuncture sessions to reduce local inflammation. He even has a hyperbaric chamber at home to maintain high blood oxygen levels.

When Davis came back in 2012, he was positioned as a backup linebacker. He regained his starting place toward the conclusion of that season. He is currently regarded as one of the greatest linebackers in Panthers history.

For his part, Davis credits two parties with helping him recover from his lengthy list of ACL injuries. He thanks the doctors and incredible medical team that helped mend his body, and he thanks his wife, who helped mend his heart and soul.[2] He knows that without those people, he would never be able to walk back onto the field and achieve greatness.

Thomas Davis might not be a household name, but for those who really know the NFL and understand the heart and soul of a player and what it takes to really secure a place in the league, Davis is a stunning example of never giving up.

1. He was the fourteenth overall pick.
2. Davis admits that he thought his career was over at certain points, but his wife convinced him otherwise: "[My wife] said, 'Well, you have to go through the surgery anyway to fix your knee. You have to go through the rehab process anyway. Why not do it in a way to potentially come back and play and see what happens?'"

18

MENTAL HEALTH IMPACTS EVEN THE STRONGEST

F ootball players are often, rightfully, seen as very strong people.

There are many reasons for this, but you get a lot of evidence of their strength just by looking at them. The vast majority of football stars are built with optimal physical presence and intimidating size, speed and power. They are able to push themselves through an entire group of people their same size —sometimes seeming easy.

Football players are definitely strong, and this is because of a resilient and devoted dedication to living and breathing the game they love so much. Football pros are driven, unlike few others. They aren't just looking to play football; they are looking to *live* it. This impacts every aspect of their lives and every part of the way they play the game.

But the NFL suffers from an issue that infects and impacts, and often destroys the lives of millions of people all over the world. The NFL has come to terms with the fact that mental health issues are a major thing many of its members have to deal with. And the league is doing more than ever before to address mental health problems. This is the right thing to do and a sign that even the strongest people in the world suffer from mental health issues. There is no shame in this, and it is not something that people should keep to themselves or hide or feel embarrassed about.

The NFL was driven to tackle mental health problems and make a difference not only because it's the right thing to do but also because it directly affected the league in some major, heartbreaking, shocking ways.

Today, more mental health resources are available to NFL players, such as mental health training, social workers, and free 24/7 hotlines with trained counselors. This is a huge step forward and an important way to help the people in the league and reach out and touch the hearts and minds of millions more.

O.J. Murdock was one of the most promising young football players in 2012 and, despite a lot of rough patches in his life, things were turning around for him. A graduate of Middleton High School in Tampa, Florida and then Fort Hays State in Kansas, Murdock could seemingly do it all.

Even though O.J.'s initial interest was football, his coach encouraged him to try track in seventh grade after noticing his speed in physical education and believing he might excel there. He was advised to attempt the 100 and 200 meters as he had asthma and had trouble running 400 meters. And with that choice, an athlete was born.[1]

Murdock was selected by the Tampa Tribune as their high school male athlete of the year in 2005 while a senior at Middleton. At the Class 3A state track meet, Murdock took first place in the 100 and 200 meters. He also caught 57 passes for 927 yards and 11 touchdowns in football. He was ranked as the tenth best wide receiver in the nation by Rivals.com.

However, Murdock's post-high school career didn't quite go as planned. Murdock embraced a football scholarship to South Carolina after receiving interest from several Division I schools. He played there for just four games before being charged with shoplifting and suspended from the team in October 2006. He was accused of stealing $425.50 worth of clothing from a Tampa department store. Murdock subsequently changed schools to Poplarville, Mississippi's Pearl River Community College, but he injured his collarbone. He was given a scholarship by Marshall, but he didn't have the necessary grades.

Murdock then left and headed back to Tampa, feeling a little down. O.J.'s mother, Jamesena Murdock, said it was a sad moment for her son.[2]

At Fort Hays State, Murdock eventually revitalized his career. Murdock caught 60 catches for 1,290 yards and 12 touchdowns as a senior in 2010, and his performance earned him a spot in the East-West All-Star Game against largely Division 1 players. A surprise invitation to the NFL Scouting Combine in Indianapolis in February 2011 also arrived in his inbox.

Murdock's experiences at the Combine and the pro day served as reminders of how his football career had changed. Murdock was not selected by a club in the 2011 NFL Draft, but the Titans gave the young, driven receiver a chance by signing him as a free agent. Then, on the second day of training camp, Murdock tore his Achilles tendon, ending his season just when it appeared like his career had taken a promising turn.

Murdock would fall into a deep depression that would lead him down a dark, dangerous path. He was still eager to play and believed in himself, but he was losing faith in his future and his chances of making good on all his promises. He pulled away, didn't speak as much with friends and family, and seemed more despondent.

Murdock would eventually take his own life, shattering those close to him and shaking up the NFL and reminding the league that something needs to be done about the mental health of its players. O.J.'s passing marked the sixth suicide in the last two years, spawning a major drive inside the league to address this issue as best it could.

Because of Murdock's passing and the suicides of others, the NFL started "It Takes All of Us," a drive to destigmatize those seeking mental health help and assistance.[3] Via PSAs, outreach to local communities, and players within the NFL, the league started making an impact on others and proving that talking about depression, anxiety, and other mental health issues isn't a bad thing. Saying that you're not okay doesn't show weakness. In fact, it shows strength.

The truth is that mental health should never be ignored. With proper outreach, care, and openness, the deaths of Murdock and others could have been avoided. The NFL made a huge step forward when it decided to talk about these things. It was a move that went beyond sports.

———————————

1. Murdock qualified for the national Junior Olympics as an eighth grader.
2. His mom would say that Murdock would spend a lot of time in his room. "He was in the dungeon," she said.
3. Some stars who filmed videos for "It Takes All of Us" include Michael Robinson, D.J. Chark Jr., Solomon Thomas, and Joey Bosa.

19

NFL'S HIGHEST SCORING GAME

"When you lose, talk little. When you win, talk less."

— TOM BRADY

While football might be one of the most exciting and engaging sports in existence, it isn't always the most high-scoring one. In fact, certain football games pale in comparison to other sports, such as basketball.

When it comes to football, a game is won by both defense and offense. That means there will be games where teams don't score an awful lot and even don't make it past the threshold of 20 points. This doesn't mean it's a bad team or bad game; it means it's one filled with intense defensive skill.

Football fans know this. They don't expect high-scoring games. Instead, they expect and want a showdown between two teams who are going to give it all they've got, press their opponents, and don't go easy on them. There is a lot of intensity in a game with great defense, which makes for a lot of excitement.

However, there *are* games when football teams are able to drive up the scoreboard and really light up their opponents. Twenty points might just be a drop in the bucket for certain teams when they are really performing at their peak ability and are able to overcome an opponent's defense.

But what happens when two teams are playing against each other and just keep racking up the points? Well, then fans are treated to something truly special—and very rare. That's when football teams are able to end games with a combined point total that is downright jaw-dropping.

As mentioned, it doesn't happen often, but some of the most impressive football games in history are some of the most high scoring too. For a number of reasons, these games broke the mold and set records that are still unbroken to this day.

All the way back in 1963, the Raiders and Oilers did something that had never been accomplished before. They were the first teams in history to pass a combined score of 100, racking up 101 with Oakland claiming 52 and Houston getting 49. Many years later, the Saints and Giants would match that in 2015. After that, the Rams and Chiefs would surpass them all when they scored 105 in 2018, which was just shy of the Bengals and Browns' combined score of 106 from 2004.

But if you want to talk about the highest-scoring football game of all time, you can't beat the November 1966 match between the Redskins and Giants. The final combined score would be 113 points, with the Redskins totaling 72 and the Giants ending with 41.[1] Ironically, the Giants were also famous for playing in the 1943 game against the Bears, which was the only to end with a 0–0 score.[2]

Games like these really aren't common, but when they happen, they are quite amazing. The games aren't any longer and still consist of four quarters of 15 minutes each. That means that both teams can pack in a lot of points in a limited amount of time. For fans of football, games like this are what make memories that will last a lifetime. Anyone watching these matchups in person knows they are seeing something special, something historic, something that may never be surpassed.

It's been some time since an NFL game has reached the heights of the ones listed above. But just wait, another 100-point game is surely on the horizon, and NFL fans will be wowed when it comes around.

1. The Redskins were able to rack up an astonishing 5 touchdowns in the first half of the game.
2. The Lions' kicker, Augie Lo, missed 3 field goal attempts that day from 32, 40, and 15 yards.

WHEN YOUR TEAM WINS IN THE LAST SECONDS, BUT THE TV CUTS THE FINAL

"When the Jets played the Raiders, it wasn't a rivalry. It was war!"

— FRANK RAMOS

Imagine this: your favorite team is playing against one of its biggest rivalries. There is a lot on the line here: you want your squad to reign supreme, not only because it will help their record and give them a better chance of winning the Super Bowl but also because it will feel ultra-nice to watch them rub it in the face of their opponents.

You turn on your TV and tune into the game, expecting nothing but explosive fireworks and a matchup that you won't soon forget. Sure enough, the game is wildly intense and both teams are giving it all they've got. The clock is ticking down and your team is up by a few points. It's a close game but, with just over a minute to go, it looks like your crew is going to secure the victory.

Then, the channel suddenly switches over to a different show. The game still had a minute to play, but your local network isn't showing it. Sure, your team was up by a few points, but a lot can happen in just seconds in football. You have no way to watch the game, no way to know who has won.

And then you find out the ultimate nightmare scenario: your team actually gave up the lead and lost in the final seconds of the game, and you couldn't catch a glimpse of it because of the network that decided to stick to a strict schedule.

That sounds horrible, doesn't it? But don't worry, it cannot happen like that anymore. That's because it *did* happen once —and it was something that angered NFL fans all over the country.

In 1968, the Raiders thought they were going to win it all. They expected to be named AFL Champions at the end of the year, thanks to the hard work and leadership of head coach John Rauch. Just one year before, the Raiders had the best season in their history, achieving a 13–1 record to qualify for the postseason play for the first time.[1]

With Daryle "Mad Bomber" Lamonica leading the way, the Raiders were the epitome of the AFL style of play. He had thrown for over 3,000 yards and 30 touchdowns in 1967 and was well on his way to another 3,000 in '68. Meanwhile, the Jets were coached by Weeb Eubanks, who had never made a postseason in his career. But the Jets had someone special: NFL superstar Joe Namath, who had thrown over 4,000 yards in the year before.

Prior to their 1968 matchup, the two teams had faced off sixteen times, with the Jets holding an 8–6–2 series advantage and the Raiders holding a 3–1–2 advantage in the past six encounters. In their first of two regular-season encounters the year before, the Jets handed the Raiders their lone defeat of the year. The two teams later faced off in one of the most brutal games in AFL history. The Raider defense had viciously attacked Namath in brutal, somewhat questionable ways that didn't sit right with many fans. In that game, a rivalry was born, and people supporting both teams were eager for a follow-up matchup. The late-season encounter would serve as a rematch between the two sides, who had become clearly envious of one another and were the two best teams in the AFL with two of its most entertaining players.[2]

The game was aired nationally on NBC and began, as with most West Coast day games, at 1 PM local time, 4 PM Eastern. The network had been pushing their special Sunday evening screening of the film Heidi for 7 PM that evening, interrupting its regular Sunday night programming in the hopes that viewers would be glued to the game by the time the film began. It was customary for football broadcasts at the time to cut away, so the finish of the Bills-Chargers game was abruptly ended to air the start of the Raiders-Jets game.

Right off the bat, the Raiders-Jets game was intense, and the bad blood was evident. The Jets got an early 6–0 lead after two field goal drives, but both sides were competitive and fierce, and the Raiders had a 14–12 advantage going into halftime.

The game kept chugging along, but it will always be remembered for the exciting, one-of-a-kind fourth quarter. In the final minutes of the game, the Jets had a 32–29 lead. Fans at home were getting anxious, knowing that the game was going to run over its scheduled time. There was a growing fear that NBC would cut away from the riveting end of the game to start their showing of Heidi. Surely, the network wouldn't do that, right?

Millions of people called in to NBC to inquire about the plans and make sure that NBC wouldn't cut away, as was usually the case. The top brass at the network actually did decide to stick with the game, even if it ran past 7 PM. However, in an ironic twist, so many fans were calling the channel that the phone lines were jammed and executives at the company weren't able to communicate with the production staff and relay their command.

So, when 7 PM rolled around, with just one minute left in the game, NBC switched over from the game to Heidi. And fans all over the country were outraged. In that one minute, they missed the Raiders coming from behind and claiming a 43–32 victory over the Jets.[3]

This would forever be known as the "Heidi Game," and it was an embarrassing moment for NBC and an episode of pure outrage for the fans of the NFL.[4] The network would apologize for the move, even though they actually broadcast the final score just moments into their broadcast of Heidi. The channel leaned into the event and even advertised the following game with an image of Joe Namath and the actress who played Heidi on his shoulders.

The channel also made something called a "Heidi phone," a hotline connected directly to the heart center of NBC that could be used no matter if the switchboards were lighting up. It allowed executives and top NBC brass to communicate with the channel—no matter what. Future television contracts also obligated that networks show the entire games to completion, meaning that an incident like the "Heidi Game" would never happen again.

---

1. The Raiders also defeated Houston, winning the AFL Championship Game.
2. Both teams had a 7–2 record entering the game, showing just how equal they were in terms of talent.
3. The Jets, powered by Namath, would later win that Super Bowl that year, getting the last laugh over the powerful Raiders.
4. Said sportswriter Jack Clary: "Short of pre-empting Heidi for a skin flick, NBC could not have alienated more viewers that evening."

A HERO ON THE FIELD AND FOR HIS COUNTRY

" *"To err on the side of passion is human and right and the only way I'll live."*

— PAT TILLMAN

I t's not common for a sports star to rise above all of that and become something more. There is great honor in being a professional athlete, but what if someone who achieves fame in that way is also able to do more for him or herself, their country, their people, and their beliefs? That is a glory and honor that is far more admirable, long-lasting, and life changing.

The name Pat Tillman is one often spoken of when you look back on the history of football. There is a good reason for that. Not only was Tillman a very talented, promising, accomplished young football star, but he was also someone who transcended the game at a very pivotal, troubling, and consequential time in American history. Through his life and shocking death, fans of football learned a lot about the man and the international conflict that took his life.

Years later, Tillman is still seen as one of the most important figures in the history of the game but not just because of the way he played on the field but also what he did when he was outside of the arena and out of his uniform.

On November 6, 1976, Patrick Tillman was born in San Jose, California. Right away, Tillman and his family knew that he had some special talents that could take him far. He was a great athlete and the eldest of three athletic brothers. In his early schooling years, Tillman guided his high school's football team to the Central Coast Division I Football Championship. He was quickly awarded a scholarship to Arizona State University as a consequence.

Tillman achieved an undefeated regular season while still in college, winning 1997 Most Valuable Player of the Year honors. Following that huge accomplishment, Pat was selected by the Arizona Cardinals in the NFL Draft in 1998, and two years later, he set the franchise record for most tackles. Tillman quickly established himself as a beloved starter. He was not only one of the best players on the Arizona roster but quickly became one of the favorite players in the league and one to watch.

He, however, experienced a complete turnaround after seeing the 9/11 terrorist assaults on American soil unfold live on television.[1] In May 2002, Tillman famously declined a three-year, $3.6 million deal with the Cardinals in favor of enlisting in the American Army.

Tillman's choice to join the American military garnered a lot of headlines, especially at the time when the entire country was still in shock over the attacks and patriotism and the calls for revenge were at all-time highs. Seeing someone who had so much success and fame put it all on the line to serve his country was the personification of true patriotism and love of country. Tillman immediately became a hero to millions of Americans from coast to coast.

Tillman decided to become an Army Ranger, and he fought hard to qualify for that position. Army Rangers are elite troops who excel in collaborative special operations missions, and Pat and his brother Kevin prepared toward becoming that well-regarded, respected ranking. They subsequently joined the Fort Lewis, Washington-based 2nd Battalion of the 75th Ranger Regiment. Then, they were sent to Iraq in 2003.

However, Pat Tillman was notable for opposing the Iraq War.[2] He was ready to go to Afghanistan, where the first war effort had started after September 11th, but he was disappointed to learn that another nation was now the main focus. He didn't understand why he was being sent to Iraq when the perpetrators behind the 9/11 attacks were hiding in Afghanistan.

After fighting hard in the war and leading his group of loyal soldiers, disaster struck and changed the Tillman family forever. Pat was killed in battle on April 22, 2005. Tillman's untimely death at the age of 27 occurred in Afghanistan on his second tour, and it was a huge shock to the country and created numerous headlines, followed by outrage, controversy, and conspiracy.

According to the first reports, Tillman was ambushed in the Khost Province in southeast Afghanistan and was slain by enemy fire. It was revealed to Tillman's family and the American public that he had gallantly hurried up a hill to drive the enemy back while also rescuing hundreds of his fellow soldiers. Tillman was immediately hailed as a hero.

Senior officers were stating that the 27-year-old should be awarded the Silver Star and the Purple Heart not long after he passed away. On May 3, 2004, he was soon remembered in a memorial ceremony that was broadcast nationwide. Senator John McCain, a POW and war hero himself, gave the eulogy for Tillman there.

A month or so after Pat Tillman's passing, the Army made a startling disclosure. Tillman was shot down by his fellow troops and was not murdered by rebels.

Although the gunshot was later deemed to be an accident, some others are not so sure. Contrary to the Army's first account of the incident, Tillman was not only shot three times in his head, but he was also hit at close distance, and there wasn't any sign of hostile fire nearby.

When Army physicians inspected Tillman's body, it was disclosed in 2007 that they were "suspicious" of the gunshot wounds on his skull. Since "the medical evidence did not match up with the scenario as described," they even attempted—and eventually failed—to persuade officials to look into the death as a possible crime.

According to the physicians, Tillman was about 10 yards away when he was killed by an American M-16 weapon. But notwithstanding the report's troubling revelations, it was reportedly buried and not made public for years.

Strangely, it was also found that Tillman's personal belongings, notably his uniform and private notebooks, had been set on fire. Additionally, individuals who saw his death were instructed to remain silent about what truly transpired.

As it happened, Pat Tillman's brother Kevin was also out that day on an assignment. Kevin, however, was absent when Pat was slain. Clearly, it was necessary to keep the secret from him as well. Kevin originally didn't know about Pat Tillman's passing, just like his mother. They believed they were missing out on information even after it was revealed that friendly fire had occurred.

In search of answers, Tillman's mother spent years battling through several inquiries and Committee investigations in order to piece together the entire case. She was also outraged by how much Army propaganda had distorted the facts around her son's demise.[3]

Pat Tillman initially gave off the impression of becoming the face of all of America's Middle East wars. Tillman, a well-groomed all-American superstar, had transitioned from being a sports figure to a hero in battle.

But the truth was more nuanced. Tillman was unusually unconventional for a military soldier, being an atheist anti-war who swiftly lost faith in the War on Terror. Additionally, he wasn't afraid to express his opinions to other soldiers while serving in Afghanistan.

To this day, people still have many theories about the death of Pat Tillman. He was an outspoken critic of the war and was becoming only more disillusioned by the conflict in Iraq. He was a young man with stark opinions and a huge spotlight to spread them. His death and the circumstances around it were suspicious, and some suspected even criminal. You can understand why people think something sinister happened in the desert that day.

But Pat Tillman was more than just a headline. He was a strong-willed, dedicated, principled young man who was about to embark on a career that would earn him millions and give him a truly comfortable and blessed life. But Tillman didn't choose to follow that path. Instead, he decided to follow a hard route and do what he thought was best for him and his country. This would ultimately lead to his passing and the legacy we speak of today.

When you speak of the life of Pat Tillman, you have to talk about his career in the NFL and all he did as a football player. But you also must mention the life he lived, the sacrifice he made, and the hard fighting of his family to know the truth.

---

1. He would later say, "My great grandfather was at Pearl Harbor, and a lot of my familyhas . . . fought in wars, and I really haven't done a damn thing as far as laying myself on the line like that."
2. At the time the rescue of fellow soldier Jessica Lynch was happening, Tillman described the military's elaborate tale as "a big public relations stunt."
3. "They had no regard for him as a person," Mary Tillman said. "He'd hate to be used for a lie."

22

SUPER BOWL'S MOST HORRIFIC INJURY

S ports are not easy.

There are plenty of sports in the world—from soccer to basketball to tennis to track and field and, yes, football—and few of them are easy. They require the athletes involved to push themselves to the limit and go above and beyond what they think possible in order to achieve their goals and secure victory for their teams.

Yes, it's hard work. Few things require as much from someone as sports. You do not only have to be mentally tuned in and quick and healthy, but you also need to have a body that is in near-perfect shape. But even if you train every day for hours on end and have your body looking, feeling, and working better than it ever has, there is still the risk that disaster awaits you on the field.

The honest and painful truth is that sports can lead to some serious injuries. Again and again, throughout the years, even the most well-trained and healthy stars have been sidelined by awful, sometimes gruesome injuries that have at times ended seasons and, sadly, ended careers too. Some of the mishaps on the gridiron are almost too painful to think about, but they need to be addressed, not only to know the history of the NFL but also to understand and respect the hard work and drive of the men who suffered them.

Be forewarned, some of these injuries aren't easy to even think about. But, sports aren't always for the squeamish.

The human body just isn't designed to take so many knocks at such a high impact speed. In the game of football, two fully grown men are running at each other at high speed. You don't have to be a rocket scientist to understand that it could end in disaster. Take Destry Wright, for example. Wright "officially" spent one season with the Pittsburgh Steelers as an undrafted free agent, but he was unable to participate in any regular-season contests because of an injury sustained on July 30, 2000, during a preseason game against the Dallas Cowboys, in which Wright fractured his right leg and dislocated his right ankle. Wright's feet were seen pointing in various directions in an on-field shot that was published, drawing attention to the injury.[1]

You may have seen the Wright injury in photos over the years. You'll know you have because of the intense, stomach-churning feeling you immediately had upon seeing it. It's not for the faint of heart and proof that football can be a painful and rough sport.

Some players, such as Terrell Owens and Jack Youngblood, have actually continued to play *with* broken bones. After breaking his leg in 2004, Terrell Owens missed the final two games of the regular season, but he was able to make a miraculous recovery in time to play for the Eagles in Super Bowl XXXIX.

Although the Eagles lost the game, T.O. Owens caught 9 catches for 122 yards, and after that performance, there is no doubt about T.O.'s tenacity.

Meanwhile, throughout his expansive NFL career, Youngblood skipped only one game. That game wasn't played after the Hall of Fame linebacker shattered his leg, contrary to what you might have assumed. Youngblood suffered a broken leg during the divisional round of the 1979 playoffs against the Cowboys, but instead of sitting out the remaining games, he made a comeback and went on to play in the Super Bowl.

Youngblood played the whole game with a fractured leg even though the Rams would ultimately lose the Super Bowl to the Steelers.

But they never had it as bad as those who have had actual physical parts of their body removed. That's what happened with Chris Simms and Ronnie Lott. Simms' story is something completely different and unique. He had his spleen removed after the Bucs' 2006 loss to the Carolina Panthers. But before he did that, he rejoined his crew on the field after having already left early.

Simms took many heavy blows during the game, rupturing his spleen and breaking some of his ribs. Simms recovered to give his side the lead, but the Bucs defense allowed it to slip away late. All that work—and a spleen—for nothing.

Then there is Ronnie Lott. After the 1986 season, Lott opted against having surgery on the tip of his left pinky finger so that he would not have to miss any time healing. Going against doctor's advice in order to be a better football player is some kind of brave, indeed.

The majority of NFL players are tough, but Lott pushed toughness to a new level.

But no one outdoes Tim Krumrie if you are talking about NFL toughness. He set the bar, and he set it high. Since then, no one has surpassed Krumrie and his toughness.

When Krumrie broke his tibia twice and his fibula once during Super Bowl XXIII, he astounded the NFL and everyone watching at home. However, Krumrie embodied a tenacity that is uncommon in today's sport.

During Super Bowl XXIII, the Bengals were taking on the San Francisco 49ers. Krumrie came off a block from 49er offensive linemen Jesse Sapolu and Randy Cross. When he placed his foot on the ground and tried to plant it, the pressure of his weight on his ankle joint made his lower leg snap above the joint. Those who played in the game alongside Krumrie said that the snap of the bone could be literally heard from feet away. Understandably, the entire game stopped as Krurmie laid on the ground.[2] The break was so severe that a splint was brought out to the field to stabilize his leg, and Krumrie was immediately diagnosed with a broken tibia and fibula.

Krumrie remained in the locker room, encouraging his team, after being removed off the pitch and declining to go to the hospital. At one point, it appeared as though he would be toasting with his Bengals teammates and would remain in the locker room cheering them on as they secured victory and showered him with champagne. The hospital was the furthest thing from his mind at that time.

Paramedics eventually persuaded Krumrie that if he didn't get to the hospital right away, his broken leg might send him into shock. Although the injury was significant, there was less concern that it was life-threatening. However, everyone around Krumrie knew that if he didn't get proper medical care, he ran the risk of ruining his leg forever and never being able to play the game of football again, nor even walk around without the assistance of a cane or walker.

When he finally did get to the hospital, the severity of the injury became more apparent, and the doctors would later say just how smart it was to seek the proper medical care needed. The doctors and medical team immediately got to work on straightening Krumrie's leg and starting the long road to recovery.

Doctors inserted a 15-inch steel rod into his leg just in time for the next regular season to begin, enabling him to extend his run of games completed, which would eventually come to an end in 1994 at 122 games. That's accurate. He shattered his leg horribly in the middle of his run of games played, had a metal rod inserted, fastened his cleats, and kept playing.[3]

As you can see, the injuries that can be sustained in football are unlike ones you can gain anywhere else. Because of the ferocity of the game and the intensity and size of the players on the field, the mishaps that happen on a football field can quite literally snap bones in half. Just ask Tim Krumrie.

The next time you watch an NFL game, take a second to think about how hard the hits are, how intense the tackles are, and how much damage the players can do to themselves in the long run. A whole lot is on the line during each and every single game.

---

1. This would mark the unofficial end of Wright's career because he would never fully recover from the injury. The photo of the injury, however, would exist in the NFL for decades.
2. Bengals head coach Sam Wyche could be heard on the sidelines saying, "Get up Tim, get up Tim," again and again into his headset.
3. Krumrie would eventually end his career after the 1994 season with 1,017 tackles, 34.5 sacks, 13 fumble recoveries, and 11 forced fumbles.

23

WHEN NFL WAS TELEVISED

Nowadays, we are all very lucky that we can watch every single football game that interests us in glorious, beautiful high-definition pictures and sound. Via ESPN, NBC, NFL Network, CBS, and beyond, there are so many options and choices for us to watch our favorite teams take on their rivals.

And it's not just the quality of the picture that makes these modern games so fun to watch. There are now cutting-edge statistics and numbers and graphics and interviews—all within the blink of an eye. The way games are broadcast to audiences today is a wonderful mix of beauty, technology, and entertainment.

But it wasn't always that way. Not by a long shot. For a very long time, games were never even shown on TV. People could listen to them on the radio sometimes and, of course, they could attend the arenas and watch them in person. But viewing games wasn't nearly as easy as it is now.

That's because television is still a relatively new invention. It has only been around for a couple of generations and a few decades. And even after it was created, television wasn't a home for football or other sports for a long time.

When football was finally shown on antique television screens, it was nothing like the games we watch now. It was radically different, harder to follow, and much more confusing and unenjoyable.

Football has come a long way in just a couple of lifetimes, and so has the way it is broadcast.

Back in 1939, most people didn't own a television. The invention was taking the world by storm in many places, and some people saw it as the future of entertainment and even knowledge and education. But others saw television as a passing fad.

Whatever it was, it sure was expensive to have a TV back in the day. In the late 30s and early 40s, a TV cost about $600, which is roughly $12,000 by today's standards. The first TV was released to people in the spring of 1939, and in a few months, a network attempted to air the very first football game.

The first game to air on television was between the Brooklyn Dodgers and Philadelphia Eagles on October 22, 1939. Now, you need to remember that the game looked wildly different than the ones you watch today. Not only was the quality of the images on screen light years behind what 2022 offers, but it was also different in terms of commentary, audience size, and just about everything else.

For the game, there were just two cameras. Compare that to today's games, where there are dozens, along with sound men and interviewers, graphic supervisors, producers, and more. And while today you can hear the commentary from several seasoned announcers for every game, this game only featured one, who was tasked with pointing the camera where it needed to be pointed.[1] All in all, the entire production team consisted of only eight people. The game's announcer, Allen "Skip" Walz, was paid just $25 for his hard work.

The game was held in New York City, and that was part of the reason why NBC chose to air that game. The Empire State Building had a TV transmitter on top with a range of nearly 50 miles, giving the network a huge boost and a way to get the picture to thousands of people across the country.[2]

The actual matchup was a Week 7 competition. Given that both clubs had had disappointing seasons the previous year, there wasn't a lot on the line. The Eagles and Dodgers had just completed a tedious 0–0 stalemate three weeks prior.

Naturally, a few anxious TV executives hoped there wouldn't be a recurrence.

With an easy victory of 23–14, Brooklyn increased their record to 3–2–1.[3] At 0–5–1, the Eagles are still winless. However, the outcome was unimportant. It was a successful broadcast, and that's all that truly mattered. The remaining Dodgers games for that season were chosen to be shown. The NFL TV revolution had begun in earnest.

In the years since that, football has come a very long way, and it has grown to dominate not only the world of sports but the world of television too. As the technology behind TV and TV production grew, so did the hold that the NFL and football games had on the industry. More and more networks got into the game and started to become a major draw for audiences. By the time the 1970s rolled around, football was one of the biggest phenomena on television.

And the Super Bowl grew and grew too. When the first game was aired, it definitely attracted an audience, but nothing like what is garnered today. Now, billions of people literally watch the NFL's biggest game every year, and the money raised via the Super Bowl is immense. And while the Super Bowl is a huge deal every single year, every football game aired on national television receives millions of viewers from all over the country and all over the world.

Watching football on TV today is the epitome of high production value. The games look great, are produced with excellence and skill, and are entertaining, well-filmed, and engaging events. They are a sight to behold. To think about how far televised football has come in a few decades is a testament to the people working behind the scenes.

As the second World War broke out in Europe in the late 1930s, Americans were preparing to see the very first televised NFL game, which was something rudimentary and basic. But it was also something that changed the world of American football forever.

---

1. "I did my own spotting, and when the play moved up and down the field, on punts or kickoffs, I'd point to tell the cameraman what I'd be talking about," Allen said.
2. Official estimates said the total worldwide audience for the game was about 1,000 people.
3. The game ran for 2 hours, 33 minutes, and 10 seconds. There were no commercials.

24

THE ICE BOWL OF 1967

 "Astroturf was a pillow compared to this."

— CHUCK MERCEIN

When you watch football today, you sometimes see games played in less-than-wonderful weather conditions. Because the game is played all over the country, typically in some of the coldest months of the year, we have seen NFL games played through rain, sleet, and snow. Watching a game in Wisconsin in December is truly intense, not just because of the game.

Millions of fans and players have pushed through some really ugly weather to be part of the game they love so much. But few games can rival one game that happened fifty years ago. This game, now dubbed the Ice Bowl, was something truly bone-chilling—literally.

On December 31, 1967, the Green Bay Packers took on the Dallas Cowboys in the coldest NFL game on record. It was the NFL Championship, the equivalent of the modern Super Bowl, and it was a day that all fans, players, coaches, and staff would remember with a shiver for the rest of their lives.

The game was played at Lambeau Field, where it was a chilly 13 degrees below zero when it started.[1] Nevertheless, about 50,000 parka-clad spectators braved the weather on New Year's Eve to see the Packers' 21–17 triumph and third straight NFL championship. Although people in that part of the country were never happy in that sort of weather or temperature, they were far more used to it than those coming from warm, humid Dallas, Texas.

The same was true for the teams tasked with playing the game too. Since the Packers were based in the frigid Wisconsin environment and practiced there, Green Bay supporters believed their team had a clear advantage against the hot-weather Cowboys from the outset. And, when the game started, it looked like they may have had a point. The early 14–0 advantage for Green Bay likely persuaded the crowd that they were well on their way to victory in what was already being called the coldest game in the history of all professional sports.

Yet, the Packers were also impacted by the bad weather.[2] Even though they were born and raised and practiced and played in that weather, the Packers were starting to get icy fingers and make cold mistakes. After two Packer fumbles, Dallas capitalized and scored a touchdown, then added a field goal and a second touchdown in the final quarter. With 4:50 remaining in the game, the Packers found themselves suddenly 17–14 behind.

The Packers kept their cool as if they had a choice. They stormed down the field under the direction of future Hall of Fame quarterback Bart Starr. The Packers were only 2 feet away from winning with 16 seconds left at a temperature of 18 below zero. Starr announced a timeout. The field resembled an ice sheet. The two running plays before this one had failed. A rushing play looked completely out of the question because no more timeouts were available. Unquestionably, a successful pass would win. The Packers could have attempted a field goal to tie things up and force overtime with even an incomplete throw stopping the clock. Vince Lombardi, the Packers' head coach, was consulted before Starr reentered the huddle.

Ken Bowman, the center, snapped the ball to Starr. Bowman and guard Jerry Kramer killed Dallas tackle Jethro Pugh together. Starr startled everyone by diving over for the touchdown once Pugh was out of the way. The Packers took home the glory with a 21–17 win over the Cowboys.

Cold games are still quite normal and expected in the modern NBA, and we see quite a few of them every single year. But even when they get cold enough to rival the Ice Bowl, precautions are taken to keep the players, fans, and coaches safe. Portable heaters, heavy jackets, and modern insulation in the arenas have all made things a bit more comfortable, even though people will still be shivering and seeing their breath as they watch the game.

The Ice Bowl has been a thing of the past for years now. But it is still talked about in the great history of the NFL because of just how intense and particular it was.[3] Back then, football was not the enormous industry and sport it is now, and games like this hadn't been witnessed by many players or fans.

The fact that the Ice Bowl happened and so many people participated in it shows that people are truly devoted to football in ways that can sometimes be considered fanatical. When you really love a sport, you're willing to put up with a lot to support it, even nearly freezing your fingers off.

---

1. The wind chill made it feel like 36 below zero.
2. Hours later, several players on both teams would be treated for frostbite.
3. The Ice Bowl ranked first all-time for the lowest average temperature for any December 31 in Green Bay: -6.5°F for the day.

THE BIGGEST COMEBACK OF ALL TIME

Let's be honest: everyone loves a good comeback story. Everyone loves rooting for the underdog, rallying behind them, seeing them rise through the ranks, overcome the odds, and pull off a win. There is simply nothing like seeing someone or a team believing in themselves, formulating a plan, and then achieving their goals because of their hard work, determination, and belief in their common goal.

Sports is a great place to find underdogs. It's not just football where this happens, either. There are underdog tales in basketball, baseball, tennis, and so many other sports. Think of all the amazing memories you have watching the Olympics and seeing teams or individuals rise against the odds and reign supreme after an unlikely start or a bad hand dealt to them. You don't get that in many areas of life, but you do get it in sports.

But perhaps no other sports underdog comeback story is as good as the one witnessed in 1993. To this day, it is still considered the most remarkable comeback story in the history of the NFL. Therefore, it only makes sense to end our book about football extremes with the most extreme underdog success in history.

To really see how great the comeback of the 1993 Buffalo Bills was, you need to understand where they came from and how they rose like a phoenix out of the ashes of the abysmal NFL season they had.

Teams can mess up and give away victories in the closing moments of a game. But just as a team can take their foot off the gas in the closing seconds of a matchup and end up losing, a squad can also be exceptionally determined until the very last minutes and make each and every second count toward a win.

At the time of this pivotal, consequential, and historic game, the Buffalo Bills weren't really at their best—not by a long shot. They had lost the last two Super Bowls, had come in second in the AFC East in 1992, and then had to play the Wild Card game.

For a majority of their matchup against the Houston Oilers on January 3, 1993, it seemed like the Bills were about to have yet another rough day to put behind them.[1] By halftime of the game, the Oilers were leading the way with a huge 28–3 record, behind 4 touchdowns passed by future Hall of

Famer Warren Moon. Things were only looking worse when the second half of the game began, as Houston had an interception, a 58-yard run, and another touchdown. The score was now 35–3, and many Buffalo Bills fans were accepting the loss before it was even called. To them, it was yet another game and yet another loss at the hands of their beloved but troubled squad.

But then things turned around. This was when the comeback of the year began.

The Bills began to rally. It started with them driving 50 yards in 10 plays and then scoring a touchdown with a 1-yard run by Kenneth Davis. Following that, Steve Christie of the Bills recovered his own onside kick to give backup quarterback Frank Reich the ball.[2] Just four plays later, Reich found Don Beebe with a 38-yard touchdown, and the score was now 35–17.

The Bills were still behind, but they weren't completely out of the game. There was a chance, as slim as it might be, to claim victory after such a dismal start.

Buffalo's defense kept the team in the game and got them possession of the ball again. Reich took full advantage of that, and he found Andre Reed for another touchdown, a 26-yard one. Then Bills' safety Henry Jones was able to grab an interception for a 15-yard return, allowing Reich to find Reed once again for another score.

Fans on both sides of the game were shocked and on the edge of their seats. In just a few short moments, the lead of the Oilers had been cut down to just 4 points. It only took 6 minutes and 52 seconds, but the Bills were most certainly in the game and, in many ways, momentum was all theirs. They could win this game if they wanted and kept playing as they had been.

All eyes were on the next few moments of the game, as Buffalo fans were beyond excited to see a side of their squad they hadn't witnessed in ages, if ever.

The Oilers attempted a field goal and, shockingly, they screwed it up. It couldn't have happened at a worse time for them. With the ball now turned over, the Bills continued to surge forward. Reich made a 17-yard touchdown pass to Reed, which brought the score to 38–25 with less than three minutes in regulation of the match. Houston was still fighting, though, and their player, Al Del Greco, made a field goal kick to tie up the score and send the game into overtime.

If that was the end of things, it would have been a remarkable game and a stunning, strong effort from the Bills. But that was not the end of things. Buffalo was tuned in, fired up, and ready to win the game after so many people thought they didn't stand a chance to come back, let alone walk away victors.

On a Houston drive, Nate Odomes of the Bills intercepted a pass to Moon. Then Davis made two 6-yard rushes, and

Christie claimed a 32-yard field goal attempt. The ball went sailing through the field goal range, and the Buffalo Bills officially won the game, 41–38.[3]

It was now the largest comeback victory in the history of the NFL. The 32-point rally was the first of its kind, unlike anything that had ever been witnessed. Stunned, Bills fans were dancing in the stands and at home. They had just seen their team, who had been counted out by everyone (including themselves), come back from literally nothing to defeat their rivals. What a game, what a win, what a huge comeback.

What an amazing moment in football history.

The Bills kept pushing forward throughout the rest of the season and had some more success again and again. In fact, the Bills made it to the Super Bowl that year, but they ended up losing to the Dallas Cowboys. It would be the third of four consecutive Super Bowl appearances and, sadly, they lost all four.

They might not have ever claimed a Super Bowl win during that era and might have repeatedly come up short and not lived up to expectations or potential. But the comeback game in January of 1993 was the perfect example of the can-do, don't-quit spirit that makes so many people dedicate their lives to sports. Everyone who enters any sort of game wants to win. However, that's not always possible, and sometimes people are going to lose even when they try their hardest.

But no one will ever stage a comeback unless they truly believe in themselves and are willing to pour their hearts out into the game for the good of their team, their fans, and the people they are playing with. The Buffalo Bills were able to rise up and create an unheard-of comeback in just 6 minutes. So what if they didn't win the Super Bowl that year? They were still able to do something that was considered impossible.

Of course, fans of the Bills will always fondly remember and speak of the game against the Houston Oilers when the Bills were able to rally and overcome nearly impossible odds. But even people who don't root on the Bills can see the beauty, stunning dedication, and skill on display in that game.

---

1. The Oilers were using what was called a Run n' Shoot offense, which was later seen as a gimmick and dropped by many other teams in the league.
2. Reich was taking over for Jim Kelly, who had sprained his knee the previous week.
3. It is important to note that the Oilers were two-point underdogs before the game.

SHARE YOUR THOUGHTS, REVIEW!

If you are enjoying this book and want to help spread the message and the stories of football, the NFL, and all the amazing legends involved in it, why not leave us a review? Writing a review for this book will help others find it, and that's the best way to really celebrate football! Spread the word and let the world know about all the incredible figures who have made football such a special sport.

Scan the QR code below to leave a quick review!

CONCLUSION

After reading all of these amazing stories, hopefully, one thing has been made abundantly clear to you: there really is no game like football.

Again and again, you have seen that football truly is a game of extremes. Its history and the history of the NFL are filled with legendary players and coaches and referees, analysts, commentators, and fans. They have been the game's champions from the very beginning and helped lead to amazing records and incredible highs and lows.

Many of the moments we have read about have not been topped in decades or generations. Through tragedy, national events, deaths, success, changes, and monumental shifts in culture, country, and sports, those who love, live and breathe football have always been ready for the next big things. They have stuck it out through thick and thin. There have been both positive and negative extremes throughout the history of football. And those who love the game have been there for it all—from record cold games to epically long blowouts and shocking comebacks.

People are always there for the game of football because football always provides. The game has changed in so many countless ways over the years, from the way it's broadcast on TV to the way the halftime show is performed to the way that the game is supported and celebrated. Much has changed about football, but the loyalty of fans, players, and coaches has not. There is a good reason for that: football always provides an incredible story. It always has, and it always will.

There have been many eras of football. Think of the early games, when the game wasn't aired on TV, and only a few thousand fans stood in the arena. Think of how elementary the game looked back then. Compare that to a few decades later, as people at home were now able to watch the game and find a team to support and stay loyal to. Skip ahead a few years more, and now millions of people were watching the game, attending them in person, and wearing the jersey of their favorite stars.

Even more years have passed, and now the NFL is a billion-dollar industry unlike any other. There are many popular sports in America and all over the world, but none of them truly rival the devotion and dedication of football. The amount of money that the NFL makes and the amount of loyalty it derives from those who love it speaks for itself. Over the years, there have been many changes to the game, but one thing has remained consistent: people love this game.

Perhaps the best story to think of as you close this book is the one that ended it: the story of the Buffalo Bills overcoming incredible odds and winning against the Houston Oilers back in 1993. Everyone had counted the Bills out and thought they were going to get trounced. Halfway through the game, it seemed those people were right. But then the Bills fought hard, rallied, and came back and found a way to win.

That says it all, doesn't it? That speaks to the spirit of those who love the game. Not just the players on the field but the fans in the stands, the supporters at home, the coaches on the sidelines, and everyone who watches the game on the edge of their seats.

There are many extremes in the game of football, but perhaps the most extreme aspect is the love that the game garners.

SOURCES

https://bleacherreport.com/articles/30811-the-last-of-the-nfls-super-teams-the-epic-80s.

https://en.wikipedia.org/wiki/1984_NFL_season.

https://www.latimes.com/sports/la-xpm-2013-nov-21-la-sp-nfl-jfk-assassination-20131122-story.html.

https://www.history.com/news/jfk-assassination-dallas-cowboys-cleveland-browns-1963.

https://www.si.com/nfl/2014/11/20/black-sunday-nfl-plays-after-jfks-assassination.

https://en.wikipedia.org/wiki/Super_Bowl_XXXIV.

https://bleacherreport.com/articles/2817227-where-are-they-now-mike-jones-made-the-most-famous-tackle-in-super-bowl-history.

https://fs64sports.blogspot.com/2010/12/1979-cowboys-come-from-behind-deny.html.

https://www.washingtonpost.com/wp-srv/sports/redskins/longterm/1997/history/allart/dw1979b.htm.

https://www.washingtonpost.com/wp-srv/sports/redskins/longterm/1997/history/allart/dw1979b.htm.

https://www.nytimes.com/2012/11/23/sports/football/jets-humiliated-by-patriots-in-a-new-york-minute.html.

https://www.espn.com/nfl/story/_/id/28066447/patriots-rb-jonas-gray-brush-fantasy-vs-reality-five-years-ago.

https://www.skysports.com/nfl/news/12040/9567626/nfl-new-england-patriots-running-back-jonas-gray-scores-four-tds-against-indianapolis-colts.

https://www.espn.com/nfl/story/_/id/28066447/patriots-rb-jonas-gray-brush-fantasy-vs-reality-five-years-ago.

https://theanalyst.com/eu/2021/12/the-biggest-blowouts-in-nfl-history/.

https://247sports.com/nfl/chicago-bears/Article/Bears-100-Looking-back-at-the-biggest-blowout-in-NFL-history-135839189/.

https://www.profootballhof.com/players/jim-thorpe/.

https://www.theguardian.com/sport/2013/aug/02/jim-thorpe-pennsylva
nia-football-hall-fame.

https://www.profootballhof.com/players/mel-hein/.

https://www.nytimes.com/1992/02/03/sports/pro-football-sports-of-the-
times-mel-hein-transcends-all-eras.html.

https://www.espn.com/blog/nflnation/post/_/id/136593/mnf-moments-
no-14-dorsett-runs-for-99.

https://www.espn.com/nfl/playoffs/2012/story/_/id/8911864/2013-super-
bowl-power-outage-stops-game-super-bowl-xlvii.

https://www.espn.com/nfl/story/_/id/22682035/washington-redskins-
issue-super-bowl-rings-1987-scabs.

https://www.hogshaven.com/2018/3/9/17099972/long-overdue-super-
bowl-rings-for-redskins-scabs-influenced-by-espn-documentary.

https://www.si.com/nfl/2016/01/25/john-parry-official-super-bowl-xlvi

https://www.si.com/nfl/2016/01/25/john-parry-official-super-bowl-xlvi.

https://en.as.com/en/2016/04/27/nfl/1461794354_354759.html.

https://www.si.com/nfl/2015/12/28/max-mcgee-green-bay-packers-super-
bowl-i.

https://www.profootballhistory.com/max-mcgee/.

https://profootballresearchers.com/archives/Website_Files/Coffin_Corner/
22-01-837.pdf.

https://www.cbssports.com/nfl/news/susan-tose-spencer-broke-glass-ceil
ing-for-women-in-nfl-front-offices-while-saving-eagles-from-disaster/.

https://www.nfl.com/author/kurt-warner-0ap3000001037948.

https://bleacherreport.com/articles/1190204-kurt-warners-grocery-store-
checker-to-nfl-mvp-story-a-tale-of-perseverance.

https://www.sportscasting.com/thomas-davis-is-the-only-athlete-to-ever-
return-from-3-acl-tears/

https://www.si.com/more-sports/2012/09/26/oj-murdock.

https://www.dailymail.co.uk/news/article-2181232/O-J-Murdock-death-
NFL-player-fifth-football-star-committed-suicide-years.html.

https://en.wikipedia.org/wiki/List_of_highest-scoring_NFL_games.

https://www.theguardian.com/sport/blog/2015/oct/01/and-you-thought-
the-bears-offense-was-bad-nfls-last-0-0-game.

https://www.nytimes.com/2000/12/10/sports/sports-of-the-times-in-afl-
days-jets-raiders-was-a-rivalry.html.

https://americanfootball.fandom.com/wiki/Heidi_Game.

https://kidadl.com/quotes/pat-tillman-quotes-from-the-american-football-player.

https://bleacherreport.com/articles/734757-20-most-gruesome-injuries-in-nfl-history.

https://www.cincyjungle.com/2014/2/2/5370744/bengals-super-bowl-history-the-tim-krumrie-injury.

https://www.nfl.com/news/nfl-celebrates-80th-anniversary-of-first-tele vised-game-0ap3000001068673.

https://books.google.es/books?id=XeJK5d1xRGQC&pg=PT169&lpg= PT169&dq=Allen+(Skip)+Walz+and+announcing+the+1939+game& source=bl&ots=mb-_n9paAD&sig=ACfU3U1sn_roMF7lboeeLaQ_iTIMi fahhw&hl=en&sa=X&ved

https://www.profootballhof.com/football-history/the-ice-bowl/.

https://www.history.com/this-day-in-history/buffalo-bills-pull-off-greatest-comeback-in-nfl-history.

Made in the USA
Las Vegas, NV
30 November 2024

13003944R00322